The Canadian 100

The Canadian 100

THE 100 MOST INFLUENTIAL CANADIANS
OF THE TWENTIETH CENTURY

•

H. Graham Rawlinson
and J.L. Granatstein

McArthur & Company
Toronto

First published in Canada by
Little, Brown (Canada)

This paperback edition published by
McArthur & Company

Canadian Cataloguing in Publication Data

Rawlinson, H. Graham
The Canadian 100:
the 100 most influential Canadians of the twentieth century

Includes index.
ISBN 1-55278-005-8

1. Celebrities - Canada - Biography. 2. Canada - Biography. 3.
Canada - History - 20th century - Biography.
I. Granatstein, J.L., 1939-
II. Title. III. Title: Canadian one hundred.

FC601.A1R38 1998   920.071   C98-931706-4
F1034.3.A2R38 1998

Jacket Design by COLLEEN O'HARA OF 4 EYES ART & DESIGN

Cover Illustration by ROCCO BAVIERA

Interior Design and Page Composition by JOSEPH GISINI
OF ANDREW SMITH GRAPHICS, INC.

Printed and bound in Canada by Transcontinental Printing

McArthur & Company
322 King Street West, Suite 402
Toronto, Ontario, Canada, M5V 1J2

10 9 8 7 6 5 4 3 2

Contents

Introduction

IT IS HUMAN TO ATTEMPT TO CATEGORIZE, TO RANK, to make lists. We want to know who is the best in every human endeavour. We seek to discover where we as individuals stand in comparison to our peers— in sports, politics, business, and art. We as Canadians often rank our nation against others, proudly bragging that we are a member of the G 7, the most powerful industrialized nations, even if the gap between Canada and its superpower neighbour is huge and growing. We enjoy lists, we pore over numerical rankings, we even make *Maclean's* annual ordering of Canadian universities its best-selling issue of the year.

The authors of this book, the first attempt to select and rank the hundred most influential Canadians of the twentieth century, have fallen victim to this compulsion. We asked ourselves, Who among our compatriots has had the greatest influence, for good and for ill, on Canada and the world? Who among us made a discovery that altered the way the world lived? Who used power to change our lives for good or ill? Who entertained us so well, so movingly, that the memory lingers pervasively? Who changed the course of history in a substantial and notable manner?

We sought to measure influence—in other words, not fame, heroism, brilliance, merit, or mere wealth or power. Fame is fleeting, but not necessarily deserved, and too many are famous merely for being famous;

heroism is gallantry raised to its peak, but regrettably its influence is ordinarily transient; brilliance can be so ill-focused as to amount to little; and merit is a word that has been debased to the point where it has lost its meaning. Nonetheless, there are the famous, the heroic, the brilliant, and the meritorious on our list—where such inclusion was justifiable—and we have also included some evil individuals whose ill will has had profound impact. Influence, therefore, is not the same as goodness, but, happily, there have not been too many harmful Canadians in this century. There are more Canadians who have devoted their lives to the mindless, ceaseless accumulation of wealth, a trait that Canadians know and sometimes admire. Rarely is money used to achieve continuing influence, and only those who had that impact are found here. It is the same with power—some prime ministers have power, but fritter it away much like lottery winners squandering the spoils; other political leaders use their power to effect permanent change. It is only the latter who interest us.

This book is by definition about individuals. We believe that history is made by people, something that ought to be a truism but is not. To many historians, history is the product of great impersonal forces—ideology, class, or social movements—and the absence of great Canadians from our consciousness seems to foster such habits in their minds. It is a striking fact that Canadians tend to have trouble naming "the greatest living Canadian." In a 1942 public opinion survey, some 40 per cent could not name anyone; in 1995, in another poll, a staggering 76 per cent failed to name a single great Canadian. This is not how we see it. Living, breathing Canadians made and make history, their actions affected us all, and this book attempts to pinpoint the hundred key players of this century.

More, we have attempted to rank the most influential from 1 to 100. We admit at once the wholly arbitrary nature of this process, to compare apples to soybeans to maple trees. We understand and accept that every reader of this book will quarrel with our choice. This disagreement is inevitable; we invite readers to make their own lists and send them to us, care of our publisher. We promise to consider them closely in preparing the next edition of this book.

In defence of our own list and rankings, we will say only that we fought and argued over them for months, and that we ransacked the efforts of literally hundreds of historians and journalists to produce a list and a ranking that we agreed on and believed defensible. We will find out, no doubt, if our defences are as strong as we believe they are.

In selecting our Canadian 100, we admit that we did not seek to create a regional, linguistic, gender, racial, or multicultural composite of Canada in the late 1990s. To do so would simply be ahistorical, simply false. For much of the twentieth century, Canada was a favoured land for white males with a British background, while francophones, natives, immigrants, and women were left out in the cold. Similarly, to be born and raised in central Canada conferred an advantage, as did having well-off parents who could provide the education or capital necessary to launch their offspring into the world. We wish that this had not been so, and we recognize that our list says discouraging and disheartening things about Canada's century; we hope and believe that these biases are changing, and we trust that when a list like ours is prepared in 2097, it will be very different.

Two rules were followed. It was not sufficient merely to be born in Canada to be included in our list. Mary Pickford may have been Toronto's gift to Hollywood, just as Saul Bellow was Montreal's to American literature; neither, however, made their careers in Canada or seemed to draw much sustenance from their upbringing. They will not be found in our ranking. Max Aitken, Lord Beaverbrook, however, was born in Canada, made his first fortune here, and, although his greatest influence was in British politics and he lived abroad most of his long life, he retained a continuing interest in and influence on Canada. He is included. In other words, to be influential in Canada meant to us that a person's career, or a substantial portion of it, had to be spent here.

The authors enjoyed researching and writing this admittedly impossible book. If our readers approach it in the spirit we wrote it, we are certain they will be engaged and provoked by it.

ACKNOWLEDGMENTS

We have been greatly assisted by Milena Ivkovic and Rick Lund who did much useful research work for us; by Dean Oliver who collected the illustrations and was in turn assisted by many others, especially Pam Hyndman, Liisa Tuominen and Rosemary Isaacs of the Ottawa *Citizen*, Joan Cooper of Quebecor, Allan Stewart of Canada's Sports Hall of Fame, Myrn O'Brien of the Dalhousie Art Gallery, and Ursula Gattoc of Ontario Hydro.

We are grateful to Kim McArthur and Sarah MacLachlan of Little, Brown Canada, and to our agent, Linda McKnight, for expertly guiding us through the publishing process.

Our greatest debts are to Catherine Salo who helped formulate the original idea and refine it later on; to Ellen Rawlinson, who served as a crucial resource on east coast questions; to Rosemary Shipton, our extraordinarily skilled editor; and to our friend William Kaplan whose carping and constant goading was enormously helpful to our work.

HGR AND JLG,
TORONTO, JUNE 1997

BORN: London, Canada West • 2 February 1867
DIED: Toronto, Ontario • 25 July 1937

KING WHEAT! THE WORLD STANDARD FOR HARD
wheat has been and remains Canadian, and it was
wheat that settled the prairies and made them rich.
Even today, in a diversified west, wheat can still bring
in $15 billion for each crop, mobilize an army of
40,000 combines in its harvesting, and employ tens
of thousands in its distribution and sale.

The man who made this possible wanted to be a
flutist and a singer. Charles Saunders, a frail, slightly
timid man, was one of five sons of William Saunders,
the druggist and self-taught horticultural scientist
who prepared the report that prompted Sir John A.
Macdonald's government to create the Dominion
Experimental Farms and Stations in 1886. The father,
named first director of the Experimental Farms, had
tutored all his sons in plant hybridization, directed
their education, and formed them in his own mould.

Except Charles. Although he had yielded to his
father's hectoring and studied chemistry at the
University of Toronto and Johns Hopkins University,
from which he received his doctorate in 1891, he
broke loose in 1893 to continue his interest in music.
With his wife, a mezzo-soprano, he ran a music
school in Toronto, taught in the city's private schools,
wrote a music column in *The Week* magazine, and
simply failed to earn a living. When a telegram
informed him in 1902 that his father, overriding his

earlier refusal to take the job, had appointed him experimentalist, a title changed to dominion cerealist a few years later, he docilely accepted his fate and moved to Ottawa. Patronage was much simpler in those days, along with familial duty.

In fact, Saunders had spent his summers at university working with his father at the Central Experimental Farm. He was a meticulous man, with the great patience his new work required. His father had been searching for a quicker maturing wheat that could prosper on the Canadian prairies, where early frost regularly bankrupted farmers. Breeding the popular Red Fife bread wheat with various Russian and Himalayan varieties held promise, but the work was slow, the difficulties formidable, and the number of samples to be tested in the thousands.

Saunders grew tiny quantities of the various crosses, and he chewed a few grains of each to determine the most elastic

varieties. "I made more wheat into gum than was made by all the boys in any dozen rural schools," he said later. Then he milled the wheat and baked the flour into bread to see which one was best. A variety called Markham, developed by his brother Percy in 1892 from Red Fife and Hard Red Calcutta, seemed promising, though many plants in the tiny sample had weak straw and failed to reproduce consistently.

Pressed by his father, Saunders persevered, selecting seed from the best plants and chewing the kernels to test for strong gluten. The resulting strain he called Marquis, a wheat that was clearly superior in 1904 when grown and tested for its milling and breadmaking qualities in equipment he had developed. Saunders then arranged for Marquis wheat to be test grown in Saskatchewan and Manitoba in 1907, 1908, and 1909, and the crop, maturing seven to ten days earlier than other strains and producing large crops, did phenomenally well, even when early freezes destroyed most of the other varieties. The next year samples went to 400 farmers scattered throughout the prairies, and by 1912, there was enough Marquis seed for all who wished to purchase it. With its faster maturity and its head resistant to heavy winds, Marquis hugely extended the area where wheat could safely be planted. By 1920 there were over 17 million acres in wheat in the West, 90 per cent of them Marquis. Thanks to Saunders, Canada had acquired its reputation for producing the best hard spring wheat in the world, its flour in demand by bakers everywhere. Thanks to Saunders, prairie farmers could plant their crops in the expectation of bringing it in at harvest time.

Charles Saunders worked at the Experimental Farm until 1922, when his always delicate health collapsed. His research work had branched out to barley, oats, flax, peas, and beans, and his achievements here had been significant as well. But now, ill and weary, he retired from his civil service post and, with his pension of $900 a year, left Canada for France to study literature at the Sorbonne, write a book of verse and essays in French, and immerse himself in music. Protests at the niggardly reward for the service he had made to Canadian agriculture led the government in 1925 to increase his annual pension to $5000, and he was the recipient of a flood of honours, including a knighthood in 1934.

Tall and frail, with a narrow, bearded face, Saunders was modest about his achievements. Who made Marquis wheat? he was once asked, and his response was immediate: "God Almighty." Certainly, but without Charles Saunders' work, God alone knows when Marquis might have been found. As London's *Daily Express* commented on his death, "He added more wealth to his country than any other man." Saunders made possible the prosperity of the prairies, and he is entitled to stand first among the most influential Canadians of the century.

2

Brian Mulroney

BORN: Baie-Comeau, Quebec • 20 March 1939

No CANADIAN POLITICIAN IN OFFICE AND OUT HAS been loathed so universally, so viscerally. His taste in clothes, his friends, his policies, his political and business links with Americans—everything about Brian Mulroney caused the Canadian gorge to rise. Yet no other prime minister so altered the country, irrevocably changing the ways in which Canadians dealt with each other and with their southern neighbour.

Mulroney was not born with a silver spoon in his mouth. His father worked for the *Chicago Tribune*'s newsprint plant in Baie-Comeau as an electrician. Both his parents were shanty Irish, hard-working, devout, and poor, but their eldest son rose far above his origins. He learned his French on the streets, entered Rotary Club speaking contests, and after two years at the local high school, went off to St Thomas high school in Chatham, New Brunswick. Then it was St Francis Xavier University in Antigonish, Nova Scotia, and the law school at Université Laval in Quebec City. Everywhere he went the loquacious Mulroney became a big man on campus, a college wheeler-dealer playing at school politics and hitting the books no more than necessary. In Antigonish and Quebec City his political schmoozing brought him to the attention of local and national Conservatives in the Diefenbaker government and, with the friends he made in politics added to his school cronies, the beginnings of Mulroney's network were in place.

He practised law in Montreal, earning a reputation as a skilful negotiator, a good storyteller who could simultaneously pat the back and jaw at the ear of both sides in labour disputes, where he represented management. Mulroney was a Tory backroom operator too, but when he ran for the party leadership in 1976, his young, very pregnant wife, Mila, at his side, he seemed to have emerged full blown as a figment of his own imagination. Financed by corporate donations, Mulroney ran well, standing second on the first ballot. He lost eventually to Joe Clark, another little-known figure, but one who had, at least, served in Parliament.

The new leader and Mulroney had known each other for years, and there was no love lost between them. From his new perch at the head of the Iron Ore Co. of Canada, an American subsidiary, Mulroney sniped at Clark, the tempo increasing when Clark threw away the opportunity offered him after the 1979 election and soon fell from power. In 1983 Mulroney finally seized the brass ring. One year later, after a triumphant romp through an election campaign that saw him in full oratorical flower, his rich voice dramatically lowered in his public addresses, the "Boy from Baie-Comeau" was prime minister. It was patronage heaven for Tories everywhere.

Mulroney's primary tasks on taking office were twofold: to restore "super relations" with the United States, unhappy after years of Canadian nationalist economic policies; and to heal the breach with Quebec, smarting over Pierre Trudeau's slash-and-burn approach to the *nationalistes*. Singing for his supper with Presidents Reagan and Bush, Mulroney pressed for a Free Trade Agreement with the United States in 1985 and achieved it in 1988. He sealed the FTA with an election fought on the issue, as his government, backed massively by business, crushed the nationalist left and the anti–free trade

Liberals. Canada's economic future was now irrevocably
continentalist, and the flood of manufacturing jobs that
disappeared after the FTA, not all attributable to the
agreement, let his critics sing "I told you so" with conviction.

The same song would soon be sung about Mulroney's
role in Quebec. He wanted to tie the *nationalistes*, shattered
by their defeat in the 1980 referendum and furious at
Trudeau's 1982 patriation of the constitution, to both the
Tory Party and Canada, a not ignoble goal. To this end, he
brought separatists into his government, gave them place
and high position, and cast his lot with those who sought a
deal that would recognize Quebec as a "distinct society."
Marathon negotiations culminated in the Meech Lake accord
of 1987, a deal that failed to win public support in English

Canada and that died in the Manitoba and Newfoundland legislatures. Undaunted, Mulroney tried again, crafting the Charlottetown accord that went down to defeat in a national referendum. The net result of Mulroney's efforts to weld a happy Quebec into Canada was the revival of the once-moribund Parti Québécois and a surge of separatist support. Moreover, thanks to what was perceived as his government's favouritism to Quebec with contracts, grants, and appointments, Mulroney left English Canada increasingly furious with its compatriots—and the leader who had pandered to them.

Electoral wrath fell not on Mulroney, who retired in 1993, but on his successor, Kim Campbell, and on Canada. The Conservatives collapsed in the 1993 election, winning but two seats. Canada's future as a united nation perhaps died as well in the surge to official Opposition status of the separatist Bloc Québécois and the emergence of Lucien Bouchard, Mulroney's law school crony and erstwhile Quebec lieutenant, as the eventual leader of the *indépendantiste* forces.

Without question, Mulroney had irrevocably altered the political landscape. Canada and the United States, for better or for worse, were now one continental economic unit. Canada and Quebec, much for the worse, were two scorpions in a bottle, locked in a death struggle that might well leave no survivor. The Irish blarney, the insatiable ambition that had propelled Mulroney to power, and the desire to secure his place in history as a more influential leader on his nation's future than Pierre Trudeau had all left Canada *in extremis*.

3

William Lyon Mackenzie King

BORN: Berlin, Ontario • 17 December 1874

DIED: Kingsmere, Quebec • 22 July 1950

IN THE LAST TWENTY-FIVE YEARS MACKENZIE KING has been dismissed by Canadians, young and old alike, as a bachelor obsessed with his mother, a leader who consulted the spirits about every political decision, and a dog-lover whose closest friend was his terrier Pat. He has become a subject of snickers, a byword for political cowardice, and an icon of Canadian uptight weirdness. But there is more to the story.

King's mother certainly was a dominant personality. The daughter of the rebel of 1837, William Lyon Mackenzie, she ran the household, tyrannizing her husband and children. Willie was the apple of Mama's eye, however, and his academic success at the universities of Toronto and Harvard, his youthful appointment as deputy minister of labour, and his election to Parliament and appointment to Cabinet gratified her. King was intelligent enough to realize that he had to break free from his mother, but until her death in 1917 in the midst of the conscription election he could not. By then, aged forty-three, he was too set in his ways to find a suitable wife.

His life, therefore, was politics. King had managed to make himself Sir Wilfrid Laurier's protégé, and on the grand old man's death in 1919 he parlayed his loyalty to Laurier into the Liberal leadership. In 1921 he became prime minister in a House of Commons where the Progressives held the second largest number of seats. By 1926 King had generally absorbed the rural MPs into his ranks. At the same time, while slashing budgets and doing little domestically, he began the process of converting the British Empire into the Commonwealth, a voluntary association of nations united only by the monarchy and by sentiment. That task took longer, but King's success was one of his greatest achievements, the foundation-stone of Canadian independence.

King lost power to the Conservatives in 1930 and regained it in 1935 while Canada, mired in depression, was entering the pre-war years. It fell to this least warlike of men to lead Canada in war. He brought a united nation into the conflict by pledging "no conscription" to Quebec and a war of "limited liability" to wary Canadians who remembered the Great War's losses. By 1942 he had sought release from his pledge against compulsion in a plebiscite, and thirty months later he was obliged to send conscripts overseas. Quebec was angry, but King still seemed the least bad political alternative. English Canadians too, while buoyed by Canada's extraordinary war effort, had little love for the prime minister who, some said, seemed too close to the Americans. Yet in 1945 Canada elected him once more.

His wartime government, arguably the greatest collection of political talents in Canadian history and a grouping he managed with consummate skill, created a booming economy but worried about the postwar downturn. How could a return to depression be avoided when the boys came home and the war plants shut down? The answer was social welfare, Keynesian economics, and a pledge of full employment. King's government put unemployment insurance and the baby bonus in place, family allowances alone costing the country half the entire pre-war federal budget. His government prepared a shelf of public works projects, and then found

that demobilization and reconstruction progressed so well
that the anticipated recession was swallowed up in a continual
boom. And there was full employment for a decade, too.

By 1945 King was over seventy, tired and worn down.
But politics and government were his only passions. The
old man hung on to office through the opening years of the
Cold War, though increasingly difficult and cranky. In 1948,
"a sick old dog" as he admitted, he passed the torch to his
chosen successor, Louis St Laurent.

What are we to make of King? He was a fussy bachelor, a man who, as poet Dennis Lee put it, "sat in the middle and played with string and loved his mother like anything." His dogs were treasured, but no more so than those owned by any pet fancier. Like countless others, he dabbled in spiritualism, especially in the interwar years, finding consolation in the idea that the soul lived on but rarely asking for advice; even then, he followed direction from beyond only when his acute political antennae gave him the same answer. And King's political nose was acute. In an era before opinion polls acquired their reputation, King was a strong leader and a superb manager, with the shrewdest grasp of any of our prime ministers of the politically possible. His idea of government was less to accomplish than to prevent—to prevent Canada from splitting asunder, to prevent war from destroying democracy, to prevent the Tories from governing. And yet he accomplished much—the Commonwealth, the foundation of the welfare state, the triumph of Liberalism.

Mackenzie King was no charismatic leader—no Churchill, no Roosevelt. But he understood his people, he knew that French and English Canadians had to get along, and he led Canada better and more skilfully than Canadians realized then or later. His impact on Canada, fifty years after he left office, lingers still.

4

The Canadian Serviceman

I~N~ THE 1990s C~ANADIANS~ HAVE WATCHED THE destruction of their national institutions with only occasional bursts of anger. The railways, the airlines, the CBC are privatized or trashed, the RCMP is sold to Walt Disney, and the Canadian Forces are damaged by the actions of a few of their own members and a frequently gleeful press and Opposition. All these institutions have been important to Canada and Canadians; arguably, though we scarcely realize it today, the military has been the most important. This entry, unique in a book honouring individuals, assesses the influence of a collectivity.

Canadians are an unmilitary but warlike people, a historian once wrote, and there is some truth in this statement. Historically, in peacetime, Canadians paid no attention to the military, scorning the regulars as parasites living off taxes, and laughing at the militia as old men and boys playing soldier. But when war began, attitudes changed overnight. Kipling put it best: "It's Tommy this, and Tommy that, but Tommy go away; / But it's 'Thank you, Mr. Atkins' when the band begins to play." In the South African War, the Great War, and the Second World War, in Korea, and in a host of peacekeeping operations and a few peacemaking ones, Canadians cheered their troops off and, it seemed, forgot about them again as soon as the boys came home.

The soldiers didn't forget. Many returned from

overseas with wounds of body and mind; all remembered the horror of combat, the fear they fought to overcome, the dead civilians in heaps. Tens of thousands failed to return and are buried in neat, austerely beautiful war cemeteries from the Somme to Hong Kong. In the South African War, Canadian dead from wounds or disease were 224; in the Great War, 59,769; in the Second World War, 42,042; in Korea, 320; and in peacekeeping operations, more than a hundred. For a small country, for a peaceful nation "far from inflammable materials," as a politician put it at the League of Nations in the 1920s, this was a terrible price to pay.

One of those dead from the Great War might have been the prime minister who brought Canadians together. One of the air force pilots lost in the bombing campaign over Germany could have found the cure for cancer. One of the sailors drowned when his corvette sank in 1942 could have written the great Canadian novel. All these dead and wounded, the humblest and the powerful alike, left families, wives, and children shattered by their loss. The psychological toll at home was possibly as great as the losses in dead

overseas. The wars also divided French and English Canadians. For historical reasons, some good and some less so, Quebec was a reluctant participant in the century's wars. Notwithstanding the powerful anti-participationist mood, some 50,000 francophones served in the First World War and at least three times that number in the Second World War. They deserve to be remembered too.

What did Canadians gain by serving? They kept war's worst ravages far from Canadian shores. They defeated Kaiserism, Hitlerism, fascism, Japanese militarism, and communist expansionism. They fought for freedom and democracy for a country that, while it was never a perfectly free democracy, was certainly more so than virtually any other nation on earth.

Moreover, thanks to the efforts of those who fought so well in this century's wars, Canada acquired her reputation abroad and her self-image. The soldiers of the Great War helped to make Canada a nation in its own mind and in the councils of the world. The autonomous dominion that emerged from the war was constructed on Vimy Ridge and in the Hundred Days. The self-confident middle power that came out of the Second World War had been created at Ortona, the Falaise Gap, and on the Scheldt, in the Battle of the Atlantic, and over the Ruhr. Our politicians and diplomats used the power that came out of the barrel of a gun (a gun made in Canada, too) to enhance Canada's role. After 1945, in the Cold War world, Canadians carved out a reputation as the inventors and the pre-eminent practitioners of peacekeeping, a small nation that sent the best soldiers, sailors, and airmen in the free world to service in NATO. Canada did these things not to expand its territory, but out of altruism. Few nations can make such claim. Still, no one should forget that Canada's stature was paid for in blood and treasure.

5

Margaret Atwood

BORN: Ottawa, Ontario • 18 November 1939

THESE DAYS, MARGARET ATWOOD'S REPUTATION precedes her. She is described variously as "the leading feminist novelist of her generation," "the archetypal first Canadian," and, by the usually restrained *Sunday Times*, as "the outstanding novelist of our age." This is breathtaking praise indeed, and suggests—whatever one thinks of what she writes—that there is a broad consensus that Canada's most famous novelist has left an indelible mark on her times.

Peggy Atwood remembers growing up in two different worlds, and the experience framed much of her subsequent work. Her father was an entomologist who packed off his family every summer for insect-hunting expeditions in remote northern forests. Winters were spent in Ottawa or Toronto, and the contrast in lifestyles between the city and the bush was striking to Peggy. The tension between natural and artificial worlds was a theme Atwood would return to again and again in her fiction.

At the University of Toronto, from 1957 to 1961, Atwood took a degree in English and wrote poetry. She published her first book of poems in 1961, then began a master's degree at Harvard. For the next decade, Atwood drifted in and out of graduate school; taught English at universities in Vancouver, Edmonton, Montreal, and Toronto; and published several highly acclaimed collections of poetry, including *The Circle*

Game in 1966. Her first published novel appeared in 1969, but Atwood was known primarily for her powerfully suggestive verse. Her stark poems put women at the centre of a precarious world divided between the natural and the human. Stridently feminist themes were never far from the surface; in one stunningly unforgettable opening, Atwood wrote:

> *YOU FIT INTO ME*
> *LIKE A HOOK INTO AN EYE*
> *A FISH HOOK*
> *AN OPEN EYE.*

She was a leading Canadian poet before she was thirty, but Atwood's reputation was made with a pair of books published in 1972. *Surfacing* was an unsettling nationalist novel, casting American influence as the primary threat to Canada's survival. It confirmed her remarkable gifts as a novelist. *Survival*, meanwhile, was a pathbreaking book of criticism: Atwood's eclectic review of Canadian literature, which emphasized victimization and survival as recurring themes in Canadian writing, became the bedrock on which serious study of a national canon was built.

The success of these efforts meant that Atwood could devote herself full time to writing. The results were spectacular: several more volumes of poetry, and more layered novels that each developed compelling women protagonists. The best of these, *Life before Man* (1979), *The Handmaid's Tale* (1985), *Cat's Eye* (1988), and *Alias Grace* (1996), attracted glowing praise from around the world.

Even those who never opened her books recognized Atwood as a public figure. Since the 1970s her frequent public readings, often published criticism, and willingness to speak out for nationalist causes have made her "a major cultural force" in Canada. She has published prose and poetry in such diverse places as *Maclean's*, *Mademoiselle*, and the *New Yorker*. She helped found the Writers' Union of Canada and used her fame to bring the work of Amnesty International to the attention of her readers. A particular personal concern was the growing Americanization of Canada, and Atwood was a crucial figure behind the success of the nationalist House of Anansi Press. She also was paramount among artists opposed to the Canada–U.S. Free Trade Agreement in the late 1980s. In sum, Atwood has been *the* public voice of Canadian letters for the past quarter century.

From her home base in Toronto, Atwood has continued to pen international bestsellers that have drawn fawning attention from critics. Among her dozens of awards are the Giller Prize, the Governor General's Literary Award, and two nominations for the Booker Prize. There is a Margaret Atwood Society—based in Florida—and regular conferences and a literary journal are devoted to her work. No living, critically acclaimed woman author can claim such consistent attention. Few Canadians have had such impact.

6

Pierre Elliott Trudeau

BORN: Montreal, Quebec • 18 October 1919

PIERRE ELLIOTT TRUDEAU DOMINATED THE
Canadian political landscape as no one else ever
could; to both his legions of admirers and his
throngs of detractors he was larger than life. His
intellect, his background, and his attitude made him
so. The question is where to rank him in any list of
influential Canadians of the twentieth century. Even
today, more than a decade after he retired from the
political spotlight, his reputation towers over his still
considerable deeds.

The Trudeau myth had its makings in the relative
obscurity in which he lived his early life and in his
sudden leap into the national psyche. Born into a
middle-class family in Montreal in October 1919,
he was raised amidst affluence after his father's
business prospered in the 1920s. His upbringing
was bilingual and bicultural long before those phrases
were popular in Canada: Trudeau was a product of
a French-Canadian father and an English-speaking
mother of Scottish descent. Although he earned
a law degree during the Second World War, he
showed little enthusiasm for pursuing a career in
that profession. Instead, he began to roam. Graduate
study at Harvard and in Paris was followed by
worldwide travel and by affiliation with several
social-democratic organizations back home in
Montreal. Comfortably well off, Trudeau shunned

any full-time career until he was in his forties, when the prime minister came calling.

In 1965 Lester Pearson needed to improve his Liberal government's deteriorating relationship with Quebec. Trudeau, along with his friends Gérard Pelletier and Jean Marchand, was an anti-nationalist, anxious about the increasingly separatist rumblings of the Quebec government. They accepted the federal challenge to go to Ottawa and, within two years, Trudeau was justice minister; a year after that, he was prime minister, swept into power on a wave of charm and optimism—Trudeaumania—that had no precedent in Canadian history.

He never actively sought the nation's highest office, yet after winning his first majority government in the summer of 1968, it was clear that Pierre Trudeau not only relished the aura and authority that came with it but was determined to leave his stamp on the country. Without doubt, his chief goal over his next sixteen years in Ottawa was reconciling his home province with Confederation. He began by making the federal government a truly bilingual one. Millions were poured into teaching Ottawa bureaucrats French. For the first time, Quebeckers ascended to senior economic posts in Cabinet and in the mandarinate. Around the country, federal money was ploughed into second-language education, and, by the late 1970s, French immersion classes were *de rigeur* for the Anglo middle class. Trudeau had created a place for French at the very heart of Canada for the first time.

However, these efforts did not succeed in stifling the growing sentiment in his home province for vastly increased power, or, failing that, separation from Canada. Trudeau's intervention in the 1980 Quebec referendum campaign prob-ably won the battle for the federalist forces, but the outcome of the war remained in doubt. Even his patriation of the British North America Act, ratified formally in 1982, did nothing to settle Quebec's restless place in Confederation. The new constitution, which Trudeau boasted would last a thousand years, remained the subject of sustained discussion, as governments and pressure groups attempted to amend it before the ink had dried. In the short term at least, the new constitution's Charter of Rights and Freedoms created a mini-revolution in the courts, and, for the first time, Canadians were afforded entrenched protection from their governments.

Trudeau's other achievements were modest. He gave only occasional attention to the national economy, and he extended, rather than redefined, the social safety web spun by the Liberals in the 1960s. He substantially overhauled the way the federal government worked, chiefly by expanding the scope and authority of the Prime Minister's Office. Through foreign investment review and cultural policy, he made an effort to check the growing American influence in Canadian society and culture. Yet these efforts were partially successful at best, as were attempts during his term in office to mount a credible response to growing western Canadian alienation.

Statistically speaking, Pierre Trudeau was Canada's third most long-lived prime minister. He alternately flirted with Canadians and enraged them, as his television-friendly style and forceful personality made him impossible to ignore. All the same, he did not create the problem of Quebec in Confederation, nor did he solve it. He did not create the modern Canadian welfare state, though he expanded it. And efforts notwithstanding, he did not fundamentally alter Canadian foreign and trade policy with the United States. Among other prime ministers, therefore, Trudeau was not as crucial to twentieth-century Canada as Mulroney, nor as durable and important as King. Still, without question, he left a major imprint on his country.

7

BORN: Lodz, Poland • 19 March 1923

Henry Morgentaler

HE IS A CONVICTED CRIMINAL, BUT ALSO A VICTIM of horrific crimes. He is a respected professional, yet he has often been a pariah in his adopted country. He is championed as a life saver and reviled as a heartless killer. For abortion crusader Henry Morgentaler, striking contradictions are a way of life. And in a nation where achievement is usually claimed by those who follow the rules, he did not.

At the risk of undertaking a crude psychological analysis, it seems clear that Morgentaler's public career had its roots in his shattered youth. He enjoyed a childhood of privilege in Poland, where his father was a labour leader of some renown. But Jewishness in eastern Europe at the end of the 1930s was a death sentence for millions. His parents and sister were murdered by the Nazis; Morgentaler and a brother barely survived Auschwitz and Dachau. Inevitably, the experience marked him for life: any lingering faith about the existence of God disappeared, and Morgentaler left Europe with a deeply ingrained commitment to human rights.

He ended up in Montreal in 1950. In no time he was an immigrant success story: Morgentaler became a doctor and started a family. As more and more of his professional attention was devoted to family planning, however, Morgentaler grew impatient with the legal restrictions on birth control. But where others worked around the law, or silently flouted it, this doctor made Canadian women's lack of reproductive freedom a personal crusade. He became a family planning specialist and stepped onto the national stage for the first time in 1967, when he advocated a repeal of the abortion law before a parliamentary committee.

Abortion was not yet a major political issue when
Pierre Trudeau's government modernized the Criminal
Code sections affecting the procedure in 1969. The deliberate
termination of a pregnancy remained a crime, except where
specially struck hospital committees approved abortions to
protect the life or health of a patient. For most Canadians,
abortion continued to be a private, personal question—
though one too often dealt with in back alleys.

That was the case until 1970, when Morgentaler, who
was openly offering the procedure at a clinic in Montreal,
was charged with illegally performing abortions. Morgentaler
and his cause were suddenly thrust into the spotlight. During
his trial, the short, bearded, bespectacled doctor openly
admitted he was still performing abortions at his clinic.
He was charged again. At once, the nearly fifty-year-old
Morgentaler seemed to discover his calling: he was an activist,
a symbol of his cause, and, in somewhat troubling fashion,
he seemed to enjoy it. Canadians did not know what to make
of this male doctor who preached women's rights. At his first
trial in 1973, he acknowledged performing "between 6000
and 7000" abortions in just a few years. It was a stunning
admission: to both pro- and anti-abortion rights advocates,
Morgentaler appeared to be deliberately provoking more
trouble. Though he was acquitted by a jury, he was convicted
and jailed by a Quebec appeal court in 1974. He became the
first Canadian to go to jail without ever being convicted by a
jury. And the Canadian abortion-rights lobby had the first—
and only—martyr to its cause.

The pro-life, anti-abortion cause also had an enemy.
Morgentaler emerged from ten months in prison a man
detested by thousands. To those who viewed him as a baby-
killer, the doctor seemed to enjoy his work and to profit
from it in a way that was evil. His public appearances, and

often his clinics, became the targets of noisy demonstrations.

But Morgentaler would not back down. He was charged again and again, and repeatedly acquitted. The Quebec government gave up, and Morgentaler, spoiling for a fight, opened abortion clinics in Winnipeg and Toronto in 1983. He was now the focus of a national debate that commanded the attention of public officials at every level of government. Many promised reform, but polls showed little hope of finding a political compromise. Threatened with imprisonment again, Morgentaler promised only to continue to end unwanted pregnancies.

In 1988 the courts finally had the last word on the issue. In a split decision, the Supreme Court of Canada ruled that the prevailing abortion law was unconstitutional on several grounds. The federal government showed little appetite for drafting replacement legislation, and the result was a legal vacuum where abortion was legal without restriction. For Morgentaler, it was an undiluted triumph.

On a personal level, victory had its costs. The abortion doctor spent over $1 million in legal fees, and his public campaign cost him two marriages. That he had a tremendous impact, however, could not be questioned. For good or ill, the number of terminated Canadian pregnancies increased from perhaps 10,000 in 1970 to well over 100,000 in 1993. From any perspective, this figure made Canada a profoundly different society. Morgentaler could take most of the credit. Though other doctors and other activists supported the abortion rights fight, only Morgentaler—committed, persistent, defiant—consistently put his own reputation, career, and even freedom on the line to fight for his cause.

8

Clifford Sifton

BORN: Arva, Canada West • 10 March 1861
DIED: New York, New York • 17 April 1929

CLIFFORD SIFTON WAS A PROFOUNDLY POLITICAL man, but never a provincial premier or a prime minister. Yet in an era in which extraordinary decisions about Canada's future were made, he exerted vital sway. As a result, he was one of the most important Canadians of the century; remarkably more influential, in fact, than many who held higher elected office.

Born on a farm in southwestern Ontario just before Confederation, Sifton moved west with his family while still a boy but received his formal education at Victoria College outside Toronto. He returned to the new province of Manitoba in the 1880s, settled at Brandon, where he became a lawyer, and was elected as a Liberal to the Manitoba legislature in 1888. Winnipeg was still a small town in the closing years of the century, and Sifton, who had talent and ambition to spare, quickly assumed a leading role in the provincial capital. In 1890 he became closely associated with the Liberal legislation that abolished French-speaking and Catholic schools in the province.

It was this issue, which outraged most of Quebec and caused the Conservative government in Ottawa no end of consternation, that first vaulted the twenty-nine-year-old Sifton to national prominence. The young Manitoban showed no interest in retreating from his position that "national schools"—Protestant and English—were the only ones worthy of state support. When Wilfrid Laurier was elected prime minister in 1896, he and Sifton negotiated a truce on the question that forced the westerner to back down only a little: Catholic Manitoban students might receive religious instruction at the end of the school day, and non-English students could receive some teaching in their native tongue. But though Manitoba had for all intents and purposes been founded only twenty-five years before by the French-speaking Louis Riel, French was accorded no special status in the deal. This was a momentous precedent: the federal government's constitutionally entrenched capacity to protect bilingual education in the provinces had been overwhelmed. In and out of Quebec, hopes that a bilingual, bicultural Canada was possible for the new century were beginning to fade.

Laurier recognized Sifton's evident abilities, however, and, shortly after the schools question was resolved, convinced him to enter his new government as minister of the interior. Accordingly, Sifton moved his family to Ottawa and embarked on his self-appointed task to make Canada prosperous. His method of doing so was to fill the great plains of the west with people. It had long been obvious that Canada needed a much larger population to support its industries and till its soil, but now Sifton took that idea and made it happen. First he rationalized and streamlined land administration policies, and forced railway companies to develop the land they owned along the westward lines. Then he mounted perhaps the largest promotion campaign ever to lure suitable farmers to the Canadian prairie. Millions of pamphlets were distributed to farmers in the American west and in England. Advertisements were bought and exhibitions mounted. While British and American settlers were most welcome, farmers from northern and eastern Europe were also recruited.

The results of Sifton's immigration campaign were staggering: between 1897 and 1917 more than 3.1 million immigrants came to Canada. Manitoba exploded in size, and Alberta and Saskatchewan appeared almost overnight. On the eve of the First World War in 1914, the distribution and make-up of Canada's population had changed dramatically. Certainly the times were auspicious for an immigration boom: the American west was filling up, many Europeans were on the move, and scien-
tific improvements like those of Charles Saunders were making wheat farming possible on most of the Canadian prairie. But even in these circumstances, Sifton's unwavering determination to seize the opportunity

guaranteed that the country would be permanently reshaped.

His success secured Sifton's position in the Liberal Party, and, as a result, he was well positioned in 1911 and 1917 to act in two of the nation's decisive moments. First, Sifton was the leading member of the Liberal Party faction that broke with Laurier over the prime minister's plan for a free trade deal with the United States. His fight against reciprocity in the 1911 election helped stop the continentalist movement and ended Laurier's career as prime minister. Later, in 1917, Sifton was the most prominent Liberal to break with Laurier again, this time over the issue of conscription for the war. His influence was significant in splitting the Liberals and in ensuring that the bitterly opposed policy would succeed. French-English relations in the dominion would never be fully healed.

Once again, Clifford Sifton had won the day. By the time he died in 1929, his idea of Canada—bigger, British, and anti-French—had largely come to pass.

9

Walter Gordon

BORN: Toronto, Ontario • 27 January 1906
DIED: Toronto, Ontario • 25 March 1987

Bᴦ ᴛʜᴇ 1950s ꜰᴇᴡ ᴇᴄᴏɴᴏᴍɪᴄ ɴᴀᴛɪᴏɴᴀʟɪꜱᴛꜱ ᴡᴇʀᴇ to be found among Canada's power brokers. The links with Wall Street and American corporate finance had grown so close, the flow of money, trade, and ideas across the border so intense, that continentalism held sway. Resisting the trend, Walter Gordon was and remained a maverick.

Born into the Toronto financial élite "with a silver adding machine in his hands," Gordon attended Upper Canada College and the Royal Military College. He then joined his father's accounting firm, Clarkson, Gordon, and during the Second World War worked in the Department of Finance as an aide to the minister, J.L. Ilsley. It was Gordon who devised the taxation formula that split revenues between Ottawa and the provinces, the formula that concentrated money and power in federal hands so the war could be paid for. Gordon knew everyone in Ottawa, politicians and bureaucrats, and he was especially close to Lester Pearson, a rising star in External Affairs.

Their friendship had consequences. When Pearson decided to leave the public service in 1948 to take the leap into politics, Gordon raised money from business friends to compensate Pearson for the loss of his pension. Then, as secretary of state for external affairs, Pearson had a hand in Gordon's appointment to chair the Royal Commission on Canada's Economic Prospects in 1955.

Gordon had been concerned for some time about Canada's growing economic dependence on the United States. Most of the country's investment funds came from the United States, and most of Canada's exports went there. Was this healthy? His royal commission looked at this question and offered a calm, dispassionate no. Gordon recommended that foreign subsidiaries employ Canadians in senior posts and offer full disclosure of their Canadian operations. He wanted large branch plants to sell shares to Canadians, and he proposed higher withholding taxes on the dividends paid by such plants to their parents. The corporate response was harsh—Walter Gordon, in effect, was a traitor to his class.

Perhaps, but he was loyal to his friends. When Pearson decided to try for the Liberal leadership, Gordon organized his successful campaign. When the Liberals were devastated in 1958, he stepped in to direct the party's recovery, and in 1963, when Pearson took power, Gordon became his finance minister. The most powerful member of a strong Cabinet, a man who knew what he had to do to restore Canada's control of its corporate and financial future, Walter Gordon was in the catbird seat.

His fall was almost instantaneous. His budget, announcing measures to control foreign investment, a program cleared with Pearson, met a fierce response on Bay Street, St James Street, and Wall Street. The U.S. government protested the discriminatory treatment directed at American firms, and, under pressure from the financial community and the Prime Minister's Office, Gordon found himself forced to backtrack, withdrawing his measures in humiliation. For a time, it looked as if Pearson would sack him, but Gordon hung on. In 1965 he recommended an early election in an effort to

secure a Liberal majority, but the campaign went wrong,
Pearson won only another minority, and Gordon was
discredited again. To sighs of relief from many around
Pearson, Gordon resigned. Although he would return to
Cabinet briefly in 1967 and upset his opponents once more
by denouncing the Americans for their war in Vietnam,
Gordon's political power was effectively finished; so too was
his friendship with Pearson, a man who, Gordon believed,
had let him down when the going became rough.

But Gordon did not go quietly into the dark night of
clipping bond coupons. Still worried about the ever-growing
American influence on Canada, he organized and financed
the Committee for an Independent Canada to lobby for a
more nationalist economic policy. Opinion polls demonstrated that economic nationalism had strong and increasing
support among voters, especially young voters caught up in a
wave of post-Centennial fervour. The Trudeau government

created a Canada Development Corporation to "buy back" Canada, and established the Foreign Investment Review Agency to guarantee that the country received benefits from foreign investment. These were weak measures, however, and Gordon became all but certain that "we seem destined to lose our independence and eventually to become part of the United States. Most Canadians do not want this," he said correctly, as he continued to fight to reverse the trends he feared.

With his wealth and his nationalist ideas, Gordon was the heart and soul of the nationalist movement that held sway in Canada after the 1960s—until the 1988 Free Trade election, perhaps irreversibly, tied Canada to its neighbour. He won the battles for public opinion, but such was the continentalist spirit of Canadian capital that Walter Gordon lost the war.

A LITTLE WOUNDED BUT NOT SLAIN

10

René Lévesque

BORN: Campbellton, New Brunswick • 24 August 1922
DIED: Montreal, Quebec • 1 November 1987

To OUTSIDERS LOOKING IN, HE WAS AN UNLIKELY
hero: short, raspy-voiced, chain-smoking. By all
reports he was often self-absorbed, frequently moody
and impatient, and sometimes a bully. Yet to French
Quebeckers, René Lévesque was heroic. His hopes and
dreams were theirs, as were his doubts and fears. In
an era of change, Lévesque was able single-handedly
to set the agenda for Canada-Quebec relations for a
quarter century and to become the dominant Canadian
provincial politician of his time.

Like Pierre Trudeau, a fellow Quebecker whom
he would come to know well both privately and
publicly, Lévesque was a politician only reluctantly.
He was the son of a lawyer from New Carlisle,
Quebec, and remembered a childhood of prevailing
tension between the French and English parts of that
bilingual community. An indifferent student, his real
education began when he followed the U.S. Army as
a war correspondent during the Second World War.
Journalism came naturally to Lévesque, and he
returned to Montreal after the war to launch a very
successful career at Radio-Canada. His passionate,
personal approach to the news was well suited to the
dawning television age, and by the late 1950s he was
known and generally admired around the province.

Lévesque joined Jean Lesage's Liberal Party of
Quebec in 1960 after failing to convince fellow critics

of the provincial government like Trudeau and Jean Marchand to do the same. His growing public profile helped him win a seat in the general election that year, and he was an obvious selection for Lesage's first Cabinet. Lévesque was an outsider in the new government, but he used his widespread popularity to push the pace of reform. He staked his career on the Liberals' decision to nationalize the province's vast electric utilities, arguing successfully that Quebeckers' right to determine their own future required control of the industry. By 1966 the Liberals were back in opposition, and Lévesque had become convinced that the federal government and English Canadians stood in the way of Quebeckers' social and economic development. This was the turning point in Lévesque's career. It was also the issue that permanently split Trudeau and Lévesque, since Trudeau fundamentally rejected any ethnically-based nationalist strategy for change. When his efforts to push the Quebec Liberals into a more militant position in 1967 failed, Lévesque quit the party. With the few hundred Liberals who followed him, he concluded that a new political vehicle was essential, and in 1968 Lévesque founded the Parti Québécois (PQ), with the express objective of obtaining independence for the province.

The new party enjoyed little success at first. In the elections of 1970 and 1973, the PQ won only a handful of seats and failed to elect its leader on either occasion. Lévesque made future success possible, however, when he purged the party of extremists and, by sheer force of personality, gave his fledgling movement respectability. That paid off in 1976, when an unpopular Liberal government was upset at the polls by the PQ. Lévesque's dream—Canada's nightmare— had come true: an avowedly separatist government was in power in Quebec. As the country teetered on the brink of extinction, its citizens held their collective breath. The newly elected premier, though, was cautious. He concentrated on progressive reform and spoke of "sovereignty-association" rather than independence. His government also made it clear that no action in this direction would be taken until it was approved in a province-wide referendum. That historic vote came in May 1980. In a humbling personal setback, Lévesque's proposal to negotiate sovereignty was rejected

by 60 per cent of voters. The result, however, left the province in a kind of limbo in which it remains: it was neither satisfied with the *status quo* nor prepared to embrace separation. The PQ government won another mandate in 1981, but the party began to crumble from within shortly after as a frustrated Lévesque personally pushed separation, the party's founding *raison d'être*, off the policy agenda. A series of high-profile Cabinet resignations led to his own retirement as premier in 1985. He died two years later, though the cause of his life remained alive and well.

It is not difficult to imagine René Lévesque, were he alive today, being amused by the irony of his listing among the most influential Canadians of the century. After all, for much of his life, Lévesque tried to create a world in which he would no longer be a Canadian. Without this patron saint of modern Quebec nationalism, however, the country he rejected would have been a remarkably different one.

11

Lionel Groulx

BORN: Vaudreuil, Quebec • 13 January 1878

DIED: Vaudreuil, Quebec • 23 May 1967

Historians are not usually very important, nor do they write for posterity. Most accept that their fate is to write for their own generation—to respond to its questions and demands. And most undertake this task in seclusion, producing impenetrable prose in their efforts to elucidate obscure subjects. Abbé Lionel Groulx, the pre-eminent historian of Quebec, was a scholar, but he frequently left the cloisters of academe to engage in public debate and to bolster his positions with the weapons of the past. He was, as Claude Ryan of *Le Devoir* wrote in an editorial on his death, "the spiritual father of modern Quebec. Everything noteworthy, everything novel on the Quebec scene has carried the imprint of Groulx's thought."

Born in the countryside near Montreal, Groulx's origins were humble. His mother scrimped to send him to the seminary, and he was ordained in 1903. He taught at the Collège de Valleyfield from 1899 to 1915, except for three years of higher education in Rome, Strasbourg, and Paris. In 1915, with the Great War already beginning to strain relations between French and English Canadians, he was named professor of Canadian history at what would soon become Université de Montréal. Already a *nationaliste* and an inspiring teacher whose warmth enveloped his students, he had helped to shape a generation;

he would mould thousands more to his way of thinking
through intellectual action.

Without formal historical training, he immersed himself
in the past, creating his understanding of history by what
he saw as the needs of the present. To Groulx, Quebec was
sinking into a degenerate pluralist stew, with the English-
speaking controlling the province's economic destiny, and
floods of unassimilable immigrants adding the scent of root-
less cosmopolitanism and corruption. If French Canada, if
Quebec as the homeland of the French in North America,
was to survive, it must rely on religion, family, and language.
His historical writings harked back to the great heroes and

miracles of the past, most notably his highly mythologized Dollard des Ormeaux, who had saved Montreal from the Iroquois in 1660. Publishing his lectures annually, Groulx pointed to Confederation as a bad bargain—after all, had French Canadians not been maltreated in Ontario and the West? Had conscription not been imposed on them in 1917 by the imperialist Anglos?

Groulx moved in the same circles as Henri Bourassa, the great nationalist leader, but by the early 1920s, breaking with the old leader, he was flirting openly with separatism in *L'Action Française*, the journal he edited. This extremism was soon replaced by slightly more moderate positions, by the call for Québécois to be *maîtres chez nous,* or masters in their own house, by the need to have French Canadians control their economic, political, and cultural destinies. The Anglos were at fault, but so too were Québécois who had lost their faith and allowed control over the economic and political levers to pass from their hands. To regain them, Quebec had to rely on Roman Catholicism, Catholic social values, family, and language to make *notre maître, le passé*, the past, our master.

The nature of Groulx's vision is perhaps best found in the didactic and emotional novel *L'Appel de la race*, which he wrote under a pseudonym in 1922. The hero, a *déraciné* francophone, married to an English Canadian, has made his legal career in English. But in his forties he becomes gripped by a malaise for his lost culture. His language gone, living in Ottawa, he struggles to regain control and, with the aid of a sympathetic priest, eventually abandons his wife to return to a crusade for his people. The "mixed marriage" of Confederation between English and French Canada, the symbolism of this bad novel makes all too clear, could not be made to work, and, in the face of its impending collapse, French Canada had to shape its own coherent identity. It was always a choice between friend and foe, between the pure and the impure, to Abbé Groulx.

In the 1930s Groulx dabbled with fascism, with the need for *un chef* to lead Quebec into "the new order which is evolving." "We shall have our French state," he proclaimed. Like many others in Quebec and English Canada in that era, he was anti-Semitic. With the coming of war in 1939 he was sympathetic to Marshal Pétain's occupied France, and as opposed to Anglo-imposed conscription as he had been in 1917. His ideas were one of the props of Maurice Duplessis' long-lived regime.

As a nationalist, Groulx was heaped with praise. The Quebec legislature (ironically) honoured him as one of the fathers of the Quiet Revolution, while Montreal named a Metro station after him. André Laurendeau, Quebec's greatest journalist, noted in an obituary comment that "we loved him dearly." The mortal remains of the Abbé were buried after a state funeral and an official day of mourning.

As a historian, Groulx's influence today lies not in his scholarship, which is little read and largely outdated, but in the ideology he espoused. Like modern Quebec historians, many of whom have been assisted by L'Institut d'histoire de l'Amérique français that he founded in 1946, he was suspicious of Canada and focused his gaze inward; unlike them, he lacked the sophisticated methodology they now use to bolster arguments that are often very similar to the master's. Above all, Groulx changed the way Québécois saw themselves.

12

Ernie Coombs

BORN: Lewiston, Maine • 26 November 1927

CANADIANS LIKE TO THINK THEY ARE KINDER AND gentler than Americans, and it may even be true. What no one ever asks is why this should be so. The reason may be Mr Dressup.

Ernie Coombs went to art school in Boston and, as a scenery painter, found himself working in children's theatre in Pittsburgh. There he met Fred Rogers and came with him to Toronto in 1963 to be a puppeteer on a CBC children's TV program. Rogers left a year later to return to the United States, where he became famous for *Mr Rogers' Neighborhood,* but Coombs remained in Toronto and in 1964 went on air as Mr Dressup on the show *Butternut Square.* After three years, Coombs' character got its own show.

Mr Dressup quickly became an institution, a daily half hour that captured up to 90 per cent of the children's audience in Canada—a stunning half-million viewers each day! To Coombs, his audience was each individual child—never a collective "Boys and Girls"—and the style, by conscious choice, was low key, slow, amiable; indeed, the approach was characterized by a quintessentially Canadian mild understatement. "If you're restrained," Coombs said, emulating Fred Rogers, "the kids will come to you...It's easy to throw something at children and know that they're going to watch it...but ultimately you've got to recognize that children deserve to get some sort of value out of watching it." Values such as manners, innocence, and simplicity. The approach worked for twenty-nine years and more than 4000 episodes, with the children of the original 1960s' viewers still watching reruns as devotedly as their parents ever did.

The TV program, produced initially in some 140 live half-hours a year, featured Mr Dressup as a commercial artist who did drawings or crafts, sang songs, or welcomed guests. His puppet characters were a four year old named Casey who lived in a backyard treehouse with his dog, Finnegan, both created by Judith Lawrence, an Australian puppeteer. Scripted, but nonetheless a meandering and seemingly impromptu half-hour, the show's best-known feature was the Tickle Trunk, a large steamer trunk full of costumes that Mr Dressup put on for various roles ranging from foolish kings to pirates. The costumes—the budget for them was $5 a show, Coombs joked, with most passed on from other CBC productions—were sometimes shopworn, but that never seemed to matter to Coombs or his viewers. TV critic Morris Wolfe noted that unlike the American *Sesame Streeet*, *Mr Dressup* "assumes that children have an attention span that extends beyond two minutes, an assumption that's reflected in structure, style and content." And Coombs basked in the praise of parents, who told him: "Yours is the only program my child will sit and watch for half an hour. It's a quiet time when the children can watch friends and not get overly stimulated." Very Canadian, that, even if the show was the product of an American and an Australian.

The devotion of children to Coombs is genuine—and it lasts beyond the teen years. When he appeared as part of his farewell tour at the University of Manitoba in early 1996, Coombs drew a standing-room-only crowd that greeted him with a huge ovation. The students listened to Mr Dressup for an hour and then lined up at a microphone to tell him how much he had mattered to them. "You were a very important part of a very happy childhood," said one. "I just want to say you're my hero," said a second. And a student from northern Manitoba told Coombs he had set a good example for children in isolated areas. "You showed that a child does not need fancy toys to play—just use your imagination. We will miss you. Thank you. We love you."

Winner of a Gemini for best performance in a children's show in 1996, Coombs taped his last *Mr Dressup* in February that year. Happily, his show will run, likely forever, in reruns.

Not until 1994 did Mr Dressup become a Canadian citizen. "I'm a Canadian legend," Coombs said, "but I'm an import." Perhaps feeling slightly guilty over his slowness in taking the citizenship of his adopted country, he added the Canadian truism that "in a way, kids are pretty universal. If you're doing something for children, I don't think you have to necessarily be a citizen of any particular place."

13

Henri Bourassa

BORN: Montreal, Quebec • 1 September 1868

DIED: Montreal, Quebec • 31 August 1952

"LE CANADA POUR LES CANADIENS." TODAY, IN ANY language, these words seem absurdly self-evident. In 1900, however, Henri Bourassa's exhortation in the House of Commons was radical and, to many, even dangerous. Here was a politician advocating a considerable change in the way Canadians looked at themselves: no longer, Bourassa believed, should Canada turn to Britain to define itself. Much of

English Canada viewed this suggestion as nearly traitorous. After all, Canada's historically intimate ties to England were a vital part of what stamped Canadians as distinct in North America. This was the age of empire: of past military conquest behind the British flag, and future security under it. Bourassa resisted this imperial ideal. In so doing he became an influential politician and commentator, and, ultimately, a prophet of a new age of national maturity.

Bourassa's speech in Parliament was typical: here was a man who said what he believed and eschewed the traditional Canadian art of political compromise. This aplomb was perhaps the result of a childhood of privilege, for Bourassa's family was among the most prominent and respected in Quebec. The almost sacred legacy of his grandfather, Louis-Joseph Papineau, the hero of the Lower Canadian rebellion in 1837–38, did not hurt his reputation, and he was lured by Wilfrid Laurier to run as a Liberal in the federal election of 1896. Though still only twenty-eight, Bourassa won easily, and quickly became a confidant of the newly elected prime minister.

The young politician's rise through the ranks of the government ended abruptly in 1899. Britain's military adventures in South Africa fanned the fires of imperial nationalism in Canada, and Laurier reluctantly agreed to send a modest volunteer force in support. Bourassa was righteously indignant: here was a war that, even if justified, had nothing at all to do with Canada. He shocked the prime minister by resigning his seat in Parliament and, when promptly returned in a by-election, he assumed the role of government critic even though he ostensibly remained a Liberal.

Bourassa's opposition to Canadian participation in the Boer War made him known across the nation—famous in his home province, infamous outside it. A provocative speaker and a passionate essayist, his speeches and writings quickly made him a towering political figure in Quebec, and his sustained opposition to Canadian involvement in British military affairs spawned a new political movement in Quebec in 1903, La Ligue Nationaliste. This first generation of Quebec nationalists was profoundly pan-Canadian in outlook: they sought independence from British policies as well as bilingual and bicultural government institutions. Yet in Bourassa's mind, Laurier, the first French-Canadian prime minister, was failing to meet these expectations. In 1910 Bourassa founded a daily newspaper, *Le Devoir*, to attack Laurier's decision to build a Canadian navy designed to bolster imperial defences. The new daily rapidly became influential in Quebec, and in 1911 it was the means for Bourassa's most enduring impact on Canadian history. Fed up with Laurier's cautious appeasement of Canadian imperialists, Bourassa agreed to fight Quebec Liberals in the federal election with a group of nationalist candidates working in quiet concert with the Conservative Party. Using fears of British imperialism to sway voters, Bourassa won enough seats to help snatch victory from Laurier.

The new Conservative prime minister, Robert Borden, however, was firmly committed to imperialism; indeed, in 1912 he pledged Britain $35 million to build three warships. Perhaps the most remarkable irony in Canadian political history was concluded: Bourassa fought Laurier because of his imperialist leanings, but the goverment that replaced the Liberals was even more committed to the empire. By the time Borden invoked conscription for the war in Europe in 1917, French-English relations in Canada had deteriorated to an unprecedented extent, and Bourassa, proven too clever by half, was again publicly supporting Laurier.

This, of course, was Bourassa's way. Too passionate to

be an effective politician, he was successful only in the short
term. His ideas were fundamentally important, however.
By the 1920s Bourassa's brand of isolationism and Canadian
nationalism were widely popular among the again-governing
Liberals. At the same time, the nationalist movement he
founded was growing, but also changing. A new generation
of Québécois, frustrated with its diminishing voice in
Confederation, was promoting a more insular Quebec
nationalism, and occasionally even separation, as the solution
to Quebec's problems. Late in life Bourassa often disavowed
this new, radical strain of political philosophy and its chief
proponents—people like Lionel Groulx. But his legacy, as
both a pioneer of pan-Canadian nationalism and an insti-
gator of narrower Quebec nationalism, was secure.

14

Pierre Berton

B Y THE END OF THE 1960s PIERRE BERTON HAD been a staff reporter at two Vancouver dailies, an editor and columnist in Toronto, a television and radio personality, and an author of controversial books on Canada's religious and social life. These endeavours made him a celebrity, but none qualified him for exceptional influence. It was not until the 1970s, when he became the country's best-known historian, that Berton changed the way people thought about Canada. His timing was good, and his sense of what people wanted was even better.

Berton was born and raised on the edge of the country in Yukon—a place shivering from the hang-over after the Klondike gold rush party. Though his family moved to Vancouver when he was twelve, Berton never fully surrendered his frontier identity. University student newspaper experience led to jobs with Vancouver dailies and, after an interval of war service, a position as a writer and editor with *Maclean's* magazine in Toronto. The late 1940s and 1950s were auspicious times to be at *Maclean's*: in the new postwar world it purposefully entrenched itself as proudly Canadian, and spurned British and American influences. Its national reputation was at its peak, and it served as both a training ground and a showcase for most of the country's leading writers. Berton held his own in this company, but in 1958 he was coaxed into moving to the *Toronto Star*, where he wrote a popular city column. By then television was well on its way to displacing other media, and it quickly became clear that Berton was perfectly suited for TV. He was opinionated, entertaining, and controversial. He was a showman—that and his trademark bow tie made him stand out in an age when everybody on television seemed to look and act the same. As a result he showed up on all sorts of programs— most notably *Front Page Challenge,* which endured for more than thirty-five years—and hosted several himself.

But television was mostly a means to an end for Berton: it gave him the freedom to pursue book-length projects. He wrote a book on the Yukon gold rush, then examined Canada's present: volumes on Canada's religious life and class structure sold well. In 1970 and 1971 he returned to Canada's past and published *The National Dream* and *The Last Spike*, which together told the story of the building of the Canadian Pacific Railway. The public response was overwhelming: both books were runaway bestsellers. Berton's eye for detail and character, combined with a patriotic narrative, made the books overnight classics. An abridged paperback version of the books in 1974 sold a staggering 175,000 copies. The CBC spared no expense in mounting an eight-hour television production based on the works, and the story's protagonist, John A. Macdonald, became a living, breathing, drinking legend before the nation's eyes. Professional historians praised Berton only grudgingly; many suggested that he did little but tell an old story in an engaging way. But in an era in which university historians were no longer interested in, or capable of, capturing wide public attention for their efforts, Berton had become the most famous historian in the country. He tapped the right mood in the nation: with the centennial rush of nationalism still a fresh memory, Canadians needed a

past that was exciting, dramatic, and, most of all, their own.

Buoyed by this response, Berton turned to other chapters in the national past. His newspaper and magazine days gave him a sharp eye for a good story and a prolific pace that embarrassed other historians. Berton also, as he unashamedly admitted, recognized a lucrative opportunity when he saw one. His subjects, like the War of 1812, the Great Depression, and Vimy Ridge, were expansive, but the stories he told about them were always personal and compelling. And sales were substantial: by the 1980s he was the best-selling Canadian historian of all time.

That success pushed Berton onto the national stage on a full-time basis. He used the platform in the 1970s and 1980s to speak bluntly on public questions, most often in favour of a more independent Canada. He admitted that his time at *Maclean's* and his research of the past had awakened previously dormant nationalist feelings. And now, with an unruly shock of white hair, he had all the right credentials to sway public opinion: his northern background seemed, in the absence of professional training, to qualify him to apply the lessons of the past to the problems of the present. Thus, with Margaret Atwood, Mel Hurtig, and others, he was a very visible architect of a new Canadian nationalism born in the 1970s: vital, progressive, and anti-American. When he wrote, many read; and when he spoke, many listened.

15

Robert Bryce

BORN: Toronto, Ontario • 27 February 1910

DIED: Ottawa, Ontario • 30 July 1997

ROBERT BRYCE, SAID AN ADMIRING COLLEAGUE IN the Canadian public service, "was a one-man band. He could do everything better than anybody else could do anything." We are always told that no one is indispensable, and that rule is always correct— except for Bob Bryce.

Born to a mining man whose life was a succession of booms and busts, Bryce trained as an engineer, graduating from the University of Toronto in 1932. But he found that economics captivated him, which might have been expected of the son of a socialist mother who came of age in the Depression. Although he had never taken a single economics course, he went off to Cambridge University to study with the great John Maynard Keynes. His career was made, for Bryce became one of the first North Americans to understand Keynes' General Theory—indeed, one of the first anywhere. Bryce became the explicator of Keynes first in London, then at Harvard University, and finally in Canada. He worked briefly for Sun Life Assurance Co. in Montreal, but soon was snatched away by the Department of Finance. There he became an instant star in the department run by Clifford Clark, in part because of his ability to explain Keynes' theory but primarily because of his intelligence, his extraordinary capacity for work, and his gift for simple prose explication of the most complicated economic matters.

The Second World War saw Bryce, just entering his thirties, play a key role in devising the statistical underpinning of the war effort, in serving on the myriad committees that devised policy on everything, including agriculture, mutual aid, price supports, and monetary aid to Britain. Overnight, Bryce could produce a thirty-page memorandum on any issue, and he could clearly explain what it all meant to ministers and mandarins. Peering owlishly through his thick,

round glasses, Bryce brainstormed his way towards the top of the heap. By 1947 he was assistant deputy minister of finance and secretary of the Treasury Board, and when the Korean War gave rearmament a huge push after 1950, he mastered defence questions, yet another string to his prodigious bow.

In 1953 the prime minister named Bryce clerk of the Privy Council and secretary to Cabinet, the senior post in the bureaucracy. He worked closely with Prime Minister Louis St Laurent, advising the Quebec City lawyer on every aspect of policy and winning his admiration and affection. And when John Diefenbaker came to office in 1957 with his paranoia about the "Liberal" civil service, Bryce instantly turned the Chief's doubts into admiration with his straightforward approach, his knowledge of every aspect of government, the soundness of his advice, and his skill in briefing Cabinet ministers and the media. It was Bryce who, analysing African and Asian opinion, pressed Diefenbaker to support South Africa's ouster from the Commonwealth, undoubtedly Dief's major foreign policy triumph. The Tory government was often an administrative shambles, but such coherence as it had sometimes seemed to be provided by Bob Bryce alone. Diefenbaker depended on him every day—yet characteristically found no room in his three volumes of memoirs to offer one word of commendation to his clerk of the Privy Council.

When the Liberals returned to power in 1963, Bryce switched over to the Department of Finance as deputy minister, where he entered on yet another difficult period serving Walter Gordon, a minister with fixed views on certain financial and investment questions. Still, Canada was in a boom period, major pieces of expensive social legislation were being put on the books, and federal budgets were expanding. No one played a more critical role in managing matters—and in working out the delicate balance with a newly nationalist and aggressive Quebec City—than the practical Bryce.

In 1970 he became economic adviser on the constitution to Pierre Trudeau, and in 1971 he went to Washington as executive director of the International Monetary Fund, where he remained for four years. Then the government named him as chair of the Royal Commission on Corporate Concentration until 1977, when his health broke down. Bryce's active career was over, except for writing an able account of the history of the Department of Finance during the Depression.

Remarkably clear thinking, supremely intelligent, Bryce embodied the best of the Canadian public service tradition. His hand was in virtually every important decision of government for almost forty years. The mandarin's mandarin, he ranks as the most influential public servant in Canadian history.

16

Doris Anderson

BORN: Calgary, Alberta • 10 November 1921

W<small>E ARE WHAT WE EAT AND READ.</small> *CHATELAINE*, the major Canadian woman's magazine, was full of recipes and, while Doris Anderson was editor for two decades beginning in the late 1950s, feminist articles. The magazine's circulation increased during this period from 460,000 to over a million, and the groundwork for the rise in political, economic, and social power won by women from the 1960s onward was laid in its pages.

An illegitimate child, Doris McCubbin grew up in her mother's Calgary boarding house. Her father eventually married her mother, but he was a difficult parent and her home life was troubled. She made her way through school and, during the Second World War, through university, propelled by her strong will and inner (and outer) toughness. Heading to Toronto to get into journalism, she found herself held back because of her gender and limited to composing advertising copy. So she left for Europe, where for a year in London and Paris she tried her hand at writing. Then she returned to Toronto and, in 1951, persuaded *Chatelaine* to take her on as an editorial assistant.

She became indispensable. Over seven years, she rose through the ranks to become successively assistant editor, associate editor, managing editor, and finally editor in 1958. She won the last position only when she threatened to resign if a less-qualified

male was appointed. Her bosses at Maclean-Hunter were amazed that McCubbin, soon to marry lawyer David Anderson, would not want to be merely a hostess and mother. Soon enough, Anderson was the mother of three boys.

She revamped the stodgy, boring magazine, turning a money loser into the company's cash cow that carried its other titles, including *Maclean's*. She found better writers, produced a more attractive design, and introduced a strong feminist slant in the editorials she wrote each issue and in the stories she commissioned. There were features on Canada's antiquated divorce laws, on child abuse, on discrimination against women in politics and trade unions, and chilling data on the wage discrimination under which women laboured—including Anderson, whose own salary, though high, was always significantly lower than that of comparable male colleagues at Maclean-Hunter. "The articles!" Michele Landsberg commented: "Incest, child battering, divorce, lesbians, and the Royal Family."

The emphasis, another writer noted, was on challenging conventional wisdom, not coddling it, through an approach that was at once feminist, woman-centred, and outward-looking. "The view," Susan Crean observed, "may have been from the kitchen, but it reached as far as world politics." The 2 million readers of her magazine were not only sensitized to women's issues but politicized about the abuse of their rights and the national need for programs and legislation to protect them and their children. *Chatelaine* ran well ahead of women's magazines in the United States—and increased its circulation while the more conventional American magazines were faltering. The creation of the Royal Commission on the Status of Women in 1967, something Anderson had demanded in print, was an indication that the times were changing and that Doris Anderson had changed them.

Although she had been successful at *Chatelaine*, Anderson failed to get the job she wanted as editor of the troubled Maclean-Hunter flagship, *Maclean's*. Women's magazines were women's work was the message from the executive offices, and, despite promises, the editorship went elsewhere. Anderson's bitterness over her treatment was sharp and remains so, to the point that it dominates two of her three novels and her memoirs. In 1977, finally, she left after disagreements with the magazine's publisher.

She turned to writing fiction and to seeking election to Parliament as a Liberal in a 1978 by-election. Although she lost, her reward was appointment to the presidency of the Canadian Advisory Council on the Status of Women. The council, full of party hacks, was little known and unimportant—until the members, caving in to pressure from Lloyd Axworthy, the minister responsible for the status of women, baulked at holding a scheduled national conference on the constitution in 1981. Anderson promptly resigned as publicly as she could, forthrightly pronouncing Axworthy "a bully" and adding, "I don't see why women should be bullied." Her departure galvanized the successful lobbying campaign to change the wording of the Charter of Rights and Freedoms as it affected women's equality rights. Anderson then became president of the National Action Committee on the Status of Women in 1982 and continued the fight for equality. "The woman's movement has no armies," Anderson once wrote. "It hoards no secret cache of deadly armaments. All we have is numbers"—and she turned those numbers into a highly effective political force.

No single woman is responsible for the increasing role of women in Canadian life. No individual deserves credit for the legal protections that have enhanced the lives of women in this country. Even so, any short list of those who led the battle has to include the very tough-minded Doris Anderson, who had the courage to call a spade a bloody shovel at a time when many of her contemporaries were satisfied to be their husbands' hostesses.

17

Emmett Hall

BORN: St Columban, Quebec • 29 November 1898

DIED: Saskatoon, Saskatchewan • 12 November 1995

LATE IN HIS LIFE, EMMETT HALL SUMMED UP HIS amazing career: "Doors opened, I fell through them." This was a typically blunt but also perceptive judgment, since Hall usually made his mark by being in the right place at the right time. But good timing or not, his influence was remarkable. In a variety of fields, Hall affected the everyday lives of Canadians of his time as no one else.

Few could have predicted that sort of legacy for Hall in the late 1950s. He was a small-town lawyer in Saskatchewan, respected but obscure. The Halls had emigrated from Quebec to catch the pre-war wheat boom half a century earlier, and now had put down deep roots on the prairie. He was nearly sixty and planned on slowing down. But then, as they say, things started to happen. Newly elected prime minister John Diefenbaker appointed Hall, an old law school classmate, to the bench in 1957.

Hall enjoyed the life of a judge and had risen to chief justice of the Saskatchewan Court of Appeal in 1961 when Diefenbaker appeared again, this time with health care on his mind. Health was the hot political question of the day, especially since Saskatchewan's Tommy Douglas had fought and won a provincial election in 1960 by promising a universal public medical care program. Doctors and insurance companies in the rest of Canada were starting to panic. "Medicare" could limit physicians' earnings and wipe out a lucrative business for the insurers. Diefenbaker hoped to find some middle ground, and gave Hall time and money to head a wide-ranging royal commission on the subject.

Hall was still little known in 1961, but doctors assumed that any friend of Diefenbaker would be a friend of theirs. They would be proven wrong. The judge was invigorated by his massive assignment and quickly demonstrated that he would run his own show. He authorized a plethora of academic studies to shed light on the relationship between health and medical costs, and called public hearings across the country. Various interest groups had their day at the hearings, but it was the plight of average Canadians that captured the nation's attention. It was evident that thousands of Canadians were not insured against sickness; the system as it existed was not working for everybody.

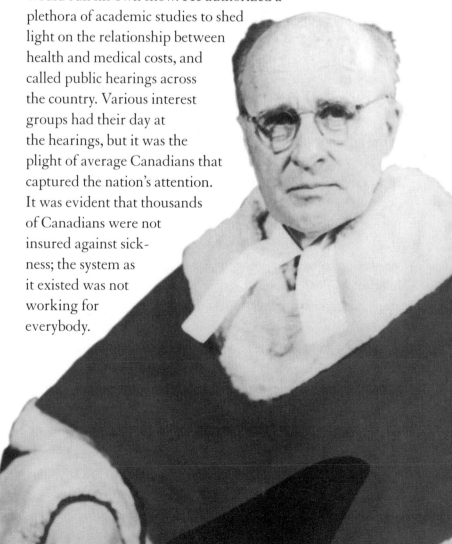

Hall gained respect with his sincere sympathy for the plight of the poor, and widespread appreciation for his glaring lack of concern for the well-paid doctors. When the commission's report was finally released in 1964, Hall's recommendation was unequivocal: a national, universal health care plan was not only affordable but essential. Doctors were livid, and Diefenbaker, now in opposition, disavowed the commission's conclusions. New prime minister Lester Pearson voiced only cautious support, but by 1965 Medicare was a popular policy. Hall, emboldened by his sudden eminence, kept up the pressure in a series of public speeches and, in late 1966, the Liberals finally passed legislation to create Canada's universal health care system.

Hall raised more than a few eyebrows in establishment circles with his partisan role in the health care debate. His behaviour was decidedly un-judgelike, especially since he had been appointed to the Supreme Court of Canada in 1962. But in the court of public opinion, Hall won a unanimous decision: here was an aging judge who was actually in step with the times. It was this reputation that made him the ideal choice to head another commission starting in 1965. Ontario wanted an in-depth review of its education system, comprehending philosophy, funding, and the future. Hall once again attacked his task with vigour; everything in the schools was up for debate. He gave a broad spectrum of educators and academics wide latitude to reconfigure Ontario education completely, and named Lloyd Dennis, a forward-thinking education consultant, as his co-chairman. Their final report, *Living and Learning*, was released in 1968, and it called for nothing short of a revolution in the way students were educated. According to Hall and Dennis, grades, exams, and homework should be abolished and a new, student-centred approach implemented that would allow learning at an individual pace. In its entirety, the report served as the touchstone for a new generation of education reformers across the country, and by 1975 many of its recommendations had been adopted.

Hall retired from the bench in 1973, but was called upon frequently by governments to investigate, mediate, and arbitrate. His reputation as a Tory, but also as a populist who put the concerns of average Canadians first, made him a uniquely qualified political problem solver. His varied experience in the public eye also gave him the ability to appeal directly to the public when it suited his agenda. He often spoke his mind on public issues, especially in defence of Medicare—a policy he had no problem calling his own. His popular, curmudgeonly style and curt manner made him a political force to be reckoned with, even in his nineties.

Emmett Hall ranks as the most important Canadian judge of his century. Of course, what is most notable about his career is not what he was, but what he was not. Hall was neither a doctor nor an educator nor a philosopher. He was never an elected politician. But in a brief public career, with a few choice opportunities, he made a huge difference.

18

Robertson Davies

BORN: Thamesville, Ontario • 28 August 1913

DIED: Orangeville, Ontario • 2 December 1995

At the height of his influence, he was a striking, unforgettable figure: six feet tall, with ample hair and beard white as snow. He was an old man, but his manners and apparel were even older. He had a piercing gaze and an imposing demeanour. To all appearances he was a bourgeois Victorian who had landed, improbably, in late twentieth-century Canada. Yet no one suggested he did not

belong; he never actually seemed out of place. Somehow, only Robertson Davies, Canadian novelist, could have pulled it all off.

That he managed to bring it off speaks volumes about his revered place in the Canadian imagination. Davies, like so many influential Canadians, enjoyed a privileged upbringing. He was sent to the best schools, then completed his formal education at Oxford—a place that suited his upper-class pretensions perfectly. His chosen vocation was the theatre, and at university and afterwards he enjoyed some success as an actor in Britain. But being on the stage, or writing for it, was a nearly hopeless career at the beginning of the Second World War, so Davies returned to Canada in 1940 to work in his father's expanding newspaper business. He wrote constantly: editorials, reviews, and plays. In the mid-1950s he attempted novels, but was known chiefly for his major contribution, as both a writer and a promoter, to the burgeoning Canadian theatre scene.

By 1963 he was respected enough to be appointed the first master of Massey College in Toronto. Academic life was well suited to Davies: his formal bearing and ancient costume, a mask that cloaked a shy personality, was positively professorial, and his thoughtful lectures were popular. The nearly two decades he spent in academe were also the peak years of his creative output; so much so that by the early 1980s he was rightly regarded as the founding father of modern Canadian literature.

In a series of remarkable novels, beginning with *Fifth Business* in 1970, the first of the Deptford trilogy, Davies changed the way many Canadians thought about themselves. He vividly demonstrated that Canada was more than a two-dimensional country—that myth, fantasy, and legend veritably oozed from the dark corners of the national pysche. Davies borrowed unapologetically from the analytic psychology of Carl Jung, and explored religion, magic, and the grotesque in Canada's past. His fully realized epic stories recounted all sorts of bizarre behaviour and, astonishingly, found much of it in the sleepy small Ontario towns of his youth.

The success of Davies' novels in the 1970s, along with those of Margaret Atwood, was the first solid evidence that something called Canadian literature, distinct from British literature and American literature, actually existed. This recognition created a new demand for teaching the subject, and Davies' sustained production ensured that new CanLit classes would have worthwhile books to read. CanLit also became the bulwark of an assertive new Canadian cultural nationalism in the 1970s and, to the surprise of many, Canada's foremost cultural export. Davies' novels, for example, are today being read in Japanese, Greek, Hebrew, and Estonian, among other languages. For these readers, Davies' Canada is almost certainly the only one they know.

Davies' international reputation was assured in 1986, when, within a few weeks, he was nominated for both the Booker Prize and the Nobel Prize for Literature. This proper, antiquated personage had brought a new understanding of Canada to the world. Since his novels are regarded as among the most spectacular of the century, he doubtless will continue to do so. But that was only part of the story: Davies also brought a new understanding of Canada to Canadians.

19

Frederick Banting

BORN: Alliston, Ontario • 14 November 1891

DIED: near Musgrave Harbour, Newfoundland • 21 February 1941

UNTANGLING THE REAL INFLUENCE OF FRED Banting is tricky business indeed. Was he a rare genius whose brilliance saved the lives of millions? Or was he a right-place-at-the-right-time chap, who falsely took credit for the work of others and never achieved much on his own? On the whole, Canadians have chosen to believe the former, preferring to exalt Banting as a hero rather than condemn him as an opportunist. If the fawning legends about him were all true, however, Banting would belong much higher on this list. The truth, as usual, lies somewhere in between: Banting was a remarkably ordinary doctor who had one or two extraordinary ideas. In ideal circumstances, one of those ideas changed the world.

What cannot be doubted is that, in 1922, a small laboratory at the University of Toronto produced an extract that prevented almost certain death when injected into the blood stream of diabetics. The extract, insulin, quickly became the standard treatment for diabetes. Here was a breakthrough of colossal significance: tens of thousands of Canadians faced death from diabetes, as did millions more worldwide. The insulin discovery would go down in history as Canada's greatest medical innovation.

Right in the middle of the triumph was Fred Banting, an uncomplicated son of small-town Ontario. Banting was an undistinguished young

surgeon in London, Ontario, who, after the First World War, was having trouble finding patients. He was working part-time as a medical lecturer and researcher when, in October 1920, he conceived a way of isolating a pancreatic hormone that all diabetics lacked. Scientists had theorized about this hormone's existence for many years, but all attempts to locate it had failed. At the University of Toronto, scientists were sceptical about Banting's ambitious ideas, but Professor J.J.R. Macleod undertook to provide research space for Banting in the spring of 1921. Macleod also assigned research assistant Charles Best to work with Banting.

In a short time, Banting and Best showed promising results using a primitive form of insulin on dogs. They had difficulty improving the recipe for the extract, however, until Macleod and biochemist J.B. Collip became involved in the research. In January 1922 the first clinical tests on humans were strikingly successful: the symptoms of the disease retreated fully in the face of insulin. When news of the medical miracle was leaked to the press, the world's gaze became fixed on Banting; after all, people reasoned, he had the idea for diabetes research in the first place.

For the doctor who had not yet turned thirty-one, it was heady stuff indeed. Banting became a national hero overnight. Soon he was the most famous Canadian ever: he won dozens of prestigious scientific awards, capped by the Nobel Prize in 1923. He scored a closetful of honorary degrees, a lifetime annuity from the Canadian government, his own research institute at the university, and a knighthood in 1934.

But insulin and the fame it brought soon became a kind of prison for Banting. He found the international acclaim and national celebrity status tiresome—he plainly preferred being called "Fred Banting" to "Sir Frederick." Within two years of the big breakthrough, he quit diabetes research altogether. Furnished with resources beyond his wildest dreams, however, he embarked on a series of ill-fated research efforts, each designed to hit another scientific home run. But with precious little real research experience, Banting struck out again and again. At times he wondered privately if his own role in the diabetes discovery had been a fluke, yet he stopped at nothing to petulantly discredit the role of Macleod and Collip, whom he despised for attempting to take some of the credit. Overall, the most famous Canadian of the 1920s and 1930s was frequently a frustrated, bitter man.

Banting died tragically in a wartime plane crash in 1941. Before and after the diabetes discovery, he lived a life of respectable ordinariness. It was interrupted, however, by that one spark of inexplicable inspiration that led to the pathbreaking diabetes research.

The insulin discovery, like so many other medical breakthroughs, was doubtless the product of several minds. A good case could be made that Banting was not the brightest of the research team, that he understood the least about diabetes, and that his scientific career after the discovery was the least distinguished. All the same, the one ingredient that could not be removed from the historical formula for insulin's discovery was Fred Banting.

20

Arthur Currie

BORN: Napperton, Ontario • 5 December 1875

DIED: Montreal, Quebec • 30 November 1933

He DID NOT LOOK LIKE A SOLDIER. He HAD A SMALL head perched on a large, indeed fat, torso, the whole supported by pipestem legs. His smooth-shaven, weak-chinned face stood out in contrast with the mustachios and firm jaws of the empire's field marshals and generals. But Arthur Currie could think clearly, understood war, and believed in trying to preserve the lives of his men. By the standards of the Great War, that made him an extraordinary commander, one who largely founded the Canadian military tradition.

After schooling in Strathroy, Ontario, Currie moved to British Columbia in 1893. He taught school, then ran a successful property speculation and real estate business in Victoria until it collapsed in the crash of 1913. The bright spot in his life was the militia, where he established a reputation both as a trainer and for his military good sense. In August 1914, when war broke out, the fortunes of this obscure lieutenant-colonel began to change.

As a friend of Garnet Hughes, the son of Minister of Militia Sir Sam Hughes, Currie was named a brigade commander in the first Canadian division to go overseas. He led his men into the maelstrom at Ypres in April 1915, became confused and possibly even fearful under the weight of the enemy attack, and did not do well. But he learned, rebuilt his confidence, and took over the division in September. Under his command, the 1st Division became widely recognized as one of the premier fighting units on the Western Front, despite fierce fighting and heavy casualties at the St Eloi Craters and the Somme.

In April 1917 the Canadian Corps, by now four divisions strong, prepared to attack the formidable German position on Vimy Ridge. Lieutenant-General Sir Julian Byng, a British officer, commanded the corps, but his plan of attack was based on Currie's thinking. The Canadian had studied recent French operations closely. His recommendations on reconnaissance, tactics, and artillery preparation, together with the briefing and rehearsal of all participants, down to the lowest private, shaped the corps' attack. The resulting success, one of the few in a hitherto bleak war for the Allies, established the Canadians' global reputation.

Currie's, too. Within a few months, Byng took command of an army and Currie became corps commander. An imperialist, Currie turned himself into a nationalist who resisted British efforts to break up his corps and parcel out its divisions. A sensible man, he resisted as much as he could the government's efforts to use him in its conscription election in December 1917. An experienced commander who understood the qualities of mind it took to lead men in war, he fought against political efforts to give his old friend Garnet Hughes a division at the front.

Currie built on Byng's work to make the Canadian Corps—with the Australian—one of the two best Allied formations, an efficiently run, ably directed fighting machine that was fierce in attack and stubborn in defence. Although his staff swore by him, he was never personally popular with the troops, perhaps because he didn't look the part and because he was aloof, shy, and cold. Currie's habit of winning battles nonetheless fostered an extraordinary spirit in his corps that his division, brigade, and battalion commanders reinforced. To many historians, in fact, Canadian nationalism was born at Vimy and, if so, Currie was its father. Through the abysmally foul conditions of Passchendaele and the open warfare of The Hundred Days that defeated and drove back the Germans in the last months of the war, Currie made his name as Canada's greatest soldier.

His reputation, however, suffered in Canada, a land that treats its heroes harshly. He was attacked by the crazed Sam Hughes, who never forgave Currie's refusal to give his son a division in France. Others criticized him for throwing men's lives away needlessly, a grotesquely unjust attack on a commander who used his guns and his brains, rather than human flesh, to win battles. In 1928 Currie launched a libel suit to clear his name and, although he won $1 in damages, the pyrrhic victory did him further damage.

Even so, Currie stands out as the man who made the Canadian Corps the embodiment of the nation. He rose from the inefficiencies of the Canadian Militia to beat the British professional soldiers at their own game. His intelligence and his ability to grasp the lessons of trench warfare gave him the tools he needed to master the horrific battlefields of France and Flanders. After the war, he tried to keep the best of his officers in a soundly organized army, but his efforts were largely confounded by politicians, anxious to cut costs and forget the war. In 1920 McGill University made him its principal, a post he filled with distinction until his death.

21

K.C. Irving

BORN: Buctouche, New Brunswick • 14 March 1899

DIED: Saint John, New Brunswick • 13 December 1992

TWO VERY DIFFERENT PEOPLE INHABIT THE LEGACY of New Brunswick's K.C. Irving. The "good" Irving, ambitious but altruistic, was an adept businessman and a creator of thousands of jobs in his home province. The "evil" Irving bullied unions and competitors as he turned New Brunswick into his personal kingdom and its citizens into his subjects. Both Irvings were impossible to ignore.

Kenneth Colin Irving was born on the east coast of New Brunswick when the new century was just months away. His father's forestry holdings ensured that the family was comfortably well off, but Irving early displayed a craving to build his own business. He started selling cars, and, in a move that became the stuff of legend, began in 1924 to compete with the giant Imperial Oil to sell gasoline to a new generation of car owners. Irving Oil Limited rapidly became the departure point for a corporate empire unrivalled in size in Canada.

Irving's success came from vertical integration. Initial profits were directed to the acquisition of more and more businesses that his companies relied on. An oil refinery would supply his service stations; ocean tankers would stock the refinery; a bus line would buy the gas from the stations. It all had an elegant symmetry to it—until New Brunswickers woke up in the 1960s to find that almost every part of the

provincial economy was controlled, if not owned, by K.C. Irving and his family.

And that is precisely where the good Irving versus evil Irving debate began. Good Irving was a committed New Brunswick resident who based his empire in Saint John and resisted the allure of more cosmopolitan addresses. He was loyal to his employees and a generous philanthropist. Good

Irving lived a simple life. He neither smoked nor drank, never flaunted his money, and mostly invested it back into the New Brunswick economy.

At the same time, evil Irving was a ruthless capitalist. His companies either crushed or acquired most competitors. They showed an uncommon willingness to resort to the courts to remove obstacles to their expansion. They were pathologically anti-union. Evil Irving systematically collected almost every major source of information in New Brunswick, including all five English-language daily newspapers. Good coverage was good business, he suggested. He could not understand why the Canadian government sought to restrict his control of the media in the early 1980s, though in the end the government backed down, unwilling to take on the Irving colossus. Evil Irving was also obsessive about avoiding taxes. He escaped to Bermuda in 1971 to dodge Canadian taxes and succession duties, and even made his children's inheritance conditional on their avoiding Canadian residency.

Good or evil, Irving was an old-fashioned capitalist who ran New Brunswick like a game of Monopoly—but it was a game he always seemed to win. When he died in 1992, Irving controlled nearly 300 different companies. He held major interests across the Maritimes and in the northeastern United States. He dominated dozens of industries—everything from oil to communications—in his home province. His personal wealth was almost inconceivable: some estimates put it at $6 billion, which ranked him among the twenty richest people on the planet.

But these numbers, if impressive, cannot begin to reveal the influence of this one man. Simply, K.C. Irving was more than the most important businessman on this list. For New Brunswickers in the second half of this century, Irving was, and remains, a way of life.

22

Harold Innis

BORN: Otterville, Ontario • 5 November 1894

DIED: Toronto, Ontario • 8 November 1952

GROWING UP ON HIS PARENTS' SMALL DAIRY FARM
near Woodstock, Ontario, Harold Innis trapped
muskrats each winter. Checking his steel traps every
morning before he made his way to school in town,
he skinned the animals, stretched out their hides on
special frames, and eventually sold each pelt for, at
best, twenty-five cents. The genesis of his great work,
The Fur Trade in Canada, lay in his own experience.

The farm boy grew into the able student who
went to McMaster University, then in Toronto, and
graduated into the midst of the Great War. Patriotic,
he enlisted in the artillery and served in France.
Wounded severely in the leg at Vimy Ridge in 1917,
he had a year-long recuperation, but used his time
to secure an MA degree from McMaster. He went to
Chicago for doctoral work and although he was not
happy with the way Americans bragged they had
won the war, he married Mary Quayle, an Ohio-born
student. In 1920, PhD fresh in hand, Innis returned
to Canada and the political economy department at
the University of Toronto, where he spent his entire
academic career.

His book on the fur trade, published when he
was only thirty-six, advanced a new hypothesis and
revolutionized the study of Canadian economic
history, hitherto a neglected field. The book, full
of detail on beaver, otter, and muskrat, traced the

development of the fur trade, Canada's first staple industry, from its origins, and considered the huge impact of that staple on Canada. To Innis, Canada had not been created in defiance of geography. Indeed, the water system formed by the St Lawrence River and the Great Lakes provided a natural highway to the fur country of the interior, and this water route had been used by French and English alike to exploit the interior and to carry the furs back to the metropolitan centres of Europe, where the profits were realized.

Thus Canada was no artificial creation; it sprang full blown from geography and trade, a natural community,

geographically distinct, and linked to Europe from its
beginnings. "The present Dominion of Canada," he said,
"emerged not in spite of geography but because of it." In
effect, Innis was arguing a nationalist case. As important,
he demonstrated that the export of staples—furs, fish,
lumber, wheat—had a huge impact on the economic, social,
and political systems of Canada, one that locked the country
into dependency on the metropolises that exploited it for its
resources. Innis' Staple Thesis became the foundation of the
Canadian school of political economy and the first major
Canadian contribution to international scholarship.

Innis moved on to the study of communications. His early
works, including his PhD dissertation on the Canadian Pacific
Railway and a book on the cod fishery, had been concerned
with the trade routes that were also the instruments of communication; his later studies looked at theoretical questions.
Empire and Communications ranged far beyond Canada, far
beyond political economy in an attempt to comprehend
the impact that methods of communication had and have on
civilization. Yet he always wrote in unusually impenetrable
prose—Innis, said historian Charles Stacey, was an expert on
communications "who was quite unable to communicate."

His scholarly achievements were immense, justifying the
suggestion that Innis was simultaneously Canada's first intellectual and the first Canadian scholar to have a global reach.
His influence was also profound on the university, which he
believed was and had to remain a place of free inquiry.
Although he served on a few royal commissions himself, he
tended to be scornful of those academics who were eager to
serve governments at every opportunity. Scholars should
teach and research, not be policy-makers, Innis believed.
He jeered at his CCF colleagues who propounded socialism
without knowing much about the problems they proposed

to treat. Yet when Frank Underhill of Toronto's history department was about to be fired for some comments he had made early in the Second World War, Innis rallied to his defence. Academic freedom, the university as a forum of ideas—those were real concepts to Innis. As his friend and disciple Donald Creighton wrote, while Innis "believed that a university could best discharge its high functions by a careful maintenance of its separateness and its autonomy," he could be fierce in his defence of academe against the ignorant attacks of outsiders.

Rumpled, tall, dishevelled, his hands stained with nicotine, Innis loved to talk, to jibe and gossip, to help his students and colleagues. He was Canada's pre-eminent social scientist, one of those rare men of original insight. If his work on Canada's natural east-west links has largely been brushed aside by continentalist economics and free trade, it is despite Innis' dour warnings.

23

Peter Gzowski

BORN: Toronto, Ontario • 13 July 1934

"So what's the weather doing up in Yellowknife this morning?" It's an easy question but a typical one, posed by a man who earned his living asking them. Judging from the success of his radio program, more than a few Canadians wanted to hear the answer. Weekday mornings, Peter Gzowski's

Morningside was compulsory listening for over a million loyal fans until his last broadcast in the spring of 1997.

Unravelling the influence of this writer-turned-broadcaster begins with this program—which was actually less a radio show and more a national conversation. Every morning, whether the chat was about politics with Dalton Camp, writing with Margaret Atwood, or the big issue of the day in a northern village with an absolute unknown, it was all about being Canadian. "I consider myself a writer," Gzowski said. "And my beat is Canada."

However you describe it, the CBC's *Morningside* was the most important radio program in Canadian history. It's hard to exaggerate its influence: for fifteen years after 1982, when Gzowski took over as host, the daily mix of interviews and discussion came to define Canadian life. More than a dozen producers micro-managed the flow, but it all seemed relaxed and unrehearsed because of Gzowski himself.

In hindsight, his career as a newspaper and magazine journalist was perfect training for becoming Peter Gzowski. He grew up in Ontario small towns in privileged circumstances, but it seemed clear from the beginning that Gzowski was going to be a writer. The University of Toronto was a place to practise the craft, but he never stayed interested enough in classes to finish a degree. Instead, he worked as a reporter at any newspaper that would take him: in Kapuskasing for a spell, then out to Moose Jaw.

In 1958 he landed back in Toronto with a job at *Maclean's*. He rose rapidly through the ranks and, in a hothouse writing environment with a host of other talents, did some of his finest work. The twice-monthly newsmagazine was just beginning to discover its Canadianness; on subjects like Quebec, hockey, and the north, so was Gzowski.

In 1969 he left full-time print journalism for a job at

CBC radio. On the airwaves Gzowski was a hit from the beginning: he had a sincere passion for the country, but was enough of a journalist to ask the right questions of his guests. His first regular show, *This Country in the Morning*, was immediately popular.

For Canadians in any field of endeavour, *Morningside* soon emerged as the national forum of record. Prime ministers, heroes, the mighty and the fallen were all interviewed by Gzowski. His favourites—the regulars—became famous in their own right.

Somehow, the show stayed intimate, the smoky-voiced host the person Canadians turned to. Whether celebrating the success of one of our own, marking the change of seasons, or mourning the death of someone we all missed, Gzowski did as much as anyone for twenty-five years to make Canada a community.

24

Ivan Rand

BORN: Moncton, New Brunswick • 27 April 1884

DIED: London, Ontario • 2 January 1969

It was a rare defining moment in Canadian history. The year was 1945, the place was Windsor, Ontario, and a protracted strike at the Ford Motor Company symbolized all the rancorous divisions between management and unions in postwar Canada. Many issues stood in the way of a settlement, but only one really mattered: Would the company recognize the right of the union to represent all workers at the plant? Both sides were unwavering: with the enthusiastic assistance of the Ontario government, Ford wanted to keep the powerful United Auto Workers from achieving gains for workers in its Canadian operation; the workers, fresh from patriotic exertions during the war, wanted what they saw as their due. The country watched and held its breath—so much seemed on the line. As weeks dragged into months, a succession of politicians and mediators failed to find a compromise.

Then, into the spotlight stepped Ivan Rand. The Supreme Court judge was appointed to arbitrate the dispute, and both sides reluctantly agreed to be bound by any terms he imposed. Rand weighed the issues, interviewed management and labour, and in late January 1946 made his decision. Though he called his settlement a compromise, Rand's judgment, approved by both sides, was a major milestone for Canadian labour: the judge refused to make union membership mandatory for Ford workers, but did impose union dues—the so-called automatic checkoff—on all employees, reasoning that even non-members would benefit from union bargaining. The Rand Formula, as it became known, guaranteed both the union's existence at Ford and its financial security. In an uncertain postwar world, the Ford agreement became the model for other Canadian labour negotiations, and the Rand Formula became an article of faith among working people.

For Rand, it was a daring, creative solution to what had seemed an unresolvable impasse. But then, finding such solutions was what Rand did for a living. He was born in New Brunswick and turned to law only after attempting a career as an engineer. An outstanding student at Harvard, he practised law in Saskatchewan and Alberta before returning to New Brunswick, where he served briefly as attorney-general in 1925–26. Rand happily left politics, however, for a successful career as counsel for Canadian National Railways. As a longtime corporate lawyer, he was a surprise choice for the Supreme Court in 1943.

Rand made his name in Windsor in 1946, but his work on the bench was also highly influential. These were defining years for the court, since the termination of appeals to the British Judicial Committee meant that, from 1949, the Canadian court was truly supreme at last. Unlike many of his fellow judges, Rand saw the new era as a chance to Canadianize the nation's law, and he delivered pioneering judgments that endure as legal landmarks. His greatest passion was civil rights cases: decisions in the 1950s on the infamous Quebec padlock law and the treatment of Japanese Canadians during the war created for the first time an implied bill of rights in Canadian jurisprudence. The notion that governments possessed unlimited authority to trample individual rights in Canada was put to rest by Rand, long before the much-hyped Charter of Rights professed to do the same.

Rand retired from the Supreme Court in 1959, though he continued to be a much-sought-after legal fixer. He was the founding dean of the law school at the University of Western Ontario, and was often appointed by governments to investigate particularly vexing problems. As more and more companies adopted the Rand Formula in Canada, and international unions took approving notice of it, his reputation was without parallel. It was eminence that was richly deserved: Rand was a creative, progressive problem-solver whose impact on his country was lasting and profound.

25

Barbara Frum

BORN: Niagara Falls, Ontario • 8 September 1937

DIED: Toronto, Ontario • 26 March 1992

"TV VIEWERS DON'T LIKE CHANGE," BARBARA Frum wrote in *Saturday Night* in a 1967 column. "The situation comedies, the quizzes, the panel shows...only have to hook firmly on to an audience to keep it. As in marriage, it's the first year that's critical; if a show can scrape through that one season, it's likely to survive...On television, it would seem, familiarity breeds no contempt." Written well before she became a regular part of the evening for CBC radio and TV audiences, those dismissive words were cutting. Yet there was truth in them—when Canadians came to know Barbara Frum, or to think they knew her because she talked for them to the great and near-great, their familiarity with her bred not contempt but growing admiration.

Her parents were from Niagara Falls, the Ontario honeymoon capital. The Rosbergs owned the largest department store, they lived well, and they were Jews, all unusual characteristrics in small-town Ontario. Born with a damaged shoulder, thanks to a clumsy forceps-wielding doctor, Barbara was raised to be independent and to achieve. Intelligent and attractive, she attended the University of Toronto and, when she was nineteen, married Murray Frum, a dentist and later very successful property developer.

Initially content to be a homemaker, Frum began to freelance as a journalist for Toronto newspapers,

Chatelaine and *Maclean's*. She made her way into television in 1967, then in 1971 became the host of *As It Happens*, the CBC's nationally broadcast radio phone-out show that pioneered the intrusive interview and, for ninety minutes a night, became a national institution. Politicians and strikers, the important and the silly—all were grist for the mill. When the British ambassador in Iceland was besieged by stone-throwing protesters, for example, Barbara was there, haranguing the poor man to talk to her before he could report to the Foreign Office. A thousand interviews a year sharpened her technique, and her silky voice hypnotized interviewees and listeners alike. "Use as few words as possible to ask your questions," she described her style, "then get out of the way."

By 1982, when CBC television was remaking its national

evening news, Frum was the natural choice to become the host of *The Journal*, the forty-minute interview and feature portion of the hour. She shone immediately. Her transparent compassion, honesty, and warmth grabbed viewers, as did her unobtrusive but comprehensive research and her tough, sometimes aggressive questioning as she pursued the truth— whatever she believed it to be. A woman with her own views, her own hates and likes, occasionally those opinions showed through. A fierce Canadian nationalist and a believer in a bicultural country, she became very partisan during the Meech Lake debacle, her efforts to save the country some- times turning into open support for the federal government's position. Her interview with Prime Minister Mulroney after Meech was viewed by many as near-pandering, and her hostility off-air to those who opposed the Free Trade Agreement in 1988 was sometimes withering. From other interviewers, such positions would not have been tolerated, but Canadians were very indulgent of Barbara Frum. Indeed, they admired her rare instances of partisanship, and when British prime minister Margaret Thatcher savaged her and rebuffed her questions in one interview, they cursed the Iron Lady for *lèse-majesté* and her snooty imperial ways.

Diagnosed with leukemia in 1974, Frum laboured in the certainty of her death. Carefully keeping her illness secret, for a time even from her children, Frum continued to push herself in her work. Her compassion for others with whom she worked at the CBC and for her friends was legendary, and the image she projected on screen was genuine. Her family wealth, high salary, chauffeured limousine, and clothes allowance from the CBC were all her due, but somehow they did not spoil her or separate her from the ordinary Canadians who called her, familiarly, Barbara, and for whom she *was* the CBC.

26

Alphonse Desjardins

BORN: Lévis, Canada East • 5 November 1854
DIED: Lévis, Quebec • 31 October 1920

Ordinary men sometimes do great things, creating institutions that shape and alter the destinies of people and nations. Alphonse Desjardins, scarcely remembered today, was one such ordinary man.

The originator of the *caisses populaires* had a useful but undistinguished career until he was in his mid-forties. A militiaman during the Riel Rebellion of 1870, then a journalist, he eventually became the private publisher of the debates of the Quebec legislature, a task he undertook as a strictly commercial venture from 1879 until 1890. He tried his best to make the parliamentary record as full and fair as he could, but he was often subject to pressures to change and amend the remarks of the provincial parliamentarians. Ottawa was more welcoming, and he became the official reporter of the House of Commons Hansard from 1890 until 1917.

Good as he was at his often stultifying job, Desjardins' real interests lay elsewhere. He worried over French Canadians' subordinate status in Canada and the flood of emigrants to the cotton mills of New England, something he attributed to the dominance of English-speaking corporations and businessmen, to usurious interest rates, and also to the lack of capital to support small Quebec entrepreneurs. Where could the money be found?

Desjardins found the answer in European

cooperatives, long a subject of interest to him. If he could create a credit cooperative in Quebec, if he could mobilize the tiny savings of thousands of individuals, then enough money could be harnessed to increase the power of all. The *caisses populaires* he envisaged would be true cooperative associations: one vote per member, cast in person at general membership meetings, but as many shares as each wished; only members allowed to make deposits; a reserve fund; directors forbidden to borrow from the association; small loans preferred and fixed maximum loans; interest rates set by the association; and the association strictly limited to savings-and-loan operations. As he said in 1907, "It is not merely cheap and facile credit which is required," but "the act and effort of obtaining it shall educate, discipline and guide the borrower."

With the enthusiastic support and participation of local parish priests and many bishops, Desjardins' scheme, begun in his home town in 1900 with a first deposit of ten cents and reserve capital of $26, began to spread through Quebec. In 1906, after his vigorous lobbying, the legislature passed the Cooperative Syndicates Act that sanctioned and regulated the *caisses*, and the movement, freed of the obligation that the sponsor of each *caisse* assume the whole risk on his own, grew rapidly. There was opposition from banks and businesses frightened of competition, but Desjardins and his friends produced a "catechism" for the *caisse populaires*, and his pamphlet's straightforward answers and instructions helped spread the cooperative gospel. As numbers grew, Desjardins realized that the strength of the *caisses* could only be realized if they came together in federations, and his last years were devoted to this cause.

The financial system begun by Alphonse Desjardins was a huge success. Taking a foreign model and adapting it to

local conditions, he created an agent of change. By 1929
Le Mouvement Desjardins, as it became known, had 1,788
caisses in Quebec (and more in Ontario and the northeast
United States) with 45,000 members and assets of $11 million.
Two decades later, assets were $225 million, and by 1995,
the *caisses populaires* in Quebec controlled $55.7 billion. The
federations, grouped together in a huge confederation, today
operate much like any large bank and provide services to the
local *caisses*. Moreover, they own insurance and trust companies, and they operate mutual funds, money management
services, and an industrial and commercial lending company.
Desjardins had created an enormous engine of growth, one
that sped the industrialization of Quebec and fostered the
idea that Québécois could be masters of their own destinies.

Alphonse Desjardins is not usually thought of as one of
the creators of the Quiet Revolution of the 1960s or the great
indépendantiste upsurge that had been so powerful in recent
Quebec. But in his quiet fostering of cooperative ideas, in his
mobilizing the savings of millions, he laid the groundwork
for Quebec independence, and his heirs have actively
pursued political and financial sovereignty.

27

Robert White

In his autobiography, Bob White tells one of his father's stories of the day four-year-old Bob went to school for the first time with his eight-year-old brother. "Don't worry about Bill," the story has Bob saying. "If anyone tries anything, I'll take care of him." Apocryphal no doubt, a story lovingly burnished by memory but probably true in its essentials. Tough, smart, combative, Bob White was always ready to take on anyone and everything.

Born into relative poverty to a Northern Irish Protestant family, White came to Canada with his parents in 1949. Settling into squalid rural accommodation near Woodstock, Ontario, the Whites worked hard for little money and, after the father was injured and could no longer handle hard labour in the fields, they lived in town. White quickly left school and at fifteen began to work on the production line in a local woodworking factory. Soon he was a union militant, and his rise through labour's ranks was meteoric. By 1959 he was president of a United Auto Workers local, and the next year he went to full-time organizing work, then to coordinator of organization, to assistant to the UAW director for Canada, and, in 1978, to director for Canada. In the hidebound union movement, already entering a period of slow decay, White was a breath of militancy and vigour.

There was more to come. A typical "international"

union, the UAW was run out of Detroit and responded to the needs of its American workers first. Canadians came a long way second, and White, already heavily involved with the New Democratic Party and caught up in the 1970s nationalist currents in Canada, was unhappy. As Canadian director, he began to press for both a "no concessions" policy to management and for more autonomy for his 120,000 workers. Stonewalled, he became increasingly restive: he and his locals were for striking, while the international leadership favoured accommodation. "They don't understand," he said to one aide. "It still hasn't penetrated that we're not another state in the United States, we're a different country." In 1984,

frustrated beyond endurance, he broke completely with the UAW and the next year became the first president of the independent Canadian Auto Workers. This was a revolutionary act for the union movement and, bolstered by victories in his new union's first negotiations with Chrysler, White quickly began to expand the CAW's reach into other sectors, including East Coast fisheries. The Canadian Labour Congress members were not happy, but such was White's charismatic appeal that he became CLC president in 1992.

He was the right man for the job. Unlike almost every other labour leader, the young-looking White had a firm grasp of public relations. In 1986, when the Canadian Broadcasting Corporation televised "Final Offer," a flattering TV program based on White's bargaining techniques, viewers were fascinated and titillated with the array of curses that showed the sheer animal drive of its protagonist. The next year he published a successful autobiography. Inevitably, White was the leader in every labour protest against the Mulroney government, and the centre of the failed Pro-Canada Network campaign against the Free Trade Agreement from 1985 to 1988.

Although White was a vice-president of the New Democratic Party and the initiator of "job canvassing," a system that encouraged workers to support NDP candidates, he was no tame supporter. He criticized the party's "disintegration" in opposing the FTA, a time that ought to "have been the New Democratic Party's finest hour." After Bob Rae's NDP took power in Ontario, a furious White led the labour movement's opposition to the government's "social contract." White's union had been a key supporter in winning the cerebral Rae the provincial party leadership and power, but now his efforts, as much as anyone's, drove the government from office. A social-democratic party was supposed to back the workers; if it didn't, if it acted first in the interests of bondholders, it merited nothing but contempt.

White tells a story of his Ulster youth: "One day I saw a rainbow so vivid that I thought it surely must have a pot of gold at its end." The rainbow disappeared behind a hill, so White climbed up, only to discover that it appeared to end beyond the next rise. "It was a while before I gave up thinking I'd find that pot of gold." The workers' pot of gold may always lie over the next hill, in Canada as in Northern Ireland, but if any labour leader has a chance of reaching it, Bob White will be the one.

Peter Newman

BORN: Vienna, Austria • 10 May 1929

THE FLAME OF POWER HAS ALWAYS BURNED BRIGHTLY in Peter C. Newman's eyes. As a journalist and popular historian, economic and political power fascinates him. His talents are such that he can get close enough to his subjects to plumb their depths—and wade all over them in the shallows. Establishments in government and business are his metier, and he has made them understandable to Canadians.

Born to a family of wealthy Czech-Jewish industrialists who lived near the Austrian border, Newman's privileged youth (six maids, a gardener, and a chauffeur) ended when the Nazis swallowed his country in 1939. Good fortune and wealth helped them escape Europe ahead of Hitler's armies and, refused entry to the United States, the Newmans came to Canada—as farmers. His father sent the shy fifteen-year-old Peter to Toronto's Upper Canada College where, discriminated against because of his accent and his religion, Newman did not flourish. But he Canadianized his accent, graduated, and went off to the University of Toronto, where he anglicized his name from Neuman. University, too, was not a notable success—except that he joined the "Untidies," the University Naval Training Division, and formed a lifelong devotion to sailing and the navy.

But it was writing that captured his attention. He found work on *The Varsity*, the student paper,

and then for five years at the *Financial Post*, the country's leading business paper. His work on business fed his fascination with the men who made the economy hum and led to his first book, *Flame of Power,* which became a bestseller. By 1959, when he was sent to Ottawa by *Maclean's,* Newman was ready to make his mark on political reportage.

The time was ripe. Journalists were still open political partisans in those days, serving the interests of their masters more often than those of the public. Newman was different. He cultivated the politicians but also the executive assistants, and he knew how to do an interview, extracting the hard news and the quirky stories that gave a story texture. The Diefenbaker government was in power with a huge majority, but the cracks were starting to show in the economy, in defence and foreign policy, and in the psyche of the prime minister. Newman had found his subject.

Renegade in Power, his devastating account of the rise and fall of John Diefenbaker and his Conservative government, forever changed political journalism in Canada when it appeared in the autumn of 1963. Here was inside information and hard judgment, political shrewdness and sparkling prose. Canadian politics, to the surprise of most readers, was just as exciting as American. The Tories fumed (to Dief, Newman was ever after "the bouncing Czech"), but the public ate it up, as his immense sales showed, just as it did his subsequent book on the Pearson government.

By 1969 Newman was editor-in-chief of the *Toronto Star*, and he turned that newspaper into the flagship of Canadian nationalism. He was a founder of the Committee for an Independent Canada, a lobby group that formed around the economic nationalism espoused by Walter Gordon. And when he went to *Maclean's* as editor in 1971, he continued to wear his nationalism on his sleeve. Under his lead, the magazine went from a monthly to a weekly, offering a current Canadian slant on the world and the nation.

Still he continued to write books, once again turning to business leaders, where his journalistic adaption of *cinéma verité* continued to work. What he did, he said, was to record his subjects "with the objectivity of a handheld camera, recording them as they are." The Bronfmans, the Canadian Establishment, Conrad Black, and the Hudson's Bay

Company were all subjects that he popularized, and his book sales and publication advances continued to lead the pack. Newman was a staple of the book trade, the author sure to be found in every home where books went unread. But it was not all hosannas. Academic historians ordinarily disliked his work, resenting his popularizations of their subjects, frowning over his perfervid purple passages. Unfazed, Newman gave as good as he got: if he didn't write popular history, Canadians would be forced to get it from Walt Disney. Take that, you professional historians. In one memorable exchange in the *Canadian Historical Review* that left his opponent battered, Newman suggested that history was too important to be left to the historians, and he blasted the academics for their boring pedantry and for forgetting that history was ultimately about stories. "I'm not dull," he told a columnist, "and I intentionally use the techniques of fiction to make history interesting." Those techniques did not make for sound history, but he was precisely right in his strictures on the professors.

Now approaching seventy, Newman still writes a weekly column for *Maclean's* in the early morning hours on his battered typewriter, with his earphones blaring Stan Kenton at him. With his fourth wife, he sails the West Coast, the very model of the active man of leisure. Heaped with honorary doctorates and awards, all carefully detailed in *Who's Who*, Peter Newman made it big in his adopted country as the chronicler of the Establishment and, most important, as the man who pulled Canadian political journalism into the twentieth century.

29

Maurice Duplessis

BORN: Trois-Rivières, Quebec • 20 April 1890

DIED: Schefferville, Quebec • 7 September 1959

HIS CHAUFFEUR WAS SURPRISED. IT WAS A WINTER afternoon in 1938 and Maurice Duplessis suddenly wanted to stop in front of a well-known Liberal club in Quebec City. The premier of Quebec was many things to many people, but never a Liberal. The car halted. Duplessis rushed in, hurried past the stunned members, and urinated in the fireplace. Then he departed.

This was obviously a deeply symbolic act, one that said much about the premier. He was intensely partisan, irredeemably petty, and habitually crude. The episode also demonstrated that for Duplessis, politics was life. That he got away with it also showed just how unchallenged this one disagreeable man's hold on power was in his home province.

For almost twenty years Duplessis was the government of Quebec, personally embodying the state more than anyone else ever had before or since. He was born the son of an unimportant Conservative politician, but as a young man from a small town he learned quickly that all politics is local. Conservatives were an endangered species in Quebec in the post–First World War era, but careful attention to the wants of the electors of Trois-Rivières gained him a seat in the provincial assembly in 1927. When Duplessis was elected leader of the party in 1933, the job was not much of a prize: the Conservatives had been out of office for thirty-six years, and immediate prospects were not promising. But the new leader quickly assumed total control of party strategy, and in 1935 he engineered a merger with reformist Liberals to make a new coalition, the Union Nationale. Duplessis made absolute loyalty to him the crucial prerequisite for membership in the alliance, and in 1936 the new party scored an upset victory over a scandal-ridden Liberal government. The Duplessis era had begun.

For Quebec, it was an era of stability and growth—yet also an era of democratic dictatorship. Except for a brief interval during the Second World War, Duplessis would rule Quebec until the day he died. For every one of those days, his eyes were fixed firmly on the past. That meant that Duplessis allowed American big business to dominate the province's economy, especially in the natural resources sector. It meant that the Catholic Church controlled Quebec's education and social services. And it meant that the Quebec government assumed a defensive, nationalist posture towards the rest of Canada: aiming for autonomy, but not separation.

But it was also the way Duplessis resisted change that made him so important. With the support of the church and big business, he organized the state as he had organized the Union Nationale: all decisions were made by him. From civil servants, Cabinet ministers, ordinary members, he demanded absolute loyalty. By developing and controlling a sophisticated patronage system so that only party supporters received government contracts, he almost always obtained what he wanted. Kickbacks were funnelled into the party's accounts, and Duplessis built up the Union Nationale into a formidable election-time force. Critics charged he was anti-democratic, and he was: ballot-box stuffing and voter intimidation were election tactics that Duplessis perfected. The cheating notwithstanding, most Quebeckers continued to support him at the polls, content, it seemed, with his traditional, inward-looking nationalist platform.

At the same time, dissidents were treated with brutal contempt, and Duplessis was personally responsible for some of the most notorious human rights abuses in Canadian history. Unions, communists, and Jehovah's Witnesses were the most famous targets. Bitter strikes in the late 1940s and 1950s at Asbestos, Louiseville, and Murdochville not only showed how out of date the traditional, anti-labour approach of the government was but initiated reform impulses that would eventually topple the regime after Duplessis died in 1959.

What did Duplessis mean for future generations? The Liberal Party was elected in 1960, defeating a government that had depended so much on one man. The Quiet Revolution started that year to reform Quebec politics and

society with lightning speed. In the turbulence, a new
Quebec nationalism—aggressive, defiant, and ultimately
separatist—took hold. Within a decade, Duplessis' one-man,
Catholic state had practically disappeared. In an important
way, however, Duplessis established the agenda for Quebec
politics for decades. His oppressive regime bottled up the
modernization impulses that spilled over in the 1960s, a
decade that would be crucial for setting the terms of the
Canada-Quebec debate. Key figures like Trudeau and
Lévesque launched public careers in response to Duplessis'
Quebec. In short, Duplessis' shadow represented clearly
and forcefully the old order, the kind of province that was
no longer wanted. What ought to replace Duplessis' Quebec,
though, is something Quebeckers have yet to agree upon.

30

Emily Carr

BORN: Victoria, British Columbia • 13 December 1871

DIED: Victoria, British Columbia • 2 March 1945

"CANADIANS," WRITER GRAHAM MACINNES SAID, "are not addicts of dancing and light wines, but of hockey and rye whisky." Emily Carr liked neither light wines, dancing, rye, nor hockey, but her bold paintings, shocking in their use of colour and in their subject matter, proved the truth of MacInnes' adage. Her fellow citizens rejected Carr, trashing her work with their hostility, humiliating her with their scorn for art that did not replicate traditional English land-scapes. Fifty years later, they'd have killed for one of her paintings.

Carr's father was English, an adventurer who had headed for the California gold rush but ended up in placid Victoria presiding over a household of nine children on his ten acres of Beacon Hill. After the early deaths of their parents, Carr's sisters were unsympathetic to the free spirit in their midst, but Emily escaped to art school in San Francisco in her late teens. There followed further schooling in London, a physical and mental breakdown that confined her to a sanitarium for a long period, and then more training in France. Her French paintings drew only scorn from her sisters and from "critics" in British Columbia, and those of her works that sold brought a derisory $5. The decisive influence on her art, however, was not her formal schooling but her trips to Ucluelet on northern Vancouver Island, to

Alaska, to the Queen Charlottes and the Skeena country.
The unselfconsciousness of the Indians fascinated her, and
she set herself the task of recording their history before the
great totem poles rotted away. The Indians befriended her,
and many ended up with her paintings and sketches in their
homes, the art that was unsaleable anywhere in Canada.
The ethnographer Marius Barbeau saw the art there, sought
out Carr in the small boarding house she ran in Victoria,
and drew her work to the attention of the National Gallery
in Ottawa.

It was a long time before recognition arrived, however. Turning her back on her art for fifteen unhappy years, Carr dealt with her tenants, raised Old English bobtail sheepdogs, forty at a time, and sold pottery to the tourist market to support herself. But in 1927, when she was already in her late fifties, her art, displayed in Ottawa, at last drew some positive notice in central Canada. She was bolstered by this attention, and she recovered her old enthusiasm from the interest of the Group of Seven in her work. Lawren Harris, especially, encouraged her to move away from Indian themes towards the British Columbia landscape. Still, there was little local acclaim for her—the burghers of Victoria scorned the fat old lady pushing a baby carriage full of her pet animals, and her art went unadmired—and into the 1940s her canvases could be purchased for as little as $25. Her first commercial exhibition, in Montreal, did not take place until the year before her death.

Nonetheless, each summer after her return from Ottawa and Toronto, Carr headed into the primeval forests in her tiny caravan to paint. She set up her studio, covered by a tarpaulin, in the woods. Accompanied by her pet monkey Woo and her ever-present parrot, her head covered in a cap, she painted with prodigious energy. Her canvases, full of towering firs, were painted in aggressive swirls of bright colour. When age and heart trouble stopped most of her painting trips, she turned to writing. Her autobiographical accounts of her encounters with natives and of her life in Victoria and Britain won her, perhaps, more renown than her painting, including a 1941 Governor General's Award for *Klee Wyck*, her first book. Klee Wyck, or "Laughing One," was her Indian name. No sobriquet was ever less appropriate for a sharp-tongued, difficult woman who burned with resentment at her rejection by stuffy Canadians, though she and her Indian friends, frequently baffled by their futile attempts to communicate across the language barrier, frequently fell into helpless giggling.

Today, Emily Carr's paintings are so high priced that only the rich can buy them. Her paintings of the British Columbia forest and coast, her studies of decaying Indian villages, still speak powerfully to Canadians who hanker after the wilderness in their souls. "She was not primarily interpreting Canada to the world," one writer said. "She was interpreting herself to herself by the symbols which the forest provided." As Emily Carr herself put it, "I was convinced that the old way of seeing was inadequate to express this big country of ours, her depth, her height, her unbounded wideness, silences too strong to be broken." She found the new way and, in the process, preserved a Canada that was fast disappearing for her compatriots.

31

Jack McClelland

IN THE SPRING OF 1960 THE TRADE PAPER *QUILL &* *Quire* surveyed the prospects for book publishing in Canada and reported the results with barely contained pessimism. Foreign titles dominated the Canadian market, and few experts who were polled saw much hope for home-grown authors. "What about the future?" the magazine queried. "With the exception of Jack McClelland, the general thought seemed to be that nothing could be done to improve the situation, indeed the market would remain static for years to come."

In the ever-cautious world of Canadian publishing, Jack McClelland was exceptional then and it seems certain he always will be. In the 1960s only he thought a buck could be made selling Canadian books to Canadians. And even when it became painfully clear that it was much easier to lose money on Canadian authors than to make it, only McClelland believed he ought to keep trying.

Canadians who today brag about the reputation their leading writers enjoy around the world often forget that, a generation ago, nobody anywhere was reading much from the Great White North. When McClelland was named president of McClelland & Stewart in 1961, taking over the company his father founded half a century before, he deliberately set out to find Canadian writers. Once he found them, he set out to sell them.

How he did it was a big part of his success. McClelland was an unlikely man of letters: by his own admission, he was a chain-smoking, hard-drinking veteran of the Second World War. One reporter was astonished when McClelland "cursed liked a sailor." But underneath it all was a salesman—doubtless the most important attribute in a publisher—and a passionate commitment to bring attention to what he viewed as quality Canadian literature. The stories are the stuff of legend: McClelland parading through the streets in a toga, or

McClelland dressing his drivers in tuxedos for a book delivery. The flash always gained his books attention, though the publisher firmly believed they should sell on their own merit.

Of course, he was right probably more than he knew: a few decades later, the authors he found are the who's who of CanLit. Margaret Atwood, Peter Newman, Mordecai Richler, and Irving Layton are just the best-known writers who published with M&S early in their careers.

By 1971 McClelland had been midwife to the birth of a new Canadian cultural industry; the problem was that the baby faced an uncertain future. Fed up with continued bottom-line losses, M&S announced it was up for sale. Word on the street was that American interests were ready to snap up the firm. The public outcry against the proposed sale was deafening, and the Ontario government had little choice but to bail the publisher out with a cheque for $1 million. Canadian books had become important in Canada.

McClelland & Stewart remained in Canadian hands, and though Jack McClelland sold his stake in the firm in 1985— to a Canadian—it continues to be the pre-eminent publishing house for domestic writers in both fiction and non-fiction.

Fifty years after McClelland entered the business, book publishing in Canada remains uniquely perched on the slippery abyss, forever balanced precariously between financial calamity and the belief that Canadian books are one cultural product we cannot do without. If the industry has not yet tumbled over the cliffs, Jack McClelland, more than anyone else, can take the credit.

32

Terry Fox

BORN: Winnipeg, Manitoba • 28 July 1958
DIED: New Westminster, British Columbia • 28 June 1981

THE HEADLINES AND THE PICTURES FROM THE
sweltering summer of 1980 recall a story of heroism
and hope. There is Terry Fox, a sunny-faced British
Columbia kid, his pained grimace staring out of a
couple of small newspaper pictures. He is literally
hobbling his way across Canada. He lost a leg to
cancer, and now, with the headstrong idealism that
only a twenty-one year old can muster, he decides
to do something about it.

Nobody cares much at first; initially, stories in the
newspapers about him are tough to find. It seems that
in the spring of 1980 cancer is nothing new, and Fox's
idea of running across Canada to raise money to fight
the disease receives only grudging support from the
Canadian Cancer Society. He heads for the eastern-
most tip of Newfoundland anyway and starts a
gruelling regimen of lonely miles. A friend driving a
van loaded with supplies is usually his only company.

It seems certain that the national news media will
"discover" Terry Fox eventually. They do when he
hits Ontario. The headlines grow more frequent, and
more and more people want to line his route to see
the man with one artificial leg and one "good" leg.
These are hot days, and this is hard work: he's always
sweating in the photographs. Surprisingly, the media
does not tire of the feel-good story and, as Fox nears
Toronto, his "Marathon of Hope" has captured the

country. Thousands of dollars are pouring in for cancer research—hundreds of these are squeezed into his hands by spectators who seem overwhelmed at the sight of him. When tens of thousands triumphantly greet Terry Fox at Toronto's City Hall, it is the lead story around the nation. A new Canadian hero has been born.

Only a handful of weeks later, a blizzard of headlines piles up again. It is August, and near Thunder Bay the summer's happiest story has turned tragic. Terry Fox is sick; doctors suspect the worst. Pictures of his worried parents taking him home to British Columbia are impossibly moving. Fox vows to return to continue the run, and millions hold their breath.

But the news is all bad: Terry Fox is dying. Nobody is

giving up hope, of course—the doctors quoted in the papers argue that if anyone can beat this wretched disease, it is Fox. "I think it's unfair. Very unfair," is all his grieving father can manage.

In the end even Terry Fox cannot win this race. Early the next summer, he dies. He is not quite twenty-three years old. Canadians from the four corners of the land weep openly. Memorials are planned, and millions continue to flow into his cancer research fund. By the time he dies, $24 million has been raised.

This money, and the money that continued to flow to fight the cancer that killed him, made sure that Terry Fox's life changed the lives of thousands of others. The annual runs held in his name in Canada and in foreign capitals around the world every September continue to grow in popularity. His legacy as the most prominent disabled athlete of his era pushed the limits of the possible for differently abled people everywhere.

These were impressive achievements for a short life; enough to earn him a ranking among the most influential of his contemporaries. But for Canadians, Terry Fox goes deeper than that. He was more than the phenomenal fundraiser, and more even than the larger-than-life hero who briefly, brightly, flashed across our collective consciousness. Fox struck a chord not for what he did but for who he was. He was the high school athlete who never emotionally recovered from losing his leg. He was the university student who could not be persuaded to give up an impossible dream. Most of all, he was someone whose dream involved conquering the Canadian landscape—the massive, forbidding stretch of territory that somehow, against the odds, unites and is part of us. He did unite us: awkwardly, fleetingly, symbolically, Fox summed up who Canadians really wanted to be.

33

Tom Patterson

"EVERYONE WAS SO ENCOURAGING ABOUT THE project," Tom Patterson recalled, because "they did not think it would happen." The project was the Stratford Shakespearean Festival, and in 1951 Canada, culture was something that existed elsewhere, and certainly not in southwestern Ontario.

Patterson was a product of the Stratford gentry, a short, balding young man who had gone off to the war and served in the Canadian Dental Corps as a sergeant for five years. His brother had been killed in action and his father had died while he was overseas, but he himself emerged unscathed. After the war, he went to university and found a job on a Maclean-Hunter trade journal, *Civic Administration*, where he was the resident expert on sewage plants.

The idea of capitalizing on his home town's name, on its Avon River and its superb park system had occurred to Patterson before the war—as a way of countering the Depression's unemployment. He had raised it again in 1946, and once more in 1951, and it was third time lucky. The mayor was supportive: "I don't know anything about Shakespeare...But if it's good for Stratford, then I'm all for it." Persuasive, enthusiastic, a natural salesman, Patterson fostered interest in the town, talked to theatre people in Toronto, and persuaded British director Tyrone Guthrie of the possibilities of Stratford. He and

Guthrie then brought actor Alec Guinness and designer Tanya Moiseiwitsch aboard. Though everyone worked for peanuts, the required funds were substantial. The money to stage the festival was raised in Stratford—$72,000 from its 15,000 citizens—and across Canada. In an era before the Canada Council existed to help the arts, this was no mean achievement.

Patterson's plan originally had been to use the town's bandshell to put on a play (not much different from Mickey Rooney saying "My Dad has a barn" in 1930s' films), but, working with a local volunteer committee, Guthrie made it a condition that things be done right. Stratford's Festival went on stage for the first time on 13 July 1953 in a huge tent, and so compelling was the production, so brilliant was Guinness in *Richard III,* that the critic Herbert Whittaker gushed that it "was the most exciting night in the history of Canadian theatre." It was, too, and it was Tom Patterson's doing. The first season had two plays over six weeks which played to 98 per cent of capacity, and the next year the season was nine weeks. Today it is six months long, and two additional theatres are used for the festival's productions, which generate 480,000 ticket sales.

Patterson was also behind the construction of a superb permanent theatre in 1957, with an innovative thrust stage and every seat within 65 feet of the actors. It was the first major theatre to be built in North America in the twentieth century.

The festival transformed Stratford. The sleepy industrial-agricultural centre was invigorated by the half million visitors who spent millions each year, leaving behind $25 million in tax revenue, and by the 500 permanent jobs created at the festival. Amazingly, Stratford largely avoided the vulgarization that could have resulted in Hamlet snack bars on every corner. Just as remarkably, Stratford transformed theatre in Canada—an art that was ripe for transformation. Shrewdly, Guthrie built on a permanent company of Canadian actors who soon assumed starring roles, generously suggesting that "Canadians can speak English clearer and better to the rest of the English-speaking world and be more readily understood than even our English actors." Very soon, trips to Stratford became a regular part of summer for tens of thousands who had hitherto believed that Shakespeare was finished with after grade ten.

For his part, Patterson had quit his job with Maclean-Hunter in 1952 to become the festival's general manager, then its director of planning, and finally director of public relations. In 1960 he created the bilingual National Theatre School in Montreal, another brilliant and innovative idea. He offered his ideas to the Dawson City Gold Rush Festival and to the West Indian Festival of the Arts. Sadly, Patterson left the festival in 1968 after a dispute over its management, his reward a very modest $100 weekly pension.

Unassuming though he was, and initially no expert on either Shakespeare or the theatre in general, Tom Patterson had transformed the Canadian cultural scene. Critics carped that Stratford produced too much Shakespeare and too little Canadian work. Locals in Stratford grumped that Patterson had become too big for his boots. Perhaps this was so, but without Patterson there would have been no festival, and without the festival Canadian culture, while it might still have blossomed, would have remained mired in the slough of cultural despond for years to come.

34

Paul Desmarais

FOR THE MOST SUCCESSFUL FRENCH-CANADIAN capitalist ever, influence can be summed up in one word: power. Because Paul Desmarais is one of the most powerful Canadians of the century, his actions and beliefs directly touch the lives of hundreds of thousands of Canadians. Yet he remains a shadowy, elusive personality, content to gain power and exercise it with minimal fanfare and only occasional controversy. His low profile, however, belies an influence that few Canadians have been able to claim.

Fittingly, Desmarais' power rests in his control of a company called Power. But for most of its existence, the Power Corporation of Canada has not manufactured anything. Nor does it provide a service. It does not, in fact, sell anything. Rather, Power Corp. exists only to own and acquire other companies. By the 1990s it owned a fabulous collection of blue-chip businesses that make and sell things in almost every sector of the Canadian economy.

The road to power began for Desmarais when he tried to make the buses in Sudbury run on time. He was a student on summer break from law school in 1951 when he convinced his parents to let him run the local transit system. The family-owned bus franchise was deeply in debt, poorly run, and on the verge of going out of business. In a fashion easier related than accomplished, the twenty-four year old assumed company management, cut costs, and made the franchise profitable by 1955. The company now belonged to him—his parents were happy to unload its debts—and Desmarais, no longer interested in finishing his degree, never looked back.

These formative years in Sudbury were crucial ones for the young Franco-Ontarian: his family was comfortably well off, not rich, but the opportunity to run an enterprise wholly on his own taught him lessons that he applied repeatedly. Chief among these precepts was that debt could cripple even the most efficiently run operation. Desmarais quickly poured profits from Sudbury into an intercity bus business in Quebec. That soon led to further acquisitions, and, by the early 1960s, Desmarais had built a mini-transportation empire. As his group of companies expanded, he perfected the art of buying undervalued businesses using his own equity rather than borrowing. He never had much liquid cash, and sometimes he had to sell a stake in his holdings to finance takeovers. But by buying the right companies at the right price, Desmarais had, by 1965, become a takeover artist *par excellence*. And, though he started with very little, he was also very rich.

By this time he was based in Montreal and was assembling significant media holdings in Quebec, including the venerable and influential daily *La Presse*. In 1968 Desmarais acquired control of Power Corp., one of the leading conglomerates in Canada. Though its roots were in hydroelectric power, Power was a vast, diversified empire by the late 1960s, with interests across the country in dozens of economic sectors. Desmarais made it even bigger, adding giant financial services companies like Great West Life Co. and the Investors Group to its core of industrial and resource sector assets. By the 1980s there was perfect capitalist symmetry to Power Corp.'s multibillion dollar web: many member companies sold products to other member companies, which in turn sold services to other member companies. Yet despite this obvious integration, Desmarais was canny enough to keep his holdings sufficiently diversified that profits remained healthy even when one sector was in recession.

The sheer size of Power, and the scope of Desmarais' personal media holdings, often draw criticism. Is too much corporate and media power concentrated in the hands of this one man? For the most part, Desmarais has been able to duck this question because his political connections are almost embarrassingly reliable: former prime ministers Trudeau and Mulroney were close to him, as were a wide assortment of Quebec premiers, federal Cabinet ministers, and senior civil servants. As the only real power capable of getting in Desmarais' way, government has consistently chosen not to do so. It helps, of course, that Desmarais maintains a low profile. And his steady support of the federalist option in Quebec—often his newspapers voice the only anti-separatist opinion in the media there—has made him a dependable ally of Ottawa.

As he neared retirement in the 1990s, Desmarais continued to tend to Power's growth. He built a major international consortium to pursue opportunities in China. He acquired a major stake in Southam Inc., making himself, Conrad Black, and Pierre Péladeau virtual lords of the newspaper business in Canada. In short, he showed few signs of slowing down. Expansion, profit, and the acquisition of power continued to be what Paul Desmarais did.

35

Adam Beck

BORN: Baden, Canada West • 20 June 1857

DIED: London, Ontario • 15 August 1925

In THIS CENTURY OF THE BUREAUCRAT, WHEN more and bigger governments have regulated and reordered our lives in countless ways, Adam Beck might properly be called one of the most important civil servants in Canadian history. Yet the description hardly begins to do him justice. For Beck so dominated his age—far more influential and better known than his political masters—that calling him a civil servant is a little like calling Mount Everest an ant-hill. By the time he died in 1925, Beck had revolutionized industrial production in Ontario, delivered cheap electricity to millions, and, perhaps most significantly, changed forever the way Canadians thought about what their governments could do— and ought to do.

None of it came without a bitter fight. In fact, from his earliest years in public life, Beck seemed to rise to the occasion when a battle loomed on the horizon. The son of a German immigrant, he was a successful cigar-box maker in London, Ontario, and mayor of the city in 1903 when he first became fascinated with the problems and possibilities of hydroelectricity. It had been known for years that power could be harnessed from Ontario's fast-moving rivers and waterfalls. The problem was getting electricity from the water to the factories where it was needed.

Beck took over the fledging hydro movement and immediately made two key strategic decisions: Niagara Falls was the best place to harvest electricity in Ontario, and a publicly owned utility was best to do the harvesting. This approach instantly made him powerful enemies, since the province's burgeoning private companies were also eyeing the falls and the potentially limitless profits that a power-hungry province would deliver.

Beck was not only unfazed by the opposition but the resistance only made him more committed to public power. Embracing the cause with startling zeal, he trekked across the province promoting the cause of cheap electricity for everyone who wanted it. For factory-owners and farmers it was an easy sell, and Beck won a political following within months. In 1905 the incumbent Liberals foolishly gambled on pleasing private power concerns, and the long-dead Conservatives were swept into office promising public hydro.

The new premier brought the province's political star into his Cabinet, but Beck was not interested in politics—except when it had to do with a public electrical utility. In 1906 the Hydro-Electric Power Commission of Ontario was created with Beck as chairman. The commission sold its first power four years later, and the war with the private sellers was on.

The outcome was by no means assured. Politics in Canada was dominated by men who had made their fortunes by privately developing natural resources, and in an era when government actually did very little, it seemed impossible that a crown corporation could serve the province's vast market for power. But Beck never once let up on his crusade: When his own government baulked at allowing him to spend millions buying up his competitors, he went straight to the people with a simple message: their own natural resources, their birthright, was in jeopardy. When attacked by the private power magnates, he painted them as corrupt millionaires.

Backed, though often reluctantly, by his own government, Beck lost some battles but won the war. By 1917 "the Hydro" was the biggest electric company in the world. More Ontarians had access to power every year, and the rates were among the cheapest anywhere. Public ownership, under the firm hand of Adam Beck, was a runaway success.

In hindsight it all sounds very heroic: here, to all appearances, was the triumph of the little guy over the capitalist

power barons. The reality was a shade more complicated. For though Beck knew that his votes came from the people, his cause lived or died because of the small businessmen who relied on cheap, reliable power to keep their factories humming. Ironically, capitalists gave Beck the support he needed to build his public monolith. But it was Beck who pushed, cajoled, and badgered to create the coalition that won public power for his province.

His efforts were enduring. By the time he died, Beck had driven most of his competitors out of business and had guaranteed a public future for Ontario Hydro. The commission would be the engine for the province's mid-century economic boom, and it brought power quickly and cheaply to most of the province. Beck's life work was also the foundation of a tradition of public ownership of monopolies in Canada. In giant sectors like transportation, telephones, and power, government regulation and control has often been demanded by the Canadian public. What Canadian governments do, and how they do it, was shaped by Adam Beck.

36

Lucy Maud Montgomery

BORN: Clifton, Prince Edward Island • 30 November 1874

DIED: Toronto, Ontario • 24 April 1942

THEY COME EVERY SUMMER WITHOUT FAIL. FROM the United States, from Britain, from Europe, and especially from Japan, they head for New Brunswick and Nova Scotia. By the thousands, they load into ferries, or they drive the new causeway across the Northumberland Strait and land in Prince Edward Island. Cameras loaded and aimed, they arrive in search of a romantic, idyllic place called Green Gables and the ghost of a red-headed kindred spirit who never existed.

Since the 1920s, many millions have flocked to Prince Edward Island, Canada's tiny perfect province, to find this place. They come because of author Lucy Maud Montgomery, who was not yet forty when she created a children's story destined to become the most influential single book written by a Canadian this century.

It almost never happened. Montgomery was a university-educated teacher and an unknown writer living an obscure existence in PEI when she finished *Anne of Green Gables* in 1905 and offered it to several publishers. One company immediately rejected it; others soon did the same. Frustrated, she vowed never to look at the manuscript again. It was only after she stumbled on it by accident two years later that she tried again, and in 1908 a Boston company agreed to publish the book.

Anne had an overwhelming, overnight impact. It sold out several printings almost immediately, and to the surprise of both author and publisher, adults rather than children were its biggest fans. Montgomery's Anne Shirley was a childhood heroine for the ages: a lonely but loving orphan with a passion for learning and a zest for life.

Sensitive about her looks, uncomfortable in a stiffly conventional society, Anne appealed to everyone everywhere who had ever felt like an outsider while growing up. Adopted by an elderly brother and sister who had wanted a boy, Anne was rejected and then embraced by the towns-folk of small-town PEI—and readers around the world were smitten. Wholesome, episodic, romantic, and set on a lovingly sketched, bucolic Prince Edward Island, *Anne of Green Gables* simply struck a chord.

The royalties from the book made Montgomery a woman of independent means, an unusual circumstance in Canada in 1908. But success was a burden: Montgomery was sentenced to a lifetime of trying to duplicate the feat of her first book. She was never able to do so, and, sadly, the life of the woman who had given the world such joy was mostly an unhappy one. In 1911 the middle-aged Montgomery married Ewen Macdonald, an unassuming Protestant minister, after dutifully waiting for her dependent grandmother to die. Her private journals reveal that he was neither her first love nor her best, but marriage was a necessary choice for most Canadian women at the time. The couple moved to a parish in small-town Ontario and Montgomery continued to write. In response to a demanding public, she produced sequels that followed Anne Shirley into maturity. These books had none of the freshness of the original, however, and the author admitted privately late in her life that she had grown to dislike the red-headed girl she had created. Burdened by periodic bouts of depression and by a husband bewildered and confused by her talent and her fame, Montgomery died in 1942 in Toronto, still known for a book written nearly forty years before.

But *Anne* lived on. Buoyed by two major film adaptations and translation into at least a dozen languages, PEI's most famous daughter continued to make new friends. In 1965 a musical based on the story premiered in Charlottetown, and it has run to packed houses every summer since. "Green Gables" is one of the largest tourist attractions in the country and the cornerstone of the island's tourism industry. A new film version of the story was an instant classic in 1985, and a television series based on Montgomery's characters was one of Canada's most successful ever.

By the 1970s and 1980s even serious students of Canadian literature were grudgingly giving *Anne* new respect. Where the book was once dismissed as superficial and melodramatic, it is now embraced by critics as a nuanced period piece, especially valuable for its perceptive portrayal of late Victorian Canadian society.

Though its style is dated, and the way of life it describes is increasingly distant, the appeal of *Anne of Green Gables* continues to grow. It is that rarest of Canadian cultural products: equally popular at home and abroad. In a bright, irresistible Canadian orphan girl, Lucy Maud Montgomery found a story whose appeal was universal.

37

BORN: Valcourt, Quebec • 16 April 1907

DIED: Sherbrooke, Quebec • 18 February 1964

Joseph-Armand Bombardier

FOR MOST OF US, THE FACT THAT CANADA HAS A northern climate is a tale more for the telling than for the living. Each winter most Canadians hibernate in heated homes, heated cars, and heated shopping malls. Winter is a distraction, a nuisance that displaces our postmodern late-century lifestyles only a little. For most of us, it is nearly impossible to appreciate just how significant the life of J.-A. Bombardier really was.

For though he did not invent the wheel, he may

as well have—at least for the millions of people around the globe whose world is white with snow much of the time. Bombardier's Ski-Doo revolutionized life in the earth's most forbidding locales, bringing the twentieth century to places that had never known it. Canada and other cold places would never be the same again.

The most remarkable thing about the life of one of Canada's greatest inventors is that he never realized his biggest dream. Growing up in the early moments of the mass transportation era in off-the-beaten-path rural Quebec, Bombardier envisioned a huge, family-sized vehicle that would end the isolation of the long winter months in villages and towns. In the horse and buggy period, but also in the dawning motor-car age, snow made most routes in Quebec impassable. Horse-drawn sleighs were slow, inefficient substitutes. Bombardier imagined a people-mover that could glide across snow and mud. He first tried a jet propeller for power, then later a track drive with front-mounted skis for steering. He was the best kind of inventor: he built everything himself, testing and retesting components in a modest workshop. In 1936 the first snowmobile was ready for the showroom.

By any measure it was a monster. Resembling nothing more than a futuristic tank on skis, the new Bombardier company's first offering was fully enclosed and featured room for ten or twelve men. The inventor clearly had commercial markets in mind, and soon the lumbering track-driven machines were a not uncommon sight on the winter highways of Quebec. Bombardier continued to perfect his invention and adapted some models for Canadian government wartime use. But even after the debut of what the inventor viewed as his masterpiece, the mammoth twenty-five-passenger C-18, sales were sluggish. When the Quebec government announced a commitment in 1947 to keep all major roads clear of snow every winter, the day of the giant Bombardier snowmobile was done.

But if Bombardier's dream of a mass transit revolution in Quebec was over, his biggest influence was still to come. A compact version of the earliest vehicles was designed almost as an afterthought; certainly, Bombardier viewed the toylike rendering of his invention with near disdain. Modelled more on a motorcycle than a bus, the Ski-Doo, first sold in 1959, used a new, reliable two-cycle engine.

Clearly, it is no exaggeration to suggest that the one- and two-seater Ski-Doos became a way of life almost overnight in the Canadian North. Entire communities that had been accessible only by air suddenly were in touch year round. The most remote Inuit nations were suddenly made closer. Indeed, the new vehicle changed the lives of native communities across northern Canada, rapidly altering hunting and migration patterns.

While it was becoming a vital transportation tool, the Bombardier snowmobile also virtually invented a new winter sport in the 1960s. The new product appeared just as the postwar consumer appetite for big, expensive thrills was growing, and soon thousands of city folks were discovering the joys of rocketing down snow-packed paths in Ski-Doos. Before long the company was offering machines with aerodynamic stylings, racing suspensions, and even on-board stereos.

Though the inventor died in 1964, his company took his product around the world. By the 1990s over 2 million had been sold. The family-owned Bombardier Inc. is today Canada's most important transportation conglomerate, with worldwide manufacturing interests in airplanes, trains, and public transportation systems. And it still sells the one- and two-passenger Ski-Doos that are as important to many of their owners today as they were nearly forty years ago.

38

Thomas d'Aquino

"IF WE ARE INFLUENTIAL," TOM D'AQUINO SAYS OF the Business Council on National Issues that he leads, "it's not because of who we are—it's because of the power of our ideas. Is free trade a powerful idea? Yes, it is!... Is deregulation a powerful idea? Yes, it is! Is the desire to reduce the size of government a powerful idea? Yes, it is!" The BCNI represents 150 of Canada's largest, richest corporations—the banks, the insurance companies, the richest multinationals, the mining giants—and it speaks for almost $1.5 trillion dollars in assets. Not because of who we are? Fat chance.

Smooth, polished, a consensus-builder of great skill, d'Aquino was not to the manor born. He emerged from modest origins in the mining interior of British Columbia to get a first-class education in Canada and abroad. While still in his twenties, he worked for Pierre Trudeau as a special assistant, and in 1972 set up shop in Ottawa as a "strategic business consultant." After a few years working for the legal powerhouse of McCarthy Tetrault, in 1981 he found his home as president of the BCNI and immediately set out to turn the little-known and largely ineffective organization around.

The BCNI, d'Aquino says, was created in 1976 "to develop constructive economic, social and international policies for the business community whether

the government likes them or not." Under his direction, the
council intended to "reconstruct" the country: "We mean
fundamental change in some of the attitudes, some of the
structures and some of the laws that shape our lives." Trade
had to be liberalized, business needed a level playing field so
it could survive in the newly competitive global marketplace,
and government had to be made to reduce its size and cease
its interference with the aims of corporate Canada. Using his
highly developed networking skills, d'Aquino jollied his
powerful CEOs along towards tough positions, derived

through task forces that mirrored government departments and priorities, and generated reports that sometimes seemed to move directly into legislation.

The Trudeau Liberals were not wholly sympathetic to the BCNI agenda, but Brian Mulroney's Progressive Conservatives, aiming to remodel the country, responded quickly to d'Aquino's lobbying. His first triumph came in 1985 when the Tories, proudly declaring Canada open for business, came out for a free trade agreement with the United States. By 1988 the deal was in place, and, in the election that followed, d'Aquino spearheaded the Canadian Alliance for Trade and Job Opportunities that spent millions publicizing the benefits of the FTA and closer economic integration with the United States. What's in it for Canadians? an election advertisement written by d'Aquino asked. "More jobs. Better jobs." Mulroney, the FTA, and the BCNI won, but that powerful promise quickly turned hollow, as manufacturing decamped to the south and unemployment skyrocketed. Corporate profits, recessions notwithstanding, did well. A triumph indeed.

Next on the BCNI program was constitutional change. A smaller, weaker, decentralized government was a positive virtue, and Mulroney's Meech Lake accord and the Charlottetown agreement were steps in the direction d'Aquino and the BCNI wanted Canada to take. Not perfect, Charlottetown was still "the best thing we've seen yet," d'Aquino argued. "It gives Canadians the opportunity to settle grievances and turn their attention to key issues such as the economy." The people were unreceptive, however, defeating the Charlottetown agreement in a referendum. For the first time d'Aquino's ambitions were checked, his *amour-propre* wounded by the personal attacks that were now coming his way.

Not for long. His next targets were Canadian social programs. To d'Aquino and the BCNI, Canada spent too much on social welfare, much more than the Americans. This made high taxes inevitable, and taxes drained away initiative and incentive. But how could Canadians be persuaded to accept the reduction of their cherished social benefits? Orchestrated by d'Aquino and the BCNI, the media tom-toms soon began to beat insistently against the rising national debt and annual government deficits. Proving that one party was as useful as another, the Chrétien Liberals responded by slashing budgets, reducing transfer payments, and cutting programs. Another triumph.

Unelected, almost unknown to the public, Tom d'Aquino more than merits the title conferred on him by journalist Murray Dobbin: "Canada's *de facto* prime minister." No other unelected person, Dobbin says, "has ever exercised the kind of influence on public policy in Canada that Thomas d'Aquino has." Of course, big business is entitled to organize itself in a democracy, every bit as much as the poor can. The power, the resources, may be different, but the principle is the same. But if the policies of business fail, who is to be held accountable? Politicians who backed the wrong horse may fall, but Tom d'Aquino and his BCNI will simply seek a better runner for the next time.

39

Wilfrid Pelletier

BORN: Montreal, Quebec • 20 June 1896
DIED: New York, New York • 9 April 1982

CHILDREN'S PIANO COMPETITIONS CAN BE WEARISOME, when ten year olds struggle through obligatory Chopin waltzes. Wilfrid Pelletier, however, did not allow his attention to wander, and a fellow jury member was once astonished to see Pelletier with tears streaming down his cheeks as one boy played. "Isn't it beautiful?" he said, emotion sweeping through him at the great sounds produced by small hands. He understood that the future of music rested in developing the skills of the young, and his life was devoted to that end.

Pelletier obviously remembered his own beginnings in music. His father, a baker, conducted an amateur band, and family members played all instruments, conducted, and taught each other. Pelletier was the percussionist at first, but he eventually graduated to the piano. At the age of fourteen, he decided, after seeing his first opera, that he had found his medium.

In 1915, with the Great War under way, Pelletier won the Quebec government's Prix d'Europe that let him go to Paris to study. The fighting in the trenches, the sound of the guns echoing on the Champs Elysée, made living difficult for the young student, but he nonetheless learned at the feet of great teachers. In 1917 he returned to North America, hired by the Montreal Opera Company as assistant conductor and then in the same role by New York's Metropolitan Opera. This was a supreme opportunity to work with the likes of Caruso and Toscanini, and Pelletier began to build a reputation. He conducted widely throughout the United States, led the Met's Sunday night concerts, and did radio work for NBC; there he established the Metropolitan Opera Auditions, which discovered many great talents. He retained his connection with the Metropolitan, where he was known to all as "Pelly," until 1950.

In the midst of the Great Depression, against his better judgment ("You owe it to Quebec," his father insisted), he allowed himself to be summoned to Montreal to organize Les Concerts symphoniques, the forerunner of the present Montreal Symphony Orchestra. It did not take him—and the local musical public—long to become enthusiastic, and in the same year of 1935 he launched young peoples symphony concerts; the next year, he inaugurated the Montreal Festivals. In the midst of the despair of the economic downturn, Pelletier had established his native city as a musical centre. What was needed now, he realized, were good local instrumentalists and singers.

In 1942 he seized the opportunity to meet this need when the provincial government asked him to establish a provincial Conservatoire de la musique et d'art dramatique. The intention, in Pelletier's mind, was to bring in the best teachers in the world to train a new generation of Quebec and Canadian artists without tuition costs. Parochial musical nationalists argued that local teachers could do the work, but Pelletier held his ground and faced them down. The flowering of Canadian music was the result.

He remained at the head of the conservatory until 1961 and acted as director of the province's Ministry of Cultural Affairs until 1970. During the same period, he led the

Quebec Symphony, conducted the Canadian première of a number of operas, made large-scale television productions, and shared the podium with conductor Zubin Mehta at the inaugural concert in Montreal's Place des Arts in 1963, an event that put the seal on Montreal's standing then as the country's greatest city. In 1966 the largest hall in the Place des

Arts was named after him, and in 1968, to his great pleasure, he became national president of Jeunesses musicales du Canada, the continuing foundation for Canada's superb youth orchestras.

Pelletier's standing in the world of Canadian and international opera was notable. But his major contribution to his homeland was in greatly enhancing musical life in Quebec and Canada. His insistence on high standards, his interest in and concern for the training of young musicians, and his coordinating efforts as an administrator were outstanding.

In September 1978, to great ovation, the aged Pelletier appeared at a concert in his honour in Montreal and conducted a piece from Verdi's *Nabucco*. Initially hesitant as he was, as *La Presse* reported, "the rhythm of the music seemed to take over. Visibly moved, the great conductor straightened his back, turned to face the audience, and led them in singing the glorious music."

40

Jack Bush

BORN: Toronto, Ontario • 20 March 1909

DIED: Toronto, Ontario • 24 January 1977

SHORTLY BEFORE HIS DEATH, JACK BUSH SPOKE about Canadian artists who were content to exhibit only in Canada: "'We're just as good as the Americans,' they say. 'Look, we're showing here, we're showing all across Canada. Canada is just as good as New York or London or Amsterdam or anywhere.' But that's got nothing to do with it. It's simply this, the difference between minor league baseball and major league baseball. If you've got enough nerve and are good enough, you can play in the majors." Bush played in the major leagues of art, the first Canadian to do so.

The pure flame of unalloyed Canadian nationalism has been brightest among the practitioners and devotees of culture. Jack Bush, the most important internationally recognized Canadian artist of the second half of this century, had no patience with his nationalist critics. He could hit the Canadian fastball and the American curve; he could play in the majors, and he did; and if Bush's attackers drew the conclusion that he was saying they could not, that was their problem.

Bush had a familiar apprenticeship. His father worked as a manager at the commercial printing and design firm Rapid Grip Co., and he took a job in the Montreal office in his youth. There he learned the rudiments of art, and when he transferred to the

firm's Toronto headquarters in 1929, his art education took a leap forward. "The Group of Seven," Bush said, "were the top boys and anybody that was adventurous at all, just ooh'd and ah'd at them and what they did." Bush did too, and his early works bore strong resemblance to the Canadian landscape school.

By the end of the Second World War, married and the
father of three, Bush was beginning to experiment with
surrealist figurative pieces, much as Paul-Émile Borduas in
Montreal. The postwar growth of the New York art scene,
covered in the U.S. magazines that crossed the border, also
began to have an impact on him, and he found like-minded
artist friends in Toronto. Men like William Ronald, Jock
Macdonald, and Harold Town began sharing an approach to
art in the 1950s and showing their abstract paintings together
in exhibitions as Painters Eleven. Nothing sold, but Ronald
soon demonstrated that his own work could do well in New
York. Thus, when the influential American critic Clement
Greenberg paid a visit to Toronto to see what was going on
north of the border, Bush was ready. Town refused to show
his work to the Yank, but Bush did. Greenberg spent a half
day with Bush, saw his work, and said, "You're so good but
what you're doing, Bush, is you're just taking all the hot licks
from the New York painters, which is so easy to do. Try
painting simpler, and thinner...If it scares you, good—you'll
know you are onto something that is your true self." Bush did
as Greenberg advised and dropped the facile brush effects.
He scared himself, but persisted. In the now hoary myth,
Clement Greenberg smote Jack Bush on the frontal lobe,
critic Barrie Hale wrote, and released the mainstream of
modernism into Canadian waters.

Bush's new work with its thin, radiant colours, irregular
shapes, and large size began to draw notice in New York, but
scorn and few sales in Toronto and Canada. Over the decade
of the 1960s, the paintings grew bolder, brighter, but still
spare, and gradually the paintings, showing Bush's remarkable colour sense, began to sell. So too did his major runs of
prints, their bold designs still startling visitors in many a
Canadian living-room. In 1968 Bush felt financially and

artistically secure enough to give up his day job as a commercial artist, finally becoming a full-time painter. No more Harvey Woods underwear ads!

He was and remained a Greenberg protégé, helped enormously by the American critic's influence. But, as Bush noted, his friend (and later co-trustee of his art works) never "picks up the phone and tells him which colour to put here and all that jazz, which is a lot of phoney nonsense." That ought to have been obvious, but the hypernationalism of Canadian culture, the crusades against New York influence and American imperialism launched by painters like Greg Curnoe and his Canadian Artists' Representation, helped create an atmosphere poisoned by nationalist envy.

A success at last, a man hailed for his art in New York, London, Europe, and, grudgingly, in Canada, Jack Bush no longer had to care what his critics at home said. He was no intellectual, but he understood that great art was art that stood the test of time. Contemporary critics pronounce some artists' work "no good," he observed, but "the reason they're so great right now is that their painting has held up." It is too soon to know if, two centuries hence, people will still fight to buy a great Jack Bush oil. They might, however, and if that is any measure of long-lasting influence, there are few Canadian artists of whom that can be said.

41

Don Cherry

BORN: Kingston, Ontario • 5 February 1934

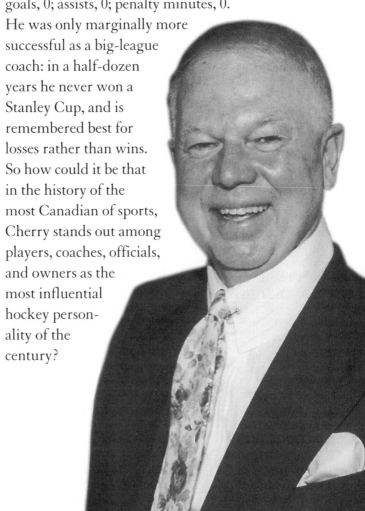

Dᴏɴᴀʟᴅ S. Cʜᴇʀʀʏ ᴡᴀs ɴᴇᴠᴇʀ ᴍᴜᴄʜ ᴏꜰ ᴀ ʜᴏᴄᴋᴇʏ player. His career statistics in the National Hockey League tell a very modest tale: games played, 1; goals, 0; assists, 0; penalty minutes, 0. He was only marginally more successful as a big-league coach: in a half-dozen years he never won a Stanley Cup, and is remembered best for losses rather than wins. So how could it be that in the history of the most Canadian of sports, Cherry stands out among players, coaches, officials, and owners as the most influential hockey person- ality of the century?

The answer begins with the fact that Cherry was not only not a star but was never really successful at all. His roots were humble. Like many who today hang on his every word, Cherry grew up a hockey-obsessed kid who just wanted to make the big leagues. He came achingly close in 1955 when, as a twenty-one year old, he played a single playoff game for the Boston Bruins. Later that year, however, an injury smashed his chances of returning to the big time. Ever hoping for more, Cherry bounced around the ranks of minor professional hockey, from Hershey to Trois-Rivières, and points in between.

He quit playing and accepted a minor-league coaching job in 1971. Three years later he began his brief NHL coaching career with the Boston Bruins. Cherry loved the attention that the big-time offered, and it showed. But the Bruins enjoyed only limited success, and after a brief stint in Colorado, he was fired for good in 1980.

Smarting from being dismissed, Cherry accepted a bit part on live hockey broadcasts on the CBC; his was one of a steady stream of new faces that television required to provide "expert analysis" of the game. No one could have predicted he would reinvent the role.

Cherry was different. Analysts were supposed to be detached; he cheered loudly for his favourite teams and players. Analysts were supposed to promote the game; he complained about "brutal" refereeing. Analysts were supposed to talk about hockey; he spoke noisily and often about whatever he wanted. Regular guys, guys who had regular dreams but who never quite made it, could relate to him; after all, Cherry himself never quite made it. And Cherry liked hockey fights. He liked to drink beer, and he sounded like he drank a lot of it. He was also proudly, fiercely Canadian and seized every opportunity to remind

Canadians that when it came to hockey, no country in the world was better. He was apparently, and actually, an average Canadian guy who just loved the game.

The proof that his message resonated was in his sky-high ratings. Television quickly gave him a star's billing: "Coach's Corner," a four-and-a-half minute show between periods of Saturday night games, quickly became a weekly status report on the state of Canada's game—and often on the country itself.

Usually, it is shouting and a lot of finger pointing. On fighting: "HOW MANY TIMES DO I HAVE TO REPEAT IT? FIGHTING IS PARTA HOCKEY." On players who refuse to fight: "THIS IS WHAT WE'VE COME TO? TURTLISM?" On foreign players: "I'M TELLIN' YA, IT BREAKS MY HEART TO SEE SOME RUSSIAN STEALIN' A JOB FROM A GOOD CANADIAN KID." On a highlight: "YOU KIDS OUT THERE, YOU LISTEN TO ME: YOU NEVER, EVER PASS THE PUCK OUT BLIND LIKE THAT." On another highlight: "WATCH HIM TAKE THE SWEDISH DIVE...THE SWAN DIVE." On honour: "YOU KIDS OUT THERE, YOU BIG TOUGH GUYS, YOU NEVER PICK ON THE LITTLE GUYS, OKAY? THAT'S THE CANADIAN WAY."

It is always outrageous, often grossly offensive. The slang and sloppy grammar raise eyebrows. The xenophobia and glorification of fighting justifiably make some people angry. But no apologies are ever offered after the fact. Always nattily attired in a gaudy suit and high-collared shirt, Cherry resembles nothing more than a cartoon mobster barking out commands to underlings.

But among fans and the media, he is almost universally revered. His openly patriotic diatribes are frequently quoted, and his style is often imitated. Those who miss him on television can buy his videos or visit one of his bars. In his own way, Cherry makes many people feel good about being

Canadian, and, hence, he has received more attention that he ever could have imagined. College courses analyse his attitudes; academic papers study his popularity. His loud opinions actually matter, even when they have nothing to do with hockey. Don Cherry has become bigger than the game; recent ratings, at least, show that more people watch him than the game itself.

In an industry that dumps yesterday's stars down the drain like expired milk, Cherry beat the odds and endured. There remains a shared sense among those that watch him that one day he will go too far. About this game or that player, he will say something too personal, too lewd, too unfair. Then television will have no choice but to discard him. If, or more probably when, that happens, he will retire from the spotlight secure in the knowledge that this minor leaguer has changed the way Canadians think about their game, and about themselves.

42

Northrop Frye

BORN: Sherbrooke, Quebec • 14 July 1912

DIED: Toronto, Ontario • 23 January 1991

HISTORY IS ALWAYS A JUMBLE OF CHANCE AND accident, but no one could have predicted that a typing contest in Toronto in 1929 would launch the career of one of the most important cultural figures in the English-speaking world. The odds were impossibly long, but when Northrop Frye's proficiency at the keyboard won him second place in a competition sponsored by the Underwood typewriter company, he decided that he liked Toronto enough to move there from New Brunswick. Shortly after, he began a degree in English and philosophy at Victoria College at the University of Toronto. Half a century later, Frye was still there, but the things he had typed had made him the legendary father of modern literary criticism.

Frye was a stellar student at Victoria, brilliant in his courses and popular in student clubs. After a brief flirtation with the Protestant ministry, he did a master's degree in English at Oxford. He returned to Toronto as a lecturer at Victoria, and embarked on an academic career without parallel in Canadian history.

He published dozens of books, but easily the most important was *The Anatomy of Criticism* in 1957. This was his *tour de force*: a remarkably ambitious, nuanced work that made the stunning claim that all literature was related in a coherent, comprehensible pattern of myth and symbol. This was no less than a revolutionary position: the notion that writers as diverse as Shakespeare, Milton, and Blake were exploring a pattern of universal symbols. Many questioned Frye's argument; many others were in awe of it. Most agreed, however, that this middle-aged Canadian English professor had made some of the most perceptive observations yet on the great authors and their works.

What Frye accomplished with this book was no less than the founding of a new discipline: no longer could literary

criticism be regarded as a branch of philosophy or linguistics. Modern criticism, and the postmodern world of deconstruction and textual analysis, all proceeded in his wake.

By the 1960s he was a world figure, and Frye solidified his academic reputation with studies of Shakespeare and the Bible. Later, he also turned his attention increasingly to books from his own country. In an era when Margaret Atwood, Robertson Davies, and others were fashioning a national canon worth reading, Frye lent his own credibility to Canadian literature. His work as literary editor of the *Canadian Forum* and his essays about Canadian culture collected in *The Burning Bush* remain required reading for anyone interested in the subject.

Acclaim changed Frye not a bit. In person, there was always something so utterly everyday about Northrop Frye that for many who knew him, it was difficult to imagine the worldwide reputation this unassuming professor possessed. He resisted all offers to leave Victoria College, and continued to read and write and type there well into his retirement. There is no doubt that Frye's was a rarefied world, wholly removed from the daily obsessions of almost everyone else. But in that world, he was a giant.

43

BORN: Yarmouth, Nova Scotia • 23 July 1885
DIED: Grand-Cascapédia, Quebec • 5 August 1955

Izaak Walton Killam

THE RICH ARE DIFFERENT FROM YOU AND ME, THE old saw goes, and Izaak Walton Killam is proof of that adage. Dour, silent, immensely wealthy, he drew national scorn when he died for leaving his immense fortune to his widow, Dorothy, and no bequests to charity. But Killam believed that, because he had made his money in Canada, he owed the country something so he deliberately did not avoid inheritance taxes. The approximately $50 million in death duties from his $100 million estate were directed by the St Laurent government to the establishment of the Canada Council, that great benefactor of Canadian culture. His wife, moreover, apparently carrying out her husband's instruction, established the Killam Trust that funds universities and scholarship. The Killams rank unchallenged as Canada's greatest philanthropists.

Killam was born to the least successful of the many Killam families in Yarmouth. All descended from pre–Revolutionary War immigrants to Nova Scotia, the others high-hatted young Walton, and although he was sent briefly away to a private school, he resented his treatment bitterly. His business career began at seventeen as bank clerk-cum-office boy in the Yarmouth branch of the Halifax Union Bank, and soon he was working at head office. There he met an extraordinary New Brunswicker, the almost equally young Max Aitken. The two became friends and, soon, associates in Aitken's Royal Securities. Aitken had figured out how to finance and amalgamate companies, and soon after the turn of the century he was too big for provincial Halifax. Montreal was the place to be, and he took Killam with him when he made his millions. Killam became rich too, and in 1919 he bought the Royal from Aitken, already immersed for several years in British politics. Now it was his turn.

Secretive to extremes, Killam built a vast empire. There were pulp and paper companies across the country and power companies in Calgary, Prince Edward Island, Quebec, Nova Scotia, New Brunswick, Ontario, Newfoundland, and throughout Latin America; there were candy and sugar companies in the Maritimes, movie houses, real estate, grain and elevator companies, and the *Mail and Empire* in Toronto; and Royal Securities itself was and remained a cash cow. Silently studying every document, Killam proved to be a master of detail. No one knew more than he did about his enterprises; no one said less.

His one indulgence was his wife, whom he married in 1922. Dorothy Johnston was an American from St Louis, a petite, energetic, beautiful woman fifteen years her husband's junior. She loved jewels, fine clothes, her five large mansions around the world—and baseball. In 1952 Killam had an expensive television cable hooked into their Montreal home so his ill wife could watch the World Series, and when the Brooklyn Dodgers were poised to move to Los Angeles, Killam put up the money so Dorothy could try—unsuccessfully—to buy the team and keep it in Brooklyn. No fool, Dorothy learned finance under her husband's tutelage, and when he died at a salmon-fishing lodge in 1955, she more than doubled the estate in ten years.

The Killam donations that she supervised were huge. Dalhousie University received $30 million, the University of British Columbia $14 million, and between them the Universities of Alberta and Calgary $16 million. The Izaak Walton Killam Children's Hospital in Halifax was given $8 million, the Montreal Neurological Institute $4 million, and, most important perhaps, the Canada Council received the funds to establish the Killam Prizes and Fellowships for advanced research in the humanities, social sciences, and science. Each year, after rigorous competition, some twenty fellowships are awarded to Canada's best scholars. Each fellow has two years of paid leave to research and write, and the "Killams" have become the nation's most prestigious academic award. The flood of books and scientific discoveries produced by Killam Fellows are testimony to the value of the program.

Considering that Izaak Walton Killam was more interested in mystery stories and fishing than in culture or scholarship, considering that Dorothy Killam was more involved in baseball than in art, the Killam benefactions were truly extraordinary. They left their country infinitely richer than they found it.

44

Ernst Zündel

BORN: Calmbach, Germany • 24 April 1939

IT WOULD BE MUCH EASIER TO THINK OF ERNST Zündel as a German than as a Canadian. It would be much easier to pretend that he occupies the lunatic fringe and that hardly anybody pays any attention to him. It would also be wrong.

Zündel is the exception that proves the rule that Canadians of influence have been mostly forces for positive change in the world. Since he first openly identified himself with neo-Nazi and anti-Jewish organizations in Toronto in 1979, he has been the public face of racial hate in Canada—and for much of the world beyond.

Zündel was part of the flood of immigrants that escaped war-torn Europe for Canada in the 1950s. He settled in Montreal, married a Québécois, and worked as a retoucher of photographs. In circumstances that remain unclear, he also became friendly with Adrien Arcand, the notorious Quebec fascist who was interned by the Liberal government during the Second World War. Arcand was an aging, obscure anti-Semite by the time he met Zündel, but the pair hit it off at once. Arcand introduced the young German immigrant to his Nazi ideas and Nazi friends, and it was here, it seems, that a career as a hatemonger was born.

Zündel kept his hate hobby secret when he first moved to Toronto in the 1960s. No one, in fact, associated him with the extreme right when he emerged from the shadows and had himself nominated for the federal Liberal Party leadership in 1968. At a convention that would eventually anoint Pierre Trudeau, he wound up without a single vote.

Working for himself, Zündel became a very successful photo retoucher in Toronto. He did work for *Maclean's* and *Homemaker's*, and earned enough to subsidize a growing

propaganda distribution business. He began by publishing pro-German rants, but descended rapidly into pure anti-Jewish hate. In the guise of history, Zündel specialized in denying that the Holocaust ever happened.

He first came to the attention of the local public and police in 1979 after organizing a series of pro-Nazi demonstrations. It became known that the basement of his downtown Toronto house was the centre of a pamphlet, book, and video distribution operation that dispatched hate materials around the globe. At the same time, there was a hidden aspect of his anti-Jewish activity that the public rarely heard about: harassing letters were regularly sent by Zündel to Jewish groups and leaders across the country. Many times, he mockingly offered to participate in a "constructive debate" on Germany and the Holocaust.

These overtures were mostly ignored, but they did result in the Canadian Holocaust Remembrance Association initiating criminal proceedings against Zündel in November 1983 for "willfully" spreading "false news." The attorney general of Ontario agreed to prosecute the case and, over the next eight years, a Zündel trial and appeal, then another trial and appeal, were heard by the courts of Ontario. Each time, Zündel was convicted.

For those sickened and disgusted by the man's message, however, this was not really a victory. The trials brought more publicity for Zündel and his ideas than he ever could have paid for himself: for days at a time, an obviously pleased Zündel made the television news and the front pages of newspapers. Whether the Holocaust actually occurred was debated in the courtroom and, inevitably, in the media as well. The Supreme Court of Canada rendered the final verdict on Zündel's legal fate in 1992. It ruled that the "false news" section of the Criminal Code violated the guarantee of freedom of expression under the Canadian Charter of Rights and Freedoms and, therefore, that Zündel was not guilty. The hatemonger had won twice: he had gained unprecedented exposure for his views through trials and appeals, and he had been exonerated by the Canadian justice system.

The notoriety pushed Zündel into the major leagues of racist and hateful publishing in the world. Neo-Nazi skinheads in Germany read his publications, and anti-Semitic American fringe groups cite Zündel as a major influence. He has been convicted in Germany, *in absentia,* of publishing hate. His worldwide mailings have increased exponentially; many suggest that "donations" bring in much more money than the production and mailing cost him. Authorities worldwide now consider him to be among the international leaders in hate literature dissemination.

Zündel's influence at home and abroad is incontestable. Though his application for Canadian citizenship has been repeatedly rejected, he has been a permanent Canadian resident since 1958. Canada is his home, and to a large degree he is a product of Canadian society.

Zündel's fellow Canadians are left with lingering doubts about how their society has dealt with him. Would his influence have been diminished if he had been consistently ignored—by Jewish groups, by the courts, by the media? Or has the publicity surrounding Zündel been a useful reminder that Canadian society has hateful, destructive elements lurking in its dark corners? Those questions haunt us all.

45

O.D. Skelton

BORN: Orangeville, Ontario • 13 July 1878
DIED: Ottawa, Ontario • 28 January 1941

THERE ONCE WAS A TIME WHEN THE CANADIAN public service was seen as a high calling both by its employees and by the citizens they served. No single person created this reputation out of the morass of patronage that had characterized the civil service until the 1920s. But by common consent, Dr O.D. Skelton is hailed as the key figure in this transformation.

The son of a schoolteacher, Oscar Douglas Skelton was an earnest, dedicated student. He won entry to Queen's University on scholarship in 1896, and over the next four years he took all the prizes as well as a bachelor of arts and a master of arts. In 1900 he went to the University of Chicago for graduate work, but soon left for England—where, passing the tough examinations, he won entry to the Indian civil service. He decided not to accept appointment and moved instead to Philadelphia, where he worked for *The Booklovers Magazine*. In 1905, married and with his wife pregnant, Skelton returned to Chicago to finish his course work in politics and economics. He received his doctorate for a critical study of socialism in 1908. Already teaching at Queen's, he soon became the John A. Macdonald Professor of Politics and Economics and established a reputation as a good teacher and scholar. He published his dissertation on socialism, wrote massive biographies of Sir Alexander Galt and Sir Wilfrid Laurier, dashed off potboilers, and produced a flood of scholarly and popular articles. In an era when even fewer professors published than today, Skelton stood out.

A strong nationalist in an era when British imperialism attracted most of his compatriots, Skelton worked for the Liberal Party during the 1911 free trade election; he opposed conscription in 1917; and he became increasingly interested in foreign policy and the "need" for Canada to recognize that, after the Great War, it was a North American nation, not a British colony. A speech that called for Canada to make its own foreign policy impressed the new prime minister, Mackenzie King, in 1922, and a year later Skelton accompanied King to the Imperial Conference as his closest adviser. The two men destroyed the idea of a centralized imperial foreign policy and laid the groundwork for a Commonwealth united only by the crown. Two years later, King made Skelton undersecretary of state for external affairs, the senior bureaucrat responsible for creating and running Canadian foreign policy.

External Affairs was tiny and ill-equipped to cope with the problems of the interwar years. Skelton began to recruit bright university graduates of "all-round ability, capable of performing in widely different assignments at short notice," both directly and through competitive examinations. He brought in able young men like Hume Wrong, Lester Pearson, and Norman Robertson, and he soon recognized that other departments needed help too. He persuaded his former student and Queen's colleague Clifford Clark to become deputy minister of finance, and Skelton and Clark were responsible for the appointment of Graham Towers as governor of the Bank of Canada. Working together to recruit the best available talent, these three built the public service and gave it its high standing, while their officers carried on the

founders' traditions of hard work and integrity into the 1960s.

For his part, Skelton served King with great skill and faithfulness until the Liberal defeat in 1930. The new Tory prime minister, R.B. Bennett, was suspicious of the Grit-appointee Skelton and planned to sack him. But Bennett quickly discovered that Skelton could answer his questions, provide shrewd advice, and do his duties with high competence. The undersecretary remained, and the principle that senior bureaucrats should have tenure was reinforced. Skelton preferred King and his policies, but he served Bennett loyally until the Depression and the 1935 election returned King to power.

No great administrator, Skelton remained what he had always been—an intellectual in the bureaucracy. He could understand why many Canadians felt a loyalty to Britain, no matter how London's policies wavered and veered, but, with his "incurable Canadianism," he instinctively preferred that Canada create its own course. He was an isolationist, a North American, certain that Britain would drag the country into war for Whitehall's interests, not Ottawa's, and fearful that this involvement would divide French and English Canada once more. King agreed with some of Skelton's reasoning, but as a politician he knew he had to get elected. That meant keeping the support of Quebec and not alienating those English-speaking Canadians who retained imperial loyalties. King succeeded when he led a united Canada into the war in 1939, but the new world war broke Skelton's heart.

His health had begun to fail in the late 1930s as he laboured under his enormous workload. The coming of a war in which he did not truly believe added to his burdens, and in January 1941, while driving home for lunch, Skelton suffered a massive stroke and died at the wheel of his car.

The creator of the modern Canadian public service was loved by those who worked with him and for him. Many in government and in the country did not agree with his views, but all understood that he had died in his country's service. He left a legacy of diligent, disciplined competence that helped immeasurably in winning Canada's war and in shaping the peace that followed.

46

Rodrigue Villeneuve

BORN: Montreal, Quebec • 2 November 1883

DIED: Alhambra, California • 17 January 1947

"HIS EMINENCE, THE CARDINAL, INVITES THE parish priests to do all that they can to facilitate to the maximum degree possible national registration... with exactness and submission, of all which is required of them by the public authorities." In August 1940 national registration was considered by many Québécois to be a prelude to conscription for yet another British war. For Cardinal Villeneuve to use his authority to urge compliance with the government's demand was seen as extraordinary, a sign of his support for the war. In religious Quebec, this was critical.

The son of a hatmaker, Villeneuve joined the Oblate Order in 1902 and was ordained in 1907. He taught at the University of Ottawa, then took doctorates in philosophy, theology, and canon law. He served as dean of theology at Ottawa until 1930, when he was made bishop of Gravelbourg, Saskatchewan. He was on the Prairies for only a brief period. In 1931 Rome recalled him to the east as archbishop of Quebec, and in 1933 the pope appointed him a cardinal.

Rodrigue Cardinal Villeneuve took command of the Quebec church in the depths of the Depression. Episcopal revenues had collapsed just as the demands on the church increased with rising labour unrest and poverty. A smooth diplomat, a lover of lavish ceremony, and a clerical conservative, Villeneuve led his flock with skill, pushing Catholic Action as a way of associating laymen and professionals with the church's urban social work and, at the same time, resisting demands for Quebec women to receive the vote in provincial elections. "A feisty, brilliant and grandstanding figure," as Conrad Black labelled him, Villeneuve was perceived as a nationalist, suspicious of what he saw as the anti-clericalist tinge of the Liberal Taschereau government and a supporter of Maurice Duplessis' efforts to topple it. In early 1936, in fact, the cardinal had to fend off Premier Taschereau's complaints that he had permitted his priests to play an active political

role in the election campaign. Duplessis soon was in charge, smashing communists and denouncing Ottawa at every turn. Villeneuve did not seem to disagree, but he was not pleased when the Union Nationale resisted his efforts to consolidate church control over French and English Catholic education.

When war came, Ottawa sent a Cabinet minister to Villeneuve to plead for his support. Perhaps to Mackenzie King's surprise, the hitherto nationalist cardinal threw in his lot with the government and the war effort. Although many of his curés and bishops supported neutrality and opposed the war, with a good number sympathetic to fascism in Italy and Spain and forthright in their anti-Semitism, Villeneuve clearly saw that Hitler was an enemy of the church and Canada; he could also understand that to oppose a war that was widely supported in English Canada would do Catholics in Quebec no good at all.

Even so, Villeneuve's efforts were extraordinary. He held huge masses in support of the army; called for prayers, penitence, and fasts in support of Allied victory; presided at the dedication of air bases; and encouraged the faithful to subscribe to Victory bonds. He even allowed himself to be photographed at the wheel of an army truck. His priests may have grumbled, but Villeneuve ruled with a rod of iron, and no one, not even the fascist-sympathizing historian Abbé Groulx, dared oppose him too openly. The church's position, as stated by the cardinal, was that "French Canada will solemnly swear never to set down arms nor relax efforts on the internal front until the triumph of the democratic ideal over the Axis powers is secure."

Nonetheless, when the nationalist Duplessis returned to power in 1944, Villeneuve cheerfully renewed his alliance with the Union Nationale premier. Duplessis clearly was more sympathetic to the church than the provincial Liberals, in power since 1939 under Adélard Godbout, had been. Had Godbout not given women the vote in 1940, threatening family solidarity and feminine modesty?

Felled by a heart attack in 1946 after a gruelling inspection of Oblate missions in the north, Villeneuve died the next year in a church rest home in California. A vain, imperious man who liked to proceed through the streets of Quebec City in a sedan chair and revelled in extravagant clerical jewellery, Villeneuve had ruled Quebec through a tumultuous period. Quebec's war effort was substantially greater than in the Great War, and much of that support must be attributed to his influence. The cardinal doubtless realized that his flock had not unanimously followed his devotion to the cause, but the results had shown that not every Québécois was isolationist. Nonetheless, his support for Duplessis and for the repression of women and radicalism undoubtedly contributed to the backlash that exploded in the Quiet Revolution little more than a decade after his death.

47

George Grant

BORN: Toronto, Ontario • 13 November 1918
DIED: Halifax, Nova Scotia • 27 September 1988

CANADA IS NOT A NATION FOR—OR OF— philosophers. The Canadian spirit is not generally introspective, nor does it soar. There is a brooding character to it, a sense that, like the weather, matters will probably get worse before they improve. The feeling also exists that poor, weak Canada cannot

control matters. Just as the nation went to war in 1914 and 1939 when someone else called, just as the United States more recently controls the country's fate, so do Canadians instinctively understand that their destiny will be decided by other forces. The philosopher who persuaded Canadians of the inevitability of this gloomy hopelessness was George Grant.

A product of a distinguished academic and Britannic imperialist family, Grant was related to the Parkins and the Masseys, and family connections played a great role in his success. His father was principal of Toronto's Upper Canada College, and he was a student there. He went to Queen's University, where his grandfather had been principal, and, though he was not especially athletic, he went to Oxford on a Rhodes Scholarship, the Rhodes Trust having long been administered by his grandfather Parkin. In England he could call on his relative Vincent Massey, Canada's high commissioner, and after the Second World War Massey would commission him, a junior academic with a new Oxford doctorate, to write the section on philosophy for his royal commission report that explored the state of Canadian cultural life.

As a scholar teaching mainly at Dalhousie and McMaster Universities, his work was slow to appear but thought to be of good quality. It was not so outstanding, however, that anyone in the body politic would ever have noticed. Grant was all but unknown until 1965, when his little book, *Lament for a Nation: The Defeat of Canadian Nationalism*, appeared.

Part philosophy, part polemic, *Lament* was the product of Grant's despair at the defeat of John Diefenbaker's Progressive Conservative government in 1963. The issue was nuclear weapons, and the way the U.S. administration of President John F. Kennedy had intervened to assist Diefenbaker's tottering government in its preordained fall from power.

To Grant, not someone who understood clearly either the politics of the time or the nuclear controversy, the bumbling Diefenbaker's ouster was tragic, not comic. To him, the Chief's political demise marked the end of the possibility of a Canadian nation, the triumph of the ever more pervasive influence of Washington over Canada's life and distinctiveness. The continentalist thrust of the Liberals, the technological force of the United States and its liberalism, had guaranteed that the dominion was destined to sink into materialism as a branch plant of American corporate capitalism. "The society produced by such policies may reap enormous benefits," Grant wrote, "but it will cease to be a nation." The same theme was developed further in his 1969 volume, *Technology and Empire: Perspectives on North America.*

Intended as a death knell, an elegy to be intoned over the corpse of Canada, Grant's *Lament* for nationalist and conservative values instead became the seminal influence in their resurgence. Although Grant often seemed to be harking back to the traditions of an era when British Canadians ruled the Canadian roost as part of a world that was painted in imperial red, he now coincided with a great burst of nationalism. Centennial year, the Vietnam War, and the efforts of Walter Gordon and others to check the inflow of American investment capital led to a new sense of Canadianism that was especially strong with the young and in the universities. Canada, Grant seemed to be saying, was about a greater good than the mere acquisition of more cars and TVs, and Canada's purpose had to be the protection and development of this good. Grant's theoretical framework and his argument that Canada was in dissolution had started a movement, and his lament turned into the motive force that powered a new nationalism. The loud, difficult, rough-hewn, and bearded philosopher became a Canadian icon.

As an academic philosopher, Grant's influence was limited, and he was never greatly admired by his peers. His arguments against technology, abortion, and euthanasia, and his belief that philosophy had to be based on an understanding of God made few converts. There would be no Grantian school of philosophers. As a nationalist, as a Red Tory, as a proponent of an alternative way for Canada, however, his importance was huge. The slow slide of Canada to the south was not stopped by Grant's outbursts in the 1960s; he was not Canute checking the tides. Yet for a time it seemed that nationalism might carry all before it and change Canada's fate. For a time, Grant's influence on the public and the politicians was immense. Even today in a much more integrated North America, Grant's lament continues to rally the nationalist Tories, the left-Liberals, and the social democrats as they ride to battle against the encroaching American hordes.

48

Ted Rogers

BORN: Toronto, Ontario • 27 May 1933

CABLE-TV CZAR, COMMUNICATIONS MOGUL, cellular telephone magnate, newspaper and magazine publishing company owner, the Canadian information highway creator—Ted Rogers is all of those things, but he is also a man carrying a huge and growing debt load, a risk-taker *par excellence*. Either he will push and prod Canada into the new millennium with his companies shaping the future, or the crash of his vast empire will shake Canada to its foundations.

Rogers' father, Ted Sr, was born to wealth in a "Fine Old Ontario Family" of Loyalist and Quaker origins, but he added to it through his own inventive genius. In the 1920s home radios were cumbersome, the sound generated sometimes exceeded by the hum of the power required. In his mid-twenties Rogers invented the alternating current radio tube, which resolved the problem, and a host of other devices. These inventions led him into radio broadcasting, notably with Toronto's CFRB, and manufacturing, and when he died at the age of thirty-nine his five-year-old boy was raised to venerate, emulate, and compete with his father.

He did. After Upper Canada College, the University of Toronto, and law school, Rogers put money into CFTO, one of the country's first private television stations, purchased CHFI-FM, and in 1967, with a fortuneteller's grasp of the future, went into

cable in Toronto, the first concerted effort to end the city's
poor reception of U.S. stations across Lake Ontario. His
Rogers Cable-TV was one of the first cable companies and,
while people scoffed, Rogers was ahead of his time. Today
his company, its reach extending from Ontario to the West
Coast, is the country's largest, with 40 per cent of the English-
Canadian market and 3 million subscribers who pay for
movie packages, sports, and other specialty channels with
ever increasing monthly fees. Cable has been and remains
the money-generating prop of the Rogers empire.

Rogers also owns the Home Shopping Network, virtually
the inventor of the cubic zirconium, and YTV, the children's

TV specialty program network. Rogers Communications Inc., the parent company founded, owned, and controlled by Rogers, in 1983 won a national cellular telephone licence and in 1986 founded Cantel, now with a million customers and, until 1995, controlled Unitel as well. In 1996 Rogers linked Cantel with the American telecommunications giant, AT&T.

In his efforts to create a giant media conglomerate and to own some of the content his cable enterprises delivered to Canadian consumers, Rogers purchased the Maclean-Hunter magazine and cable-TV empire in 1994 for $3.1 billion. In the same year, he bought 62.5 per cent of Toronto Sun Publishing Corporation, a publisher of tabloid newspapers in Toronto, Ottawa, Edmonton, and Calgary, weekly papers and magazines, and 60 per cent owner of the *Financial Post*. In 1996, to raise cash, Rogers sold off the Sun chain and other non-core assets amounting to more than $800 million.

The Sun sale showed that once again Rogers' acquisitions had begun to outrun his capacity to borrow. In 1981 he had been on the brink of financial disaster when, after selling off "everything we could just to keep afloat," he was rescued by $300 million raised for him by U.S. junk bond king Michael Milken. The lesson did not sink in. Free-spending and unable to avoid risk, Rogers' companies in the mid-1990s laboured under a massive debt that was said to amount to just under $5 billion. Shareholders, watching the price of Rogers' stock on the Toronto Stock Exchange plunge, were beginning to grumble, and the need to lower debt was clearly driving the sell-off of assets. It was all relative, of course—a share purchased in 1983 for $7 was worth some $100 in 1996 dollars.

Apparently unruffled, perhaps because his own yearly salary was regularly in the $700,000 range, Ted Rogers pressed ever onward. His Rogers Communication Inc. in 1996 began touting WAVE, a new product that, for $55 a month, provides high-speed access to the internet. Upgrading of the cable network will make WAVE potentially available to all its cable subscribers, but newer technologies are already coming on-stream.

Greatly assisted by his close links to the Eatons and the Bassetts, his lifelong connections with the Progressive Conservative Party, and his ability to employ Canadian nationalism as a way to whip the Canadian Radio-television and Telecommunications Commission into supporting his ambitions, Rogers had made his company into Canada's largest media corporation. For more than three decades, his power has been immense, his influence reaching virtually every home in the land. The collapse of his company, if it should ever take place, similarly would be felt all across Canada.

Rogers' health is beginning to break down—he had an aneurysm in 1988 and a quadruple bypass in 1992—but he continues his workaholic brinksmanship. Married for more than three decades to the daughter of a British peer, Ted Rogers took the modest broadcasting company he inherited and turned it into a Canadian competitor to international media empires. Canadians must dominate at home to compete internationally, he says, adding with the characteristic faith of the visionary, "The best is yet to come."

49

Phyllis Lambert

BORN: Montreal, Quebec • 24 January 1927

"PHYLLIS CAN BE A VERY DIFFICULT PERSON TO work with," someone who knows her well once said. "She wants everything to be too perfect and monitors everything with intense care." Perhaps that explains why her entry in the *Canadian Who's Who* is one of the longest in the annual volume, listing every single award she has won. But because Phyllis Bronfman Lambert is very rich, her co-workers and the public are willing to make allowances. And rightly so. Her money has been used to the great benefit of Montreal and Canada.

Lambert, the daughter of Seagram's founder Sam Bronfman, was educated in Montreal and at Vassar College in New York State. Surrounded by wealth, her relations with her notoriously difficult father were troubled. She found refuge in sculpture and in a 1949 marriage to a Harvard-educated French banker. But the marriage foundered after five years, and her life and career were made when she saw the architectural design proposed for Seagram's New York headquarters on Park Avenue and decided it was terrible. She persuaded her father she was right, launched a search for an outstanding architect, and settled on Ludwig Miës van der Rohe. "As far as I was concerned," she said years later, "my father was going to do this or I was never going to speak to him again." The resulting thirty-eight-storey bronze-clad tower, while hugely expensive, was instantly hailed as a masterwork, and old Sam was impressed despite himself. Inspired by her triumph, Lambert went off to the Illinois Institute of Technology to study architecture, winning her degree in 1963.

Her career flourished in both Chicago and Los Angeles. One of her few Canadian commissions was the award-winning Saidye Bronfman Centre in Montreal, a Jewish community centre named after her mother, and she consulted on Miës' Toronto-Dominion Centre in Toronto. But her greatest architectural achievement was the renovation of Los Angeles' Biltmore Hotel which helped rejuvenate a whole area of that city.

After her father's death, she returned to Montreal to live in 1973. Quickly, Lambert became interested in the conservation and preservation of the city's architectural heritage. Developer-speculators were knocking down treasured buildings and tossing up undistinguished apartment blocks, she observed, adding that "our cities look like we went to war...It's human greed, pure and simple." In response, she created a charitable foundation, Heritage Montreal, in 1975 and became a "heritage-aholic." She eats, sleeps, and breathes conservation, a friend says. Her impact was considerable, because her name instantly caught the attention of city councillors; her concentration and ability were formidable; and her wealth let her buy buildings to prevent their destruction. In 1974, for example, she purchased the once grand but then derelict residence of Lord Shaughnessy, one of the Canadian Pacific Railway's giants. Heritage Montreal undertook some eight projects a year, one of which saved blocks of workers' homes, turning them into cooperatives.

Her crowning achievement, however, was the Canadian Centre for Architecture, which opened in 1989. It was created to provide an independent study centre and museum to further the understanding of architecture and to help establish architecture as a public concern. Using the Shaughnessy House as its core, the superb grey stone building designed by architect Peter Rose surrounds it, enhances it, and provides ample exhibition, library, and research space. The building, its remarkable collection of 500,000 items gathered and paid for by Lambert, and its library of 130,000 volumes were estimated to have cost more than $100 million; more important than the philanthropy, the centre and its collection constitute a priceless national and world resource. As critical, the centre's construction instantly sparked the restoration and enhancement of the surrounding area.

Difficult though she may be, Bronfman obviously enjoys using her wealth for public good. With her close-cropped brush-cut and tight-lipped, severe face, she looks like a member of the French resistance, one writer noted perceptively, though perhaps the "architectural resistance" might have been more apt. "We are able to build too easily, too fast," she says. Buildings can be planned quickly and erected with great speed. As a result, when buildings are knocked down in a day, the permanence provided by architecture is lost. To Lambert, architecture should provide a sense of place and community, offering a reflection of the specific past of each area. Her efforts for Heritage Montreal and the Canadian Centre for Architecture amply fulfil her stated aims. As an observer noted of the CCA: "Nothing on this scale has ever been created by an individual in Canada before. Wouldn't it be nice if some of our other millionaires treated it as a precedent?"

50

Igor Gouzenko

BORN: Rogachovo, Russia • 26 January 1919

DIED: Toronto, Ontario • 25 June 1982

For almost half a century, the Cold War shaped the world. Billions were spent on weapons, millions of men and women were mobilized to serve ideological interests, and only by a hair's breadth did the world escape annihilation. To say this all began in Canada stretches credulity, but there is some truth in that claim, for it was Igor Gouzenko, a cipher officer at the Soviet Union's embassy in Ottawa, who in September 1945 forcibly warned the Western democracies that their Soviet ally had continuing aims of its own.

Born near Moscow in the terrible days of the Russian civil war, Gouzenko was a bright student who made his way through the Soviet school system with ease. He studied drawing and drafting in Moscow and attended the Architectural Institute of the University of Moscow. Nominated for a prestigious academic fellowship in June 1941, his education was derailed by the German attack on the Soviet Union. Instead of becoming an architect, Gouzenko took training in codes and ciphers and served in the headquarters of army intelligence (GRU) as a cipher specialist. In 1943 Lieutenant Gouzenko, soon to be followed by his wife, Svetlana, was posted to the Soviet Union's legation in Ottawa.

Deeply involved in the war, Canada still provided a startling contrast to wartime Moscow. People spoke

freely, there were goods in the stores despite rationing, and food was plentiful. But as a GRU officer, Gouzenko found that his work required him to betray the Canadians he had come to admire. His task was to encode and decipher messages to and from Moscow, messages detailing espionage requests from GRU headquarters and the answers provided by spy networks run in Canada. In September 1945, scheduled to be posted back to Moscow, Gouzenko decided to defect.

Carefully gathering up telegrams and documents that proved nuclear and military espionage, Gouzenko left the embassy and set out to visit newspapers, which ignored him, and government offices, which did the same. The government feared creating a diplomatic incident by taking in a man who proclaimed that "Russian democracy was different from ours"; the press simply missed the boat. Terrified, the Gouzenkos began to fear they had made a mistake. Not until embassy officials kicked in the door of their apartment while the Gouzenkos hid next door with a friendly RCAF sergeant did the Ottawa police get involved. They were quickly followed by the RCMP and the Department of External Affairs, which had been advised by the Canadian-born British intelligence officer, Sir William Stephenson, to "get your man at once." Safely hidden away with his wife and child, his revealing documents translated, Gouzenko had become very important indeed.

The result of Gouzenko's defection to freedom was a royal commission that in early 1946 heard testimony from those implicated in the embassy documents. The expulsion of Soviet "diplomats" and the conviction of eleven Canadians, including a Montreal member of parliament, followed soon after. More important, the proof of Soviet ill-will and the evidence of high-level spy rings in Britain and the United States provided by Gouzenko played an important part in galvanizing Canada's senior partners, especially as Prime Minister Mackenzie King sensibly shared everything Canada learned. Gouzenko's knowledge of Soviet codes—some also believe he brought code books with him when he left the embassy—proved as invaluable to the West as his revelations about the GRU spy network. Moreover, the evidence of

Soviet spying led Ottawa to create the security machinery necessary to deal with the new situation of ideological confrontation.

Afraid of Soviet vengeance, Gouzenko lived under an assumed name as a Canadian citizen. He wrote an account of his life and defection, *This Was My Choice*, which sold well, and in 1954 his novel about the brutality of Stalinist Russia, *The Fall of a Titan*, won the Governor General's Literary Award. But over the years Gouzenko, who appeared on the media with a bag over his head to confound the KGB's hitmen, became increasingly difficult to control. He continued to find spies in Canada and the West long after his evidence had grown cold, and his RCMP handlers found his constant complaints enervating. By the late 1970s his health had begun to break down and, suffering from diabetes and blindness, his death in 1982 was a release.

A man of culture and high intelligence, Igor Gouzenko was deliberately belittled by those who called him a mere cipher clerk and denied the importance of the spy rings he uncovered. They were wrong. His courageous actions in September 1945 alerted Canada and the West to the danger posed by Soviet communism, and this revelation was critical to a world in awe of the superb Soviet resistance to Hitler. The Cold War certainly would have occurred without Gouzenko, but it might have taken longer to wake up the democracies to the new threat they faced.

E.W.R. Steacie

BORN: Westmount, Quebec • 25 December 1900

DIED: Ottawa, Ontario • 28 August 1962

SOME BUREAUCRATS STAND OUT BECAUSE OF THEIR suspicion of bureaucracy. Dr E.W.R. Steacie, the president of the National Research Council for a critical decade after 1952, was one such worrier. He wanted government to put more money into scientific research in Canada, and he recognized that science would lose some of its freedom as a result; no government would simply pump in money without wanting to ensure that it was wisely spent. But Steacie understood that science had to be driven by the interest of researchers and that nothing could be more fatal than to control, direct, and shape it. Bureaucracy and bureaucrats must be kept in their proper place. His tough-minded vigilance put Canadian scientific research on the right path at a critical time in its development.

Ned Steacie was the son of an army captain who was killed at Ypres in April 1915. He thought of being an officer too and went to the Royal Military College for a year before he decided that the military was not for him. Instead, he went to McGill University, was captivated by science, and went on to complete a chemical engineering degree in 1923 and a PhD in physical chemistry in 1926. His progress thereafter was steady—the faculty at McGill, a research fellowship in Europe that took him to Germany and London, more teaching in Montreal, and in 1939 an appointment as director of the Chemistry Division at the National Research Council in Ottawa.

Already a prominent researcher in chemical kinetics and free radical chemistry, where his 200 papers and three books created a body of work characterized as "monumental," Steacie's tasks in Ottawa became increasingly dominated by administration. His intention was to convert the NRC's industrial research focus in chemistry into a pure and applied

research direction. But the declaration of war a few months after his arrival in Ottawa put him to work on military research.

In 1944 he became deputy director of the Anglo-Canadian Atomic Energy Project in Montreal, a post that brought him into intimate contact with the greatest secrets of the war and, after revelations of Soviet spy rings reaching into the laboratory in September 1945, with the impending Cold War. Steacie understood clearly the military imperatives of secrecy, but when he was president of the NRC he arranged for a Soviet Academy of Sciences–NRC scientific exchange program to attempt to knock down some of the barriers. Scientists, both Soviet and Western, he believed, needed the greatest possible freedom if the scientific method was to survive.

At the Chemistry Division after the end of the Second World War, he developed a successful plan for postdoctoral fellows to come from overseas to work with the Canadians in the NRC. In 1950 Steacie became vice-president of the NRC and, two years later, president. His role was to encourage the production of more researchers, to build up laboratories for industrial research, and to encourage Canada's industries to do more research themselves.

One of his first jobs was to persuade Prime Minister Louis St Laurent of the need to provide much more money to extend and improve scientific research in the universities, and he also secured support to extend his postdoctoral fellowship program into academe. He pressed university engineering departments to do more research, using funds provided by the NRC, and by the end of the 1950s he had increased government financial support tenfold and helped to establish the support structure that allowed university research to flourish in ways that would have appeared inconceivable a quarter-century before. At the same time, he created a scheme to encourage research in industry with an NRC program that provided matching grants to interested companies. Characteristically, Steacie insisted that the projects were to be in areas that interested industry, not those of direct concern to government. Government, he believed correctly, ought to encourage research, not plan, organize, or coordinate it.

As head of the NRC, Steacie spoke widely across the country. Atypically for a scientist, he realized the importance of the humanities and social sciences in providing the academic atmosphere that allowed research to flourish. He was, however, a man with a tart tongue, and he could not bear the superior airs that humanists, especially those with negligible achievements of their own, too often affected in the presence of scientists. As one of his friends observed, "his intolerance of pretension could...occasionally find a refreshingly forceful outburst." A practical, pragmatic man of action, Steacie's impact on science and scholarship earned him an enduring stature as Canada's pre-eminent scientific statesman.

52

Clifford Clark

BORN: Martintown, Ontario • 18 April 1889
DIED: Chicago, Illinois • 27 December 1952

THE GREAT CRASH OF 1929 WIPED OUT CLIFFORD Clark. The vice-president of S.W. Strauss & Co., a firm of American urban real estate financiers and developers, had enjoyed a large salary and the lifestyle that accompanied it, but the Depression swept it all away. Strauss had built its wealth on mortgages, and the wave of defaults destroyed it. Was Clifford Clark the right man to be Canada's deputy minister of finance?

Too small to be of much use on the family farm, Clark had been sent off to Queen's University in 1906 where, like his mentor O.D. Skelton, he won all the prizes. Skelton impressed Clark with his judgment, intelligence, and integrity, and Skelton obviously saw the same qualities in the eastern Ontario student, for he found him a Harvard fellowship in 1912. In 1915, his Harvard MA in hand and a never-to-be completed doctoral dissertation in process, Clark returned to Queen's to teach economics. He published a little, taught a lot, and decided by 1921 that he needed more money than university teaching could pay. That was the rationale for his leaving to join Strauss & Co. for $10,000 a year, some five times his university stipend. The years in Fat City ended with Clark in debt and his health broken. It would take him years to pay off his creditors.

Friends found Clark a job at Queen's in 1931,

but in the summer of 1932, Skelton, then at the top of the External Affairs bureaucracy, brought him to Ottawa to work on the preparations for the Imperial Economic Conference. His long, brilliant paper on monetary reconstruction impressed all, and Prime Minister Bennett, urged on by Skelton, decided that Clark was the man to lead the Department of Finance. Bennett had called his friend Charlotte Whitton to ask about Clark: "I know he's a Grit but I want him here," Bennett said, adding that "he stood out head and shoulders above all but the tops of the U.K. delegation" at the recently concluded conference.

The finance department had been a penny-ante operation since its creation in 1867, a government bureaucracy that dealt with nickels and dimes and wharves and post offices. But with the Depression strangling trade and killing employment, fiscal and monetary policy were suddenly critical. Clark began by pressing for a central bank, secured Bennett's support for a royal commission to investigate the question, and by 1935 had the Bank of Canada in place with his choice, Graham Towers, as governor. The two filled Ottawa with bright and able economists and, along with Skelton's external affairs recruits, completely changed the face of the public service and the way government in Canada functioned.

Orthodox in his economics, Clark was willing to learn. When one of his men, Robert Bryce, argued that Keynesian theory had its points and that deficit financing might be a proper way to proceed in hard times, Clark initially was unimpressed. But by 1939, the Depression continuing, he had changed his mind. The last peacetime budget was the first to be deliberately stimulative, the first mildly Keynesian budget. Would it have worked? No one could say, for the war changed everything, hugely increasing revenues and expenditures. The days of wharves and post offices were gone as Clark saw the Gross National Product double in six years and government spending rise tenfold to $5 billion a year. That Canada's wartime finance was the model for all the belligerents was a tribute to him.

Clark also directed the turn to social welfare. He could see the social worth of family allowances, for example, but he saw even more clearly that putting money in the hands of mothers each month would help to create demand in the postwar reconstruction period. The orthodox economist was gone, replaced by the crusader for government to give people money to help keep the economy moving and unemployment low. Again, the results exceeded expectations, as Canada moved smoothly from war to peace, reintegrated veterans and war workers, largely controlled inflation, and increased trade. It wasn't wholly Clark's doing, but it could not have been accomplished without him. Clifford Clark had made himself the indispensable bureaucrat.

In constant pain from a bad back, Clark continued to work himself hard, though he could frequently be discovered flat on his back on his office carpet in a vain search for relief. Except for occasional visits to the Five Lakes Fishing Club, a favourite mandarin haunt in the Gatineau near the capital, his life was work. The advent of the Korean War, with its inflationary pressures and the need to find the money for rearmament, finally did him in. On a visit to Chicago to give a paper, he died suddenly, leaving his colleagues in near total shock. The indispensable man had gone too soon, but Clifford Clark had surely demonstrated that the inability to manage one's own finances was no measure of overall capacity. None of his successors in the decades since his death would equal him in shaping the course of Canadian government.

53

Paul-Émile Borduas

BORN: St-Hilaire, Quebec • 1 November 1905

DIED: Paris, France • 22 February 1960

"BREAK PERMANENTLY WITH THE CUSTOMS OF society, disassociate yourself from its utilitarian values," the pamphlet shouted. "Refuse to live knowingly beneath the level of our psychic potential. Refuse to close your eyes to the vices, the frauds perpetrated under the guise of knowledge, of services rendered, of favours repaid." These words are from *Refus global*,

the 1948 manifesto written by Paul-Émile Borduas and signed by him and his artist friends. *Refus global* hit like a hurricane, angering the clergy, the Quebec government of Maurice Duplessis, the press, and artists who reacted against modernism. Within a few months Paul Sauvé, the otherwise progressive minister of social welfare and youth, fired Borduas from his teaching post at the Ecole du Meuble, and in Duplessis' Quebec almost no one objected. Even the editor of *Le Devoir* rejected Borduas' position and lent him not a whit of support. The firebrand of Quebec art was on his own.

Born to pious parents of modest circumstances, Borduas had intended to be a religious artist. He trained with the great Ozias Leduc in St-Hilaire, studied in Montreal and Paris, and returned to Canada in 1930 just as the Depression dried up church finances and work. To survive, Borduas taught drawing, and in 1937 found a post at the Ecole du Meuble, a provincial art and crafts school. A natural teacher, he began to gather disciples around him. He soon fell under the influence of surrealism and his style of painting changed dramatically. To Borduas, a man who had turned away from the Catholicism of his youth, surrealism became his new faith, an idea best expressed through what he called *Automatisme*, spontaneous painting inspired by stream-of-consciousness writing. His students and friends followed him, and Les Automatistes, a group that included Jean-Paul Riopelle, were born. Borduas and friends argued and fought about Marxism, psychoanalysis, and art, and their exhibitions began to draw notice by 1946 in New York, Paris, and Montreal. "At last," one critic cheered after a Montreal exhibition, "at last Canadian painting exists." The *Refus global* in 1948, a mimeographed pamphlet printed in only 400 copies, turned the cultural group into a revolutionary movement—in the eyes of the Quebec establishment.

Borduas' manifesto, ostensibly about aesthetics, was one of the first challenges to the traditional values of French-Canadian society. Quebeckers were "a little people huddled to the skirts of a priesthood viewed as sole trustee of faith, knowledge, truth and national wealth," he wrote, "shielded from the broader evolution of thought as too risky and dangerous." The influence of church and state had to be toppled, replaced by freedom, spontaneity, and "creative anarchy"; only then was hope possible. Scorned as a madman by some, a radical and atheist by others, Borduas was driven into poverty, a martyr to liberty but one almost completely unable to support his wife and three children. His art continued to draw increasing interest, however, and he won prizes in Montreal if few sales.

Soon he was working, living, and exhibiting in the United States, a freer society where painters like de Kooning, Rothko, Motherwell, and Pollock became influences on him, though his lack of English hampered direct communication. His work was almost completely abstract now, featuring textured paint of many colours exploding on the canvas. He found buyers in New York, and the great public institutions began to buy. In 1955 he returned to live and work in Paris.

His Parisian final years were not happy. He missed Montreal and Canada, pronouncing himself ready to give up Paris "and everything good in the world for a comfortable little corner, if it was in Canada." But he continued to paint furiously, and his paintings were purchased by the Martha Jackson Gallery in New York and the Dominion Gallery in Montreal. No one doubted his place now, but Paris was not home. "I belonged first to my village," he wrote in 1959, "then to my province; next, I considered myself French-Canadian, and after my first trip to Europe, more Canadian than French; Canadian (simply Canadian, no different from

my compatriots) in New York, and lately North American.
From now on, I hope to 'possess' the whole world." It was
not to be, for Borduas died in his studio in Paris at the age of
fifty-four. A great painter, his work still prized, Borduas the
man is remembered above all for his 1948 manifesto. Fifteen
years after its publication, the ideas in *Refus global* were
accepted everywhere in Quebec and the influence of Roman
Catholicism had collapsed. To some, "modern French
Canada began" with Borduas, and the great shove he gave
to the traditional Quebec values and virtues helped topple
the old ways. The Quiet Revolution and the development
of the Québécois nation, to some, truly began with Borduas
and his *Refus global*.

54

BORN: Davidson, Saskatchewan • 19 May 1917

Gordon Robertson

PUBLIC SERVANTS OBEY THE WILL OF THEIR POLITICAL masters, but there can be no denying that those who draft policy and present options to ministers and prime ministers have substantial power. The memoranda of bureaucrats, discovered much later by researchers poring over old files, frequently turn out to be the key documents that shaped the country's direction.

Only twenty-four when he joined the Department of External Affairs in 1941, Gordon Robertson had already attended the universities of

Saskatchewan, Oxford, and Toronto. There were no overseas postings for him, however; instead he went almost directly to the Prime Minister's Office and then to be an assistant to Norman Robertson, the undersecretary of state for external affairs. These jobs involved him directly in the highest affairs of state—and in some of the thorniest problems. A liberal man but a realist, Robertson understood that a civil servant could not go where the government chose not to proceed. When the question was whether or not to deport all Japanese Canadians, citizens included, back to Japan, Robertson did what he could to ameliorate the policy, and it was a triumph, he believed, when only those adjudged disloyal were to be forced out; the others had a choice of a kind. Half a century later, his advice now in the public domain, journalists without much understanding of the pressures and bitter attitudes of an earlier era denounced those policies and those who recommended them.

After the war, there was continuing service in the PMO and the Privy Council Office and then, at age thirty-six, appointment as deputy minister of northern affairs and national resources and commissioner of the Northwest Territories. In effect, Robertson was the supreme ruler of 40 per cent of Canada, at once lieutenant governor, premier, Cabinet, and speaker of the council of the NWT. As such, he dealt with everything from sewage to schools to liquor prices. He also was responsible for moving a community of Inuit from northern Quebec to Resolute Bay, NWT, in 1953, again actions that were sharply attacked forty years later. Critics charged that the Inuit suffered greatly and had been moved without sufficient supplies simply to bolster Canada's claim to the high Arctic. Robertson's defence—life in the North was always harsh and the relocation was in the best interest of the Inuit—fell on deaf ears, however true it was.

Robertson's stewardship of the North was seen as a great success and he was rewarded with the top post in the public service, clerk of the Privy Council and secretary of the Cabinet. For the next dozen years he served Lester Pearson and Pierre Trudeau during the challenging years of the Quiet Revolution and through successive administrative reorganizations that saw the number of advisers at the prime ministerial beck and call expand tremendously. Shrewd, cautious, a source of ever sound advice, Robertson was greatly prized. But after the 1974 election, Trudeau moved Michael Pitfield into the clerk's post and Robertson became secretary to the Cabinet on federal-provincial relations. His advice was not always listened to by Trudeau, who had his own views on constitutional change and Quebec.

In 1980, a private citizen at last, Robertson headed the Institute for Research on Public Policy, a think tank based in Ottawa. As the Canadian constitutional crisis began to reach the boiling point after the failure of the Meech and Charlottetown accords, Robertson spoke out frequently. To him, Canada's options seemed limited: either Quebec separated or Canadians accepted the premise that Quebec needed more powers than other provinces. Asymmetrical federalism, however, clashed with English Canada's opposition to any special place for Quebec and with the powerful notion that all provinces were and must remain equal.

Whatever Canada was or would become, Gordon Robertson had been one of those who had shaped it. He had made much wartime policy, had guided the development of the Far North, and had carved out the federal government's constitutional position in a critical era. Though denounced for his sins by a historically uninformed and politically correct present, he had offered balanced and sound advice to a succession of leaders from King to Mulroney.

55

Wilfrid Laurier

BORN: St-Lin, Canada East • 20 November 1841

DIED: Ottawa, Ontario • 17 February 1919

IN DEPORTMENT AND DRESS, ORIGINS AND OUTLOOK, Wilfrid Laurier was a product of the Victorian era. Throughout a long, highly successful public career, his was a horse-and-buggy, top-hatted world. Yet if Laurier was the last important Canadian of the nineteenth century, he was also the first important Canadian of the twentieth.

If the young Laurier had had his way, there never would have been a Canada. He was born in a village near Montreal the same year that the French and English provinces of Canada were reunited by British decree. For Laurier, this arrangement only confirmed that the English of British North America still aimed to dominate the French. The Confederation scheme of the 1860s was viewed as more of the same, and he spoke out passionately against the plans for a new nation.

But Laurier could never be accused of being a slave to previously held opinions. In 1874 he made his peace with Confederation and won election to Parliament as a Liberal. Better than most, Laurier read the public mood and saw that Confederation was here to stay. He rose rapidly in the party ranks, for he was a late nineteenth-century political rarity: a French-Canadian Liberal, educated at McGill University, who spoke and understood English perfectly. He also possessed a gracious, self-effacing

charm which, while gaining him few close friends, also made for few political foes. Even so, Laurier was as surprised as anyone when party leader Edward Blake named him his successor in 1887.

Few expected Laurier to last. This, after all, was the age of Sir John A., and no Liberal leader, least of all a French Catholic, was likely to defeat the long-serving prime

minister. But when Macdonald died in 1891, Laurier looked
very good in comparison with a succession of colourless,
squabbling Conservatives, and he was elected prime minister
in 1896. The Macdonald era was truly over at last, and the
country had its first French-Canadian prime minister.

Against all expectations, Laurier lasted in the country's
top political job for fifteen years, a consecutive streak
unmatched before or since. These were times that defined
the century: the West began to fill up with immigrants,
the Canadian economy began to boom like never before,
and the first cautious steps along a more independent path
for Canada were taken. Most important, Laurier kept the
country together, proving a masterful student of the tactics
Macdonald invented and Mackenzie King would later
perfect. When facing a tricky decision, he would preach
caution, delay, and refuse to commit. His vague pronounce-
ments on many subjects often pleased no one, but angered
few. This strategy brought Laurier and his goverment
through a series of crises: the Manitoba schools question,
the Boer War, and the naval issue all threatened the fragile
unity of the country. With tact and a deft reading of the
public mood, Laurier survived—if just barely.

It helped that he elevated capable lieutenants and gave
them real authority. Henri Bourassa, Clifford Sifton, and
Mackenzie King, all ahead of Laurier on this list, each
were given crucial career boosts by the prime minister.
Laurier was always shrewd enough to know when power
should be shared.

Near the end, however, his instinct failed him: in 1911,
as he approached seventy, Laurier agreed to fight an election on
the Liberals' proposed reciprocity treaty with the United States.
It was a good deal—a far better deal for Canada than the
Mulroney trade pact of 1988—but the aging prime minister

underestimated the extent of anti-American sentiment among voters. After a bitter, emotional election campaign, he was defeated at the polls by Robert Borden's Tories.

In opposition, Laurier's final years would be eventful. The war that began in Europe in 1914 provided the context for the most serious threat yet to national unity when Borden decided to impose military conscription in 1917. Quebec was horrified, and Laurier, painfully but honourably, fought the policy in the general election that year in the face of certain defeat. The Conservatives won the day, Laurier's party disintegrated around him in English Canada, and a few thousand reluctant soldiers were rushed to the battle front in time for the armistice. Quebec never forgot, however, and the Liberal stranglehold on the province that lasted for generations was assured.

Laurier died in 1919 while still party leader. At the time, he was planning the rebuilding of both his party and the country. But the Canada Laurier knew had changed. New provinces with burgeoning populations had shifted the balance of power in national politics. Lessons learned in the Great War had altered the way Canadians saw the world. Gasoline-powered cars had already begun to revolutionize transportation across the country. These were twentieth-century developments, and they would be left to others to deal with.

56

Conrad Black

BORN: Montreal, Quebec • 25 August 1944

AS TELEVISION SIGNALS ZIP AROUND THE GLOBE AT the speed of light and the internet brings the world to millions in seconds, the venerable newspaper seems like yesterday's news—in more ways than one. People are reading less, the received wisdom goes, and the inky, bulky daily newspaper is destined to disappear

altogether. It seems a little odd, therefore, that every time Conrad Black adds to his collection of newspapers in Canada, the hue and cry is deafening.

In gambling that the received wisdom is absolutely wrong, Black has spent the last dozen years assembling a newspaper empire with few rivals around the world. As a result, what Black thinks influences millions of people here and around the world.

He started by influencing only a handful of English-speakers just outside Montreal in Knowlton, Quebec. The *Eastern Townships Advertiser* did not seem like the beginning of a media empire in the late 1960s, but Black, a bright student frustrated with formal education by his early twenties, wanted to be the boss. With a few partners, he began building a modest chain of small dailies and weeklies in Quebec in the 1970s.

The turning point for the still precocious capitalist came in 1978, when a generous inheritance, some crafty lawyering, and brilliant tactics won him control of Argus Corporation, a blue-chip Canadian holding company. The thirty-four year old was thrust into the spotlight for the first time, and his penchant for empire-building became apparent: Black liquidated most of Argus' assets and poured his newfound wealth into newspapers. In 1985 good timing and fat pockets allowed Black to seize control of London's *Daily Telegraph*, the largest-circulation quality daily in Britain. A thorough streamlining helped him recoup his investment in a few years, and he embarked on paper-buying sprees in Australia and the United States.

The role of newspaper proprietor fit Black like a glove. To all appearances, he was born to be a press lord: he leapt at every opportunity to weigh in on public issues, and he collected high-flying friends as he did newspapers. Margaret

Thatcher, Black was proud to admit, was a particularly close acquaintance.

For Canadians, the chickens came home to roost in 1996, when Black acquired control of Southam Inc., a chain of major Canadian dailies. Combined with his previous holdings, Black overnight became the most important news provider in the country.

In 1997 the statistics are breathtaking: worldwide, he owns more than 500 newspapers. He is personally worth several hundred million dollars. He controls an absolute majority of English-speaking papers in Canada and about 40 per cent of daily circulation. He owns a handful of French dailies in Quebec and the influential *Saturday Night* magazine, based in Toronto. At a time when newspapers around the world are showing sluggish profits and declining readerships, Black keeps building and building. Usually, he announces his acquisitions with a spate of firings and layoffs, but nobody, anywhere, is as bullish about newspapers as he is.

It all sounds like a Canadian success story, but Black has always been far too outspoken to win many friends among those who read his papers. Nor has he ever been afraid to bash in print those who disagree with him. His legendary willingness to sue those who write about him means that his detractors have had to choose their words very carefully. One certainty is that as long as people are reading newspapers, Conrad Black will be the one Canadian whose opinion will not be ignored.

57

Bertha Wilson

BORN: Kirkcaldy, Scotland • 18 September 1923

THERE IS A STORY ABOUT BERTHA WILSON THAT
has been told so many times around Canadian law
schools that it's the stuff of legend. It was 1954
and the thirty-one-year-old, married wife of a
Presbyterian minister was chatting with the dean of
the Dalhousie University law school about entering
the undergraduate law program. It was a brief
conversation. "Madam, we have no room here for
dilettantes," the dean told Mrs Wilson. "Why don't
you just go home and take up crocheting?"

She ignored the advice, and it was a happy thing:
years later, Wilson would be regarded as one of
Canada's most distinguished jurists. For that, and also
for carving out a place for other Canadian women in
that most male of professions, she demands a prominent place on this list.

It is a long way from the Scottish Lowlands to the
Supreme Court of Canada, and for Bertha Wilson it
was a remarkable journey. In 1949, newly married,
university educated, but with no apparent intention
of doing anything but be a minister's wife, Wilson
emigrated with her husband to the Ottawa Valley.
She worked at a collection of odd jobs and aided in
her husband's ministry. Law school, by 1954, was an
opportunity to further her education; actually prac-
tising law was a vague and distant goal at best.

She forced her way into Dalhousie over the dean's

objections and graduated with honours in 1957. But things
didn't get any easier. After dutifully following her husband
to a new posting in Toronto, she was lucky to land a job with
Osler, Hoskin & Harcourt, a blue-blood Bay Street firm.

Wilson soon demonstrated a first-rate capacity for legal
work, and her bosses were impressed. But the only woman
lawyer in the firm was not introduced to many clients.
Instead, she was consigned to the background, preparing
briefs and arguments for other lawyers. Wilson made the
best of her ghettoization, and it soon became apparent that
the firm could not do without her. Within a few years she
had emerged as the quintessential "lawyer's lawyer"—paid
to give advice to other lawyers in the firm. She was made a
partner in 1968 and given the title "research director."
Outside her firm, not many lawyers had heard of Bertha
Wilson, but there were persistent rumours swirling in the
Toronto legal community that Oslers had a secret legal
weapon: a mysterious woman who was the brain behind its
most important briefs.

Wilson stepped out of the shadows and into the spotlight
in 1975, when she was appointed to the Ontario Court of
Appeal. She was the first woman to scale such judicial
heights in the province and, like most women entering a
previously all-male preserve, she had not only to be brave
but also to be good.

She soon proved she was both. Wilson earned a reputation
among her peers as someone who knew the law intimately
but was prepared to make sensitive, caring judgments. The
friendly, cheerful judge—liked by almost everyone—was also
not afraid to present a women's point of view in her decisions,
even when doing so provoked sharp criticism from her
colleagues on the bench.

For this Wilson was noticed, and she was a natural choice

as the first woman appointed to the Supreme Court of Canada in March 1982. Her presence alone proved that justice would never quite be the same in Canada, but she was much more than a token: Wilson found her judicial voice on the top court.

More than any other judge, Wilson used the new Canadian Charter of Rights and Freedoms as a powerful tool to strike down laws that trampled individual rights. Often, she found herself on the losing side of split decisions, as more cautious members of the court were reluctant to upset the centuries-old tradition of allowing Parliament to do whatever it wanted. Her biggest triumph came in 1988, when her decision in *R.* v. *Morgentaler* set off a legal earthquake that is still reverberating in courts around the country. Wilson joined the majority in striking down Canada's abortion law, but by making an overtly feminist argument, she established a key precedent.

Wilson retired from the bench in 1991. With the odds stacked against her, she had reached the very pinnacle of her profession. It was a profession that had finally made room for women and women's perspectives—and for that, Bertha Wilson could take her fair share of the credit.

58

Stephen Leacock

BORN: Swanmore, England • 30 December 1869
DIED: Toronto, Ontario • 28 March 1944

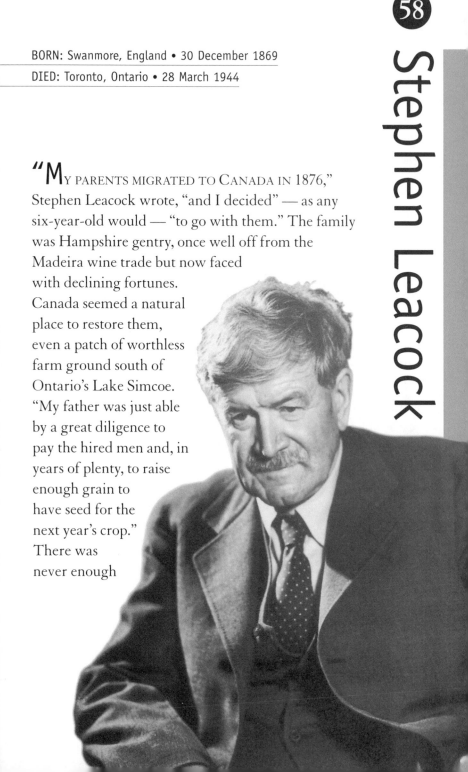

"MY PARENTS MIGRATED TO CANADA IN 1876," Stephen Leacock wrote, "and I decided" — as any six-year-old would — "to go with them." The family was Hampshire gentry, once well off from the Madeira wine trade but now faced with declining fortunes. Canada seemed a natural place to restore them, even a patch of worthless farm ground south of Ontario's Lake Simcoe. "My father was just able by a great diligence to pay the hired men and, in years of plenty, to raise enough grain to have seed for the next year's crop." There was never enough money, but there were pretensions to status, and young Leacock was sent to Toronto's Upper Canada College. His brothers too received a good education, and there was not a trace of wistfulness in Leacock's later comment that they had been "driven off the land, and have become professors, business men, and engineers, instead of being able to grow up as farm labourers."

Leacock attended the University of Toronto, taught unhappily at his old school for eight years, then went to Chicago to study with Thorstein Veblen and earn his PhD. Then it was marriage, McGill University's Department of Political Economy, and a successful, if ill-paid (and notoriously ill-dressed) career as an academic, with textbooks, monographs, and academic papers to his credit. "The emolument," he wrote, "is so high as to place me distinctly above the policemen...and other salaried officials of the neighbourhood, while I am able to mix with the poorer of the business men of the city on terms of something like equality." This was not enough for Leacock, however, who in truth was not much of a political scientist or economist. His métier was the comic sketch that applied exaggeration and incongruous juxtaposition to commonplace situations. He began publishing newspaper pieces and eventually collected them himself in a privately published volume in 1907. A visiting British publisher read the book, published him in London, and the rest is history.

From 1910 to 1925 or so, Leacock had a deserved reputation as the funniest writer in English, the man who brought Canada to the world. His fifty-seven books sold in the hundreds of thousands, he undertook successful speaking tours that literally had audiences laughing themselves silly, and he earned huge sums—which he promptly threw away on stock speculation. He was funny in the distinctively droll

Canadian way, and he remains so today. Consider Leacock's comment in *Sunshine Sketches of a Little Town* on the 1911 election in his mythical Mariposa, the Ontario town of Orillia, where he had a summer place on Lake Couchiching. The Liberal Bagshaw tells his gullible electors that "I am an old man now, gentlemen, and the time must come when I must not only leave politics but must take my way towards that goal from which no traveller returns." A hush fell over the crowd. "It was understood to imply that he thought of going to the United States." Mind you, elections were serious business in Mariposa, with the great debate on reciprocity focused on "the price of marsh hay in Missinaba County" and the fact that the "average price of an egg in New York was decimal ought one more than the price of an egg in Mariposa." The people of Orillia were not amused at being caricatured, and Leacock suffered dark looks from the locals for years.

His wonderful book aside, Leacock was a participant in the election of 1911, supporting the Conservative Party's efforts to defeat free trade with the United States by writing propaganda—and being paid well for his efforts. His professorial colleagues were not impressed, one telling his class that all economists were free traders. But, sir, a student cried, Dr Leacock is a protectionist. "I repeat," the reply came, etched in acid, "all economists are free-traders."

Fundamentally imperialist in outlook, Leacock worried over the Americanization of Canada and over the influx of immigrants filling up the West and crowding the city slums. Sometimes he was viciously cruel in his comments, referring once to the "hungriness of the Hungarians and the dirtiness of the Doukhobours," and his fear that Canada would never be able to make citizens of these people. Paradoxically for someone with such an Anglo and Tory outlook, he wrote a book on social problems at the end of the Great War which suggested social security measures and guaranteed work as the only way to counter the dehumanizing impact of modern corporate society on Canadian men and women. Leacock as "Red Tory"?

A bundle of contradictions, Leacock was a superb humorist with a strong melancholic streak. His academic work and his preaching on empire and immigration, however, are all but immaterial. Leacock endures because he was the pre-eminent Canadian humorist of all time and, as such, he is immortal.

59

BORN: Edmonton, Alberta • 21 July 1911

DIED: Toronto, Ontario • 31 December 1980

Marshall McLuhan

AT THE OUTER EDGE OF AN OLD MILLENNIUM, splashy ads in the highbrow *New York Review of Books* peddle a new Marshall McLuhan CD-ROM. Internet web pages dedicated to his ideas boast cult followings around the world. His image, his voice, and his slogans mingle on communication paths that were scarcely conceived of when a serious, middle-aged English professor from Canada first shook up the world. It is all very fitting.

Today McLuhan remains the most famous communications theorist on the planet. At home, he is that rarest of Canadians: a legend of such staggering proportions that who he actually was and what he actually said is buried under an avalanche of myth and confusion. The trick for historians pondering his influence is uncovering the man himself: Who was McLuhan? And did he really matter? Yet detaching the man from the myth is an impossible and probably fruitless endeavour. Simply, McLuhan is important precisely because he was a myth; in his own time and today, people around the globe are drawn to the *idea* of McLuhan, regardless of, or even despite, what he actually wrote and said.

McLuhan was the son of a real estate agent, and his formative years in Edmonton and Winnipeg provide few clues to suggest a future of path-breaking intellectual achievement. He excelled at the

University of Manitoba, however, and completed a doctorate in English at Cambridge in 1942. Appointed a professor of English at the University of Toronto, he gained a reputation as a forceful literary critic in the 1940s, but in 1951 he hinted at his changing interests when he published *The Mechanical Bride*, a book on the power of advertising in a consumerist society. By 1964 the publication of *Understanding Media* and

The Gutenberg Galaxy had demonstrated his success in applying literary criticism to communications technology.

The books gained McLuhan a wide following, but few Canadians, and only a handful of dedicated scholars in other places, have actually read any of them. That is not surprising, considering that he showed little deference to the conventions of written argument and had a frustrating, often impenetrable style.

That didn't matter. In the public mind, McLuhan's enduring intellectual legacy boiled down to one basic proposition: the way we communicate is at least as important as what we communicate. "The medium is the message" was an underwhelmingly simple suggestion, but it was an appealing one. That culture was being ambushed by ever improving communications technology, creating a "global village," had common sense appeal. Revolutionaries, intellectuals, and literary critics awakening to the possibilities of postmodernism found in McLuhan a kind of anti-hero. In a world renewing itself with dizzying speed, Marshall McLuhan alone seemed to see the big picture—although no one could really say so with certainty.

He was a worldwide celebrity by the late 1960s, an overnight sensation created by the same forces that his work described. Installed as the head of his own Centre for Culture and Technology at the University of Toronto by the 1970s, McLuhan continued to test his ideas publicly, but the world was starting to tune out. Soon his communications theory disappeared from popular discourse almost as quickly as it had appeared. His seminal influence continued, however, as communications and media studies emerged as distinct fields of study.

By 1990 he was back. Though he had in fact died a decade earlier, the new ways in which information was criss-crossing the universe hurled the planet into yet another communications revolution and gave McLuhan the mantle of prophet. He saw it all coming, many suggest, and today he is again in vogue as the foundational philosopher of technology and postmodernism—though the caricatures of his work usually presented are at best gross simplifications.

Even as his popularity ebbed and flowed, Canadians have always maintained a special relationship with McLuhan. He is more than a native son; his work has long been a reference point, an article of faith for succeeding generations of Canadians who have attempted to define their space in the cosmos. As political borders have become increasingly contested, a McLuhanesque communications state is now an almost universally accepted description of what defines us.

60

Maurice Strong

BORN: Oak Lake, Manitoba • 29 April 1929

A RAPACIOUS BUSINESSMAN WHOM ENVIRONMEN-
talists decry for the damage he and his kind do to the
Earth? The point man on a host of environmental
crusades, the leading spokesman for the idea that
economic development and environmental integrity
need not be antagonistic? Maurice Strong, to his critics
and admirers, is either one or the other, but perhaps he
is a bit of both. What no one doubts is that he matters.

Born in rural Manitoba to a frequently unemployed Canadian Pacific Railway worker, a man
whose proudest possession was a Loyalist heritage,
Strong is the exemplar of the self-made capitalist.
After a few years of high school, he ran away to sea
during the Second World War and briefly worked as
a fur trader in the Northwest Territories, learning an
Inuit language in the process. Then he worked in the
securities business, for oil companies, and in Africa.
In the mid-1950s, still in his twenties, he found a job
with Dome Petroleum in Calgary and began to earn
serious money, dealing in stock options and running
financial risks every day. Within a few years, labelled
a financial genius by everyone who knew him, Strong
was in Montreal at the helm of Power Corp., a fast-
growing conglomerate with the best of ties to the
Liberal Party both in Quebec City and in Ottawa.

Power Corp. paved the way for Strong's next
career as a Canadian bureaucrat. Summoned by

Prime Minister Pearson to reorganize and galvanize Canadian foreign aid, Strong expanded operations into French Africa, a tactic that served Canadian interests as the difficulties with Quebec's role in La francophonie reached a crescendo. As important, with Pierre Trudeau's help and interest, Strong found the money to raise Canada's aid from roughly 0.4 per cent of GNP to 0.7 per cent. His job took him around the world and introduced him to the movers and shakers.

Naturally, the idealistic and entrepeneurial Canadian,
a man acceptable in corporate boardrooms and at the United
Nations, seemed the ideal person to run the 1972 UN
Conference on the Human Environment and, after its relative
success, to lead the UN's new Environmental Program
created to monitor ecological issues. Then Strong returned
to Canada to run Petro-Canada, the quasi-nationalized oil
company, a company that in Alberta in the period was not
viewed with much favour. "The private sector," Strong
groaned, "thinks you are an oddball or a socialist, and in the
rest of the community you are suspect because you are a businessman." His work as chair of the Canada Development
Investment Corporation in the early 1980s did little to ease
that confused perception of his role and approach.

But to the United Nations, Strong was still a very attractive figure, precisely because he combined business skills, a
conscience, and charisma. In 1984 New York called on him
to manage famine relief in Africa, a huge job of enormous
importance. As Stephen Lewis, at the time Canadian ambassador to the UN, put it, "Whenever there was a critical
moment, Maurice would appear in the country and, magi-
cally, the bottleneck would disappear." Estimates suggested
that 35 million survived who might have starved because of
Strong's program. He then organized the 1992 Earth
Summit, again to global plaudits, and in 1997 a new UN
secretary general called on him to shape the world organization's administrative reform. This was power *and* influence.

How could anyone dislike this giant? Some of the difficulties arose from his activities in Colorado where, with his
second wife, he has been involved in various activities
involving the paranormal and the flakier environmental
groups, while at the same time he has been promoting
schemes that aim to exploit one of the West's largest

untapped aquifers. Strong maintains that he wanted to develop the scheme in an environmentally safe way, but there are doubters aplenty who charge that Strong's philosophy seems to be "think globally, dig locally." Other critics point to some apparently dubious stock promotion schemes and suggest that Strong's efforts in the environmental area are marked consistently by a too-cozy relationship with the corporate world, a combination that produces much talk and far too little action to rein in the greediest corporate exploiters.

Whatever the truth of the allegations, Strong has lost none of his lustre to Canadian governments. Bob Rae's New Democratic Party government seduced him away from his corporate concerns and New Age spirituality to take over Ontario Hydro, a giant utility that was mired in debt. Strong's remedies were sweeping, but their impact for good or ill remains unclear. So too does the overall legacy of his long career as a public bureaucrat and corporate tycoon. There can be no doubt that he did much good in his UN roles; there is no denying that he made millions by riding skilfully along the interface between the corporate and the public. Maurice Strong remains all but unique in Canada as a master of the public and the private boardrooms. And there is still a slight, if dwindling, chance that the UN might call him to be a "Mr. Fix-it" secretary general. This is the role, some say, for which he has been running all his life.

61

Neil Young

BORN: Toronto, Ontario • 12 November 1945

A CASE COULD BE MADE THAT NEIL YOUNG surrendered his eligibility for this book in the spring of 1966, when he left Toronto in a car bound for Los Angeles. For most of the next three decades, the singer lived in California and became that rarest of breeds: a popular musician whose popularity endured. However, if he was *in* the United States, Young was never *of* the United States. While building a remarkably innovative and influential career, he returned home often and, in art and life, remained profoundly Canadian.

There is no question that Young's formative roots were in Canada. Born in Toronto just after the Second World War, Neil was the son of Scott Young, a respected journalist and author. The Youngs lived in or near the city until Neil was fourteen, and his parents' marriage collapsed. Seeking a new start, his mother moved to Winnipeg with Neil and his older brother. Young began high school on the prairie, but he never finished. What gained his attention most were the new kinds of music coming out of England and the United States; a quiet teenager, he neverthe-less formed a band as soon as was able to play the guitar, and he came to know future notables like Joni Mitchell and Randy Bachman who shared his passion. Young was soon playing locally at any place that would have him. He left Winnipeg and arrived in Toronto in 1965, ready to chase a musical dream.

The Toronto folk scene was at its creative peak when Young arrived. He embraced the hippie counterculture in Yorkville and was drawn to the folk music that spilled from every coffee house. Unlike many rock musicians of the era, Young did not reject folk, and he sang in both styles wherever he could in Toronto. Just as he was beginning to be noticed, though, Young set out for California.

The west coast was in musical ferment in the late 1960s, with a communal atmosphere among players that could never last. But before it ended, Young and American Stephen Stills formed Buffalo Springfield, a group whose hit song, "For What It's Worth (Stop, Hey What's That Sound)," became an overnight classic—one of the 1960s' anthems that perfectly captured its era. The band's first album introduced a new kind of upbeat folk-rock and it sold quickly. It was 1967, and the twenty-two-year-old Young had achieved wealth and celebrity beyond his wildest expectations.

But Buffalo Springfield was not built to last. The pop star lifestyle took its toll on the band, and the members soon went in different directions. The break-up was a fortuitous development for Young, however; he was barely more than an adolescent, but he now possessed the resources and the reputation to try new things on his own.

Thirty years on, what he tried stands as one of the singular achievements in contemporary music. In more than thirty albums Young proved that it was possible to link the sophisticated lyricism of folk with the energy of rock. His distinctive voice gave all his music an eerie credibility, and his willingness to borrow from different styles made him something of a pioneer, since, for all its revolutionary rhetoric, most mainstream rock since the 1970s has explored only the narrowest range of the possible. Perhaps his daring was best

demonstrated in 1983, when Young was sued by his record company for producing an album that was "not characteristic of Neil Young."

Still, hits like "Southern Man," "Helpless," and "Heart of Gold" made him unforgettable to millions of fans. And an on-again, off-again relationship with Crosby, Stills, Nash, and Young, the one supergroup of the 1970s that mattered, gave his other solo efforts continued exposure.

Through it all, Young's songs were deeply emotional and personal. Many referred plainly to his childhood in Canada, and the message for other artists back home was clear: Canada was an acceptable place for a rock star to come from. Young also made frequent trips home, often to perform, to collect awards, and to receive honorary degrees. His fame gave him a political platform, and Young—the detached foreigner—did not hesitate to bash or praise the United States when he saw fit.

In the 1990s Young is still producing top-selling records. Unlike most others of his generation, he continues to explore new musical avenues, and he is often referred to as a seminal influence by newer stars.

A recent incident sums up his significance. In the summer of 1995 Eddie Vedder of the grunge rock giants Pearl Jam suddenly became ill on stage. Young, backstage but nearly fifty, was pressed into emergency service as the frontman for the group. Though the band and most of its thousands of screaming fans were less than half his age, he finished out the set on lead vocals and lead guitar. Perhaps only Neil Young could have pulled it off. Without a doubt, only Neil Young would have been asked.

62

Davidson Black

BORN: Toronto, Ontario • 25 July 1884
DIED: Beijing, China • 15 March 1934

THE QUESTION WAS A STARK, UNSETTLING ONE:
Did humankind evolve from apes? Just about
anyone in the nineteenth century could understand
the query, but none could answer it with any degree
of certainty. Charles Darwin had an opinion, of
course, but there were only passionate theories and

no real consensus as the 1900s dawned. The stakes were colossal: all of Western civilization was premised on the idea that God in heaven had put people on earth. So, if "your uncle was a monkey," as many would have it, the way you looked at the world would be turned upside down.

Young Davidson Black graduated into a world grappling with this issue when he left the University of Toronto in 1909 as both a doctor of medicine and a master of arts. He found a job as an anatomy professor in Cleveland, but he quickly made it clear that he hoped to immerse himself in the most famous scientific pursuit of his time: the search for the "missing link" between humans and apes. Convinced that the earliest human beings came from China, he sought the chance to ply his trade there.

Opportunity came in 1920 when the new Peking Union Medical College hired Black as an anatomist and neurologist. This was an unlikely base for cutting-edge archaeology: the medical school was a Rockefeller charitable project, aimed at schooling "primitive" Eastern students in Western medical techniques. It was also a career move of dubious wisdom, since Black was beginning to acquire a reputation as a teacher and a scholar. Yet to China he went, where he worked his teaching duties around attempts to convince his U.S. backers that paying him to dig up the earth in search of early human—or pre-human—remains was worthwhile.

Archaeology is painstaking work at the best of times, but with uncertain backing, Chinese political and military instability, and nothing but educated hunches, what Black found is truly breathtaking. After beginning excavations in various remote sites across China, Black concentrated his work at Chou K'ou-tien, a site atop underground caves just twenty-five miles outside of Beijing. There, in 1927, a break-through occurred when a tooth was discovered. After some consideration, it was enough for Black to declare a new genus of ancient humanity, which he named *Sinanthropus pekinensis*.

The new discovery has greeted cautiously by the world-wide scientific community. After all, could the most controversial theory about human development be confirmed by a single tooth found in a cave? The answer was no, but Black continued to investigate the site. On 1 December 1929 a nearly complete skull was found that affirmed Black's hypothesis that a new species had been found—more man than ape, but more ape than man. It was suddenly clear that Darwin had been on to something after all.

Stories of the discovery of "Peking Man" filled the newspapers and sent archaeologists streaming into China. Black became an instant celebrity, but he left China only to discuss his theories before academic audiences. He wrote extensively on the new species, and was able to put previously misunderstood discoveries into a context that affirmed much of what Darwin had claimed decades earlier.

Black died suddenly in 1934, still a young man but widely recognized and honoured in the annals of science. His foresight and tenacity, the chief attributes of any gifted archaeologist, made his contribution a lasting one: there was little serious doubt after the 1930s that modern humans had evolved, in some way, from more primitive species. For that, the world was a different place.

And while it seems likely that someone, sometime would have discovered the link had Black never gone to China, it might have been well into the 1950s before it occurred. Instability in China and the Second World War interrupted excavation for at least twenty years. Certainly, without Black, and without Peking Man, the triumph of twentieth-century modernism in all fields of human endeavour would have been less complete.

63

Henry Wise Wood

BORN: near Monroe City, Missouri • 31 May 1860

DIED: Calgary, Alberta • 10 June 1941

IN EVERY GENERATION SINCE CONFEDERATION, THE vast Canadian prairie has produced a political personality who defined the times. Louis Riel and Tommy Douglas, for example, were each larger-than-life characters who dominated their respective eras. When impact rather than myth is measured, however, the most influential of them all was a modest, oft-forgotten farmer who did not arrive in Canada until his forties.

Henry Wise Wood was already a successful cattle rancher when he came to Canada in 1904 from Missouri. He had worked his parents' land for several years, but as the head of a growing family he wanted to earn his own prosperity and security. The Alberta prairie was the "Last Best West" in North America, and Wood's was the final generation to break new ground and join in Canada's wheat boom.

Wood joined the United Farmers of Alberta when it was founded in 1909. He had observed with interest the power that American populist organizations had exerted on behalf of farmers, and he was suspicious of the influence that banking and manufacturing interests wielded in the Alberta government. In 1915 the mature, tall, almost completely bald farmer who had just become a British subject was elected vice-president of the UFA. A year later he was president.

The new leader soon learned that though crops

were plentiful and demand was high, many Alberta farmers
still struggled to make a living. This incongruity squared
perfectly with Wood's long-held belief that farmers were
systematically exploited by other social groups. In search of a
general approach to this problem, Wood read widely, trying
to develop a theory of social relations that might help farmers
get their due. He was attracted by the notions of class in the
writings of Marx, but his progressive Christian upbringing
and commitment to democratic government made him
uncomfortable with Marx's class conflict solution. As an
alternative, he gradually developed a model of political

decision-making he called "group government," in which groups organized by economic interest would meet and govern in the interests of all. Conflict, in his scheme, was to be replaced by cooperation.

Farmers found group government a compelling concept and the UFA president a compelling leader. Wood's personal reputation grew to the point where he was widely viewed as the most powerful man in Alberta, and pressure mounted for him to lead the UFA into electoral politics. In 1919 the UFA did jump into politics, with reform of the system as its stated goal. In a province dominated by agriculture, the movement was an immediate success at the polls. In 1921 the UFA won a majority victory, and it remained in power until 1935. Wood declined an invitation to head the government; he was content, it seems, to be the philosophical leader of the movement and to maintain his position outside the political arena.

He also remained in the background when the Progressives, a loose coalition of farmers mainly from Alberta and Ontario, won sixty-five seats in the federal election of 1921. Wood helped shape the platform for the new party and directed his well-organized UFA locals to support it. When it finished second behind Mackenzie's King's Liberal Party, the outlook seemed bright for the reformers both in Ottawa and in Alberta.

But radical change was not to be. The Progressives heeded Wood's advice and refused to become the official Opposition; by the next election, the party was fatally split by King's wooing of the moderates. It disappeared completely within a few years. Back in Alberta, the UFA, once in power, made little effort to change the way the political system worked. "Group government" was never seriously considered, and soon the UFA appeared almost indistinguishable from the Liberals or the Tories.

Wood remained in charge of the farmers' movement and turned his attention to the major postwar concern of Alberta grain growers in the 1920s: the marketing of wheat. When efforts to get both the federal and the provincial governments to regulate sales failed, Wood helped create the Alberta Wheat Pool—a farmer-owned cooperative that kept the sale of the crop in the hands of producers.

By the time he retired from the UFA in 1931, he was, according to his biographer, the "uncrowned king of Alberta." The description was an apt one. Wood single-handedly established the farmers' movement as a dominant force in prairie politics for twenty years. More important, he changed the rules of Canadian politics for good. Though his group government idea—a rare, made-in-Canada political invention—never got off the ground, he helped smash the traditional parties' hold on power in the West. In Alberta, and also in Ottawa, a rich tradition of third-party protest had been established. No longer could the central Canada–based parties take the West for granted. Social Credit, the CCF, the NDP, and the Reform Party all inherited the tradition Wood began, and provincial and federal politics would never be the same.

64

Northern Dancer

BORN: near Oshawa, Ontario • 27 May 1961
DIED: Chesapeake City, Maryland • 16 November 1990

ONCE UPON A TIME ON A FARM OUTSIDE A SMALL town in a northern land called Canada, a brand new baby came into the world. A rich, important man called Mr Taylor owned the farm where the baby was born. He named the newborn Northern Dancer. The year was 1961, and there were high hopes that one day he would grow up to be a racer, just like his father and mother.

As he grew, Dancer trained and trained, but not many people thought he would ever be very fast. The reason? He was too small. "There's no way he'll ever run fast," said the man who looked after him. "He's short, and chunky...and SLOW!" The words stung Dancer. More than anything, he wanted to run fast.

He practised running every day, often with other youngsters at the farm where they lived. It was no use: the more Dancer trained, the more it seemed he would never run fast. This made him angry. One day, when he was out on a long drive, Dancer lost his temper and hurt one of his feet. The man who looked after him cleaned his foot and bandaged it, but the man was annoyed.

Before long, the man talked to Mr Taylor, and Mr Taylor made his decision: "Let us get rid of Dancer," he said. "He will never run fast. We will sell him to anyone who wants him."

By then it was 1962, and on the appointed day Dancer and the others that Mr Taylor did not want were taken to be sold. As the day went on, many of them were sold and taken away to live in faraway places. Many people came to look at Dancer to see if they wanted to buy him. But they were not impressed: "He is so small," they said. "He is not at all like his father or mother."

By the end of the day, nobody had bought Dancer, and Mr Taylor had to take him back to his farm.

"Nobody wanted Dancer," Mr Taylor told his wife when he returned home that night. "I guess we will let him run some races anyway. I don't think he's very fast, but we'll see."

Once again, Dancer was angry, but this time he kept his anger inside. "I'll show them," he said to himself. "I'll show them that I can run fast—faster than anybody in the WORLD!"

Dancer's first race came in August 1963. He was the smallest, but he won easily. Nobody was even close. A few weeks later he won again. In the next few months, Dancer ran seven races and he won five of them. The man who looked after him was not angry with him any more: "I thought you were too small," he told Dancer one day, "but even though you are small, you are very fast."

Mr Taylor was watching Dancer's races, and later in 1963 he decided to take him to the United States. Dancer was nervous—after all, the racers in the United States were very famous, and most of them were known to be very fast. "Don't worry," said the man who looked after him. "Just run as fast as you can."

And that's what Dancer did. He won one race in the United States, and then another. Suddenly, he was famous. Many people wanted to take his picture. Mr Taylor was happy, and Northern Dancer was happy too.

When he turned three years old, Dancer started going to some of the most famous races in the world. All the fastest racers in the world wanted to win them. There was lots of pressure on Dancer: now, all of Canada was cheering him on. People said he was the fastest racer that ever came from Canada. Mr Taylor tried to relax him: "Just race as fast as you can."

On 2 May 1964 Northern Dancer won the Kentucky Derby, the most famous race in the world. He was the first Canadian to win the race, and no one had ever raced it faster. He won the Preakness, another big race. Then he lost a race called the Belmont Stakes. But Mr Taylor was happy: "You have done very well. You are a great racer, but now it is time to go home."

Back at home, there was one more race. In Canada, millions of people wanted to see Northern Dancer, the racer they had heard so much about. At a famous race called the Queen's Plate, they stood and cheered for Dancer for a long time. Now, nobody said he was too small. Nobody said he was too slow. After the cheers stopped, Dancer won the race.

All the races had made Dancer tired. Mr Taylor decided that Dancer deserved a long rest. He built a special place on the farm for him and told the man who looked after him to give Dancer anything he wanted.

It was a nice, comfortable life. Many people came to visit: they all wanted to see the fastest racer Canada had ever had. Some people said that because of Northern Dancer, many more people were now interested in racing. A lot of people said Northern Dancer was one of the most important Canadians ever.

Northern Dancer had many, many wives and many, many children. It made him very happy when some of his children grew up to be very fast. Northfield, True North, and Nijinsky were just some of his children that were great racers. But none of them was as fast as Northern Dancer.

When he was quite old, Dancer moved to the United States, just like many older Canadians do. He wanted to go there to relax and enjoy the nice weather. Mr Taylor built him a cozy place there, and Dancer continued to have more children. He rested, dreamed about all those glorious races, and lived happily ever after.

65

Frank Scott

BORN: Quebec City, Quebec • 1 August 1899

DIED: Montreal, Quebec • 30 January 1985

FRANK SCOTT ARRIVED HOME IN 1923 FEELING depressed. After four years and two degrees at Oxford, he had returned to Montreal to find the city dull, ugly, and backward. This was undoubtedly a reasonable judgment: compared with mother England, Montreal after the Great War was a drab place indeed. In arts and architecture, politics and personalities, the city was profoundly colonial from top to bottom. But, ironically, for Scott, improving this unhappy circumstance meant making Canada *less,* not *more* like the mother country. In fields as varied as law, politics, and poetry, he would spend the rest of his life working towards this goal.

Scott settled down to a teaching job at Lower Canada College in 1923, but he was restless. He began a law degree the following year at McGill, but initially showed more interest in writing poems than learning the law. He and fellow student A.J.M. Smith founded *The McGill Fortnightly Review*, a small, pathbreaking magazine intent on reinventing Canadian poetry in the modernist style. Canadian poetry up to then had been romantic, rigidly Victorian, and imperialistic in outlook. Through his own verse but also through encouraging the work of others, Scott pursued a modernist, nationalist agenda and, almost single-handedly, changed the way Canadian poets approached their subjects.

At the same time, Scott was learning to appreciate the niceties of constitutional law. In 1928, newly married and now editor of the avant-garde journal *The Canadian Mercury*, Scott was named professor of federal and constitutional law at the McGill law school. The roles of legal scholar and modernist poet hardly seemed complementary, but for Scott they were each part of a larger project: to develop an independent, vibrant Canadian culture.

The Depression wracked the Canadian economy while Scott was still a young man, and the experience affected him

profoundly. His poetry became more socially engaged, and the British socialism he had flirted with a decade before re-emerged in a series of published essays. Committed to a progressive, socially conscious Canada, Scott, Frank Underhill, and others formed the League for Social Reconstruction in 1931—a group of progressive academics who aimed to create "a social order in which the basic principle regulating production, distribution and service will be the common good rather than private profit." These were nearly revolutionary words in the early 1930s, and Scott paid a professional price for his political activism when he was passed over for the deanship of law at McGill several times in the 1940s and 1950s for being too "radical." In 1933 Scott helped prepare the Co-operative Commonwealth Federation's Regina Manifesto. Much of the theoretical socialism that Scott had been pushing found its way into the CCF's political platform, and eventually a central bank, central economic planning, and medicare would all be adopted by the mainstream parties.

His involvement in the CCF confirmed his role near the centre of national politics. Scott campaigned widely for Canadian neutrality before the Second World War, and was the national chairman of the CCF from 1942 to 1950. But in the 1950s his attention turned increasingly to his home province. He represented the plaintiffs against the government in the Supreme Court of Canada over Quebec's infamous "padlock law"—which gave the provincial government police-state authority to quell leftist dissent—and he emerged as the leading English-Canadian interpreter of French-Canadian politics and culture. He continued to publish poetry and to translate the best French-Canadian verse into English. All the while, he remained a leading Canadian legal scholar and the braintrust of the national CCF.

In 1961 the long-delayed appointment as McGill's dean of law was finally his. He spent much of the decade as a member of the Royal Commission on Bilingualism and Biculturalism, a project that defined the terms of political debate in Canada for the next quarter-century. In the 1970s and early 1980s Scott continued to write poems and political pieces, his commitment to equality and social justice evident in both.

When Frank Scott died in 1985, there was no great achievement for which he alone was responsible, no climactic moment when he alone made the difference. Instead, his was a lifetime of influence: in law, politics, and poetry, Scott led his country.

Antonine Maillet

Antonine Maillet

BORN: Buctouche, New Brunswick • 10 May 1929

THE PRICE OF FAME CAN BE HIGH. IN 1995 A FIRE broke out in Antonine Maillet's Montreal kitchen. She called the fire department which, quite properly, asked for her name and address. The reply was Antonine Maillet of 735, avenue Antonine Maillet, the street named in her honour after she won France's Prix Goncourt. Not surprisingly, the operator believed the call was a prank and, when matters were sorted out and the engines finally arrived, the kitchen was beyond saving.

Acadia's greatest writer was raised in small towns in New Brunswick, where her parents were teachers and storekeepers. Her education was in local schools, classical colleges, and, eventually, at Université de Montréal and at Laval, from which she received a doctorate in literature in 1970. Briefly a nun, she lived and worked in Paris, toiled for Radio-Canada, and all the while wrote about what she knew and loved—her embattled people, her struggling *nation,* and the will to survive.

Almost all her work, from her first novel through her plays and her television and radio dramas, relies on a fictionalized version of small-village Acadia. Her prose is written in Acadian, a combination of modern French, sixteenth-century dialect, and localisms. Her doctoral dissertation had traced the impact of Rabelais on Acadian French, and she identified hundreds of words that survive nowhere else but in the Acadian patois. In one of her stories, she didactically noted that Rabelais had a vocabulary of one hundred thousand words, many of which disappeared in France but persisted in Acadia. This heritage of language, she said, is "tucked away" in Acadia's "own unconscious, ancestral memory...this language...is alive in us." It is kept alive in Maillet's work, sometimes self-consciously in its evoking of national sentiment. To her, Acadia still exists because of its storytellers.

Maillet's best-known works are *La Sagouine*, which made her name in Canada, and *Pélagie-la-Charette*, which won her acclaim in France and throughout *La francophonie*. The first, roughly translatable as "The Slattern," is the story of a cleaning woman who tells her story as she scrubs the floor; a story of prostitution, poverty, marriage, and strong opinions about the class system of Acadia. Maillet is always on the side of *les pauvres* and never on that of the tightfisted élites (including the clerical élite, which is viciously satirized), and her charwoman is the perfect symbol for her. Naive and wise, passive and resistant, the collective representation of the Acadians though an anti-Evangéline figure, *La Sagouine* won tremendous acclaim on its publication in 1971. The book was brought to life in a brilliant one-woman stage and radio performance by Viola Léger.

Pélagie-la-Charette is a historical saga, the tale of the epic return to Acadia from Georgia by a woman and her children and hangers-on. This 1979 novel, which has sold more than a million copies around the world, is the fictional return of Evangéline after the 1755 expulsion, a triumph over adversity that consciously sets out to recreate the history and mythology of Acadia and establish its cultural distinctiveness. The Prix Goncourt was her reward, the first ever given

to a writer who was not a native of France. Its coincidence with the 375th anniversary of Acadian settlement made it all the more special. For Maillet, the recognition in France was recognition of the Acadian language, praise for the popular speech of Buctouche.

Although Maillet lives in Montreal, she remains an Acadian and a nationalist and to some extent an outsider. The *Guide cultural du Québec* (1982) gives her an entry, but adds that it had to break its rule to exclude Acadians to do so.

Nonetheless, she is closer to the Québécois than to the English-speaking. In 1986 she spoke of the danger that Moncton might become an English city, but then she contrasted the three hundred English-speakers who turned out to celebrate the city's anniversary with the eight thousand Acadians. "The English could not ignore that." What did that prove? "It proves that there's a vitality in the Acadians that the English people in Moncton no longer have." Yes, there is a reason to fear assimilation, but given Acadian history, it is possible that "we'll be able to assimilate the others. When Rome conquered Greece, it was Greece that assimilated Rome!" If that ever occurs, it will likely be the product of an Acadian cleaning woman and her creator.

Andrew McNaughton

BORN: Moosomin, North-West Territories • 25 February 1887

DIED: Montebello, Quebec • 11 July 1966

MEN LOVED ANDY MCNAUGHTON. NO SOLDIER IN this century was so admired by those Canadians he served with and led; no general rose so high and fell so far. And yet, despite losing his overseas command, McNaughton was able to turn himself into the indispensable man by constructing wholly new careers for himself as politician, diplomat, and stout warrior for Canada on international boards and continental commissions.

McNaughton's father ran a trading post in the still-rough country that had been fought over during the Riel Rebellion. There was enough money—and enough concern for education—for Andy to be sent off to Bishop's College School in Quebec when he was thirteen. He did well there and at McGill University, where he studied electrical engineering, completed his master's degree in 1912, and joined the teaching faculty. Two years later, just before the outbreak of war, McNaughton set up his own engineering practice.

The Great War put paid to that. A militia artillery major, newly married, McNaughton went overseas as a battery commander in the first contingent. He had a good war, escaping death though being twice wounded, fathering three children on leaves to visit his wife in England, and rising rapidly in rank. By 1916 his specialty was counterbattery work, the location and destruction of enemy artillery,

a task he undertook with scientific zeal and great success. By 1918 Brigadier-General McNaughton commanded the Canadian Corps' heavy artillery, and he used his guns "to pay the price of victory...in shells, and not in the lives of men." Intelligent, confident, sure of the value of the scientifically trained in battle, McNaughton was at the peak of his powers.

With the peace, he joined the Permanent Force. He took staff courses in England, commanded on the West Coast, and in 1929, at the age of forty-two, became chief of the General Staff, Canada's top soldier. McNaughton's rise had been meteoric, but the Depression forced him to rely on stratagems to keep the army alive. To help deal with the huge numbers of out-of-work men roaming the country, he devised a scheme to use unemployed men to construct a military infrastructure across the land. Labouring for a pittance, the "Royal Twenty-Centers" became a breeding ground for revolution, and McNaughton became a political liability. In the dying days of R.B. Bennett's regime, he was shunted off to lead the National Research Council. At his insistence, he was on secondment from the army, so he retained "the chance of coming back in emergency if required."

The emergency arrived in 1939 when Hitler invaded Poland. Mackenzie King gave McNaughton command of the 1st Canadian Division, writing that "no better man could be selected," and for a time it seemed so. Popular with the troops, who liked his lack of airs, and skilful in presenting the Canadian position in discussions with the British, McNaughton was an inspiring figure compared with the Colonel Blimps who led in the dark days of the war. Soon he was a corps commander and, in April 1942, commander of First Canadian Army. To McNaughton, the Canadians were "a dagger pointing at the heart of Berlin," and he resisted any attempts by Ottawa or London to break up the army so his men could get battle experience. By 1943 this stand had become a liability, and Ottawa insisted on sending one and eventually two divisions to Sicily and Italy. McNaughton's obduracy, combined with increasing doubts about his ability to train his men and his fitness as army commander, led to his ouster in late 1943, a combined operation plotted by British and Canadian generals and by J.L. Ralston, the defence minister. Andy would not get to lead his beloved army against the Hun.

Returned to Canada, the general entertained leadership offers from the Conservative Party and considered taking the post of governor general, but in November 1944 when Mackenzie King called, he eagerly became defence minister and replaced his enemy Ralston. The issue was conscription. McNaughton, as a scientific soldier, did not believe in compulsion, but when he could not find sufficient volunteers to meet reinforcement needs at the front and he was faced with the threat of resignation by senior commanders, he had to accept conscription. Gravely damaged by the crisis, McNaughton lost a by-election in Ontario and failed to be elected in the 1945 general election. His political career, like his military career, had ended in abject failure.

Incredibly, McNaughton was undeterred and he bounced back, much to the good fortune of his country. Mackenzie King appointed him Canadian chair of the Permanent Joint Board on Defence, Canadian representative on the United Nations Atomic Energy Commission, president of Ottawa's Atomic Energy Control Board, and Canadian permanent representative at the UN. All these posts he filled with skill and energy, and the old soldier proved a remarkably effective diplomat. In January 1950 he became a Canadian member of the International Joint Commission, a post he held for twelve years and the scene of his last battle. McNaughton decided that the deal negotiated with the United States to develop the power of the Columbia River favoured the Americans, and he fought against it with determination, only to lose once more.

Fierce in battle and argument, devoted to his country above all, McNaughton's career as soldier and public servant was remarkable. Born just after the North-West Rebellion, he ended as a diplomat of the nuclear era. A fine scientific mind, a powerful charismatic leader, McNaughton believed that once he had worked through an issue and taken a stand, others would automatically agree that he was right. Unfortunately for him, unfortunately for Canada, the world didn't work that way. It might have been better if it had, but Andy McNaughton deserves high marks for grit, determination, intelligence, and his unswerving nationalism.

68

Oscar Peterson

BORN: Montreal, Quebec • 15 August 1925

It is hard to imagine the Canadian jazz scene without Oscar Peterson. Undoubtedly, without him, there would still be summer jazz festivals across the country, and smoky clubs in Montreal and Toronto would still compete for customers by showcasing musicians who emulate the greats. But without Peterson, something of the star quality of jazz in Canada would be missing. With him, the knowledge that one of the all-time greatest came out of Canada makes every club here just a little more exciting.

Peterson was born Canadian but grew up in a world that few Canadians have ever known. He was black and English-speaking in a province that was mostly white and French; he was, therefore, as different as he could be. Anti-black racism was part of daily life for Peterson's family, who lived and played and worked in places whites rarely went. His father, a West Indian immigrant and railway porter, pushed all his children into music, but Oscar was special from the beginning. He played more than one instrument but showed a natural flair for the piano. At fourteen, he won a national piano contest sponsored by the CBC. Soon he had his own weekly program on a local Montreal radio station and was playing at local clubs.

Jazz arrangements were his specialty, though Peterson would later recall that jazz was the only real choice for a black piano player in the 1940s. He also remembered being turned away from many gigs because of the colour of his skin. Promoter Norman Granz discovered the precocious pianist in Montreal, and Peterson debuted at Carnegie Hall in September 1949. In a line-up of stars, the Canadian stole the show. Here was a true virtuoso: Peterson's apparently effortless playing, with dazzling interpretative flourishes rarely seen in one so young, almost

brought the house down. His career was made that night. Most of the next ten years saw him performing with Granz' Jazz at the Philharmonic tours, playing behind and in front of such luminaries as Ella Fitzgerald, Dizzy Gillespie, and Lester Young.

Success brought international fame and fortune and the chance to tour with his own trio. But Peterson continued to make his home in Canada. He moved to Toronto in 1958 and briefly operated a world-famous jazz school there in the 1960s. He also became one of the most successful recording artists of his time—by 1997 he had made almost 100 albums on his own and backed other artists on dozens more. By the 1970s Peterson was easily the most successful jazz pianist on the planet.

In the world of jazz, no other Canadian could come close to that kind of claim. Though critics sometimes scolded Peterson for a failure to innovate, packed orchestra halls, shelves full of Grammy and Juno awards, and ever increasing record sales showed that his popularity with fans had not waned.

Peterson also maintained a high public profile in his native land. In 1983 he spoke out against the dearth of coloured faces in television advertising in Canada. In 1986 he began teaching music part-time at Toronto's York University, and in 1991 he was named the school's chancellor. Even in the 1990s this was a breakthrough of sorts, since few Canadians of colour had ever been appointed to leading positions in universities.

Peterson has been influential on many levels. He is the best-known black Canadian ever, and has doubtless been a role model in ways impossible to measure. His success has ensured a vibrant jazz scene across Canada. Today, and for almost fifty years, jazz for most Canadians begins and ends with Oscar Peterson.

69

Lester Pearson

BORN: Toronto, Ontario • 23 April 1897
DIED: Ottawa, Ontario • 27 December 1972

"A BIG MAN FROM A SMALL COUNTRY"—THAT WAS how an American newspaper characterized Mike Pearson when he was Canada's foreign minister. It was true: Pearson's intelligence, charm, diplomatic skill, and persistence made him a star on the international stage and, as he rose, so did his sometimes reluctant middle-power nation.

The son of a clergyman, Pearson was bright and athletic. He played baseball and hockey with great skill, he studied occasionally, and he made his way to the University of Toronto just as the Great War erupted. Quick to enlist, Pearson served first with a hospital unit in the Balkans and then transferred to the Royal Flying Corps, where a combination of a nervous breakdown and a bus accident in the blackout ended his military career. After demobilization, he completed his degree at Toronto and made his way to Oxford. His most notable success was playing hockey—in Europe he was called "Herr Zigzag" for his weaving skating style, an apt metaphor for his life. Returning home, he joined the history faculty at his alma mater, married a student, coached sports, wrote the examinations for External Affairs, ranked high, and joined the department in 1928. He had found his career.

Pearson discovered that he had to work hard in Ottawa, that his opinions on events and personalities

were sound, and that his service was recognized. He realized too that he was ambitious. At the Canadian High Commission in London he watched the democracies quail before Hitler and Mussolini, and he became a good Canadian neutralist, for a time washing his hands of Europe's quarrels. But by the time war broke out, he had swung around, seeing clearly that the Nazis had to be stopped.

The war gave him his opportunity to shine. Although Norman Robertson, not Pearson, became undersecretary when O.D. Skelton died in 1941, Pearson played a critical role in policy-making in Ottawa until, in 1942, he went to Washington as the number two in the legation; there Pearson ran the mission as he had the high commission in London. In 1945, after helping to create a host of international agencies and boards, he became ambassador to the United States and, in 1946, undersecretary of state for external affairs. Working with Louis St Laurent, the very able foreign minister, and a superb collection of bureaucrats, he laid the groundwork for

Canada's emergence as the leader of the middle powers and the creation of the North Atlantic alliance. In 1948 he joined the Cabinet as foreign minister.

Rich and powerful in a world still devastated by war, Pearson's Canada not only had clout but used it. There was financial and material aid to Europe, there were troops for the Korean War and NATO, there were tough negotiations with Washington in an era, Pearson said, when the time of automatic good relations had ended. And when Britain, France, and Israel colluded in an attack on Egypt in 1956, Pearson rose to greatness. Working the corridors and telephones at the United Nations in New York, Pearson saved the British and French bacon by cobbling together a peacekeeping force—the first such UN operation—that supervised the Anglo-French withdrawal and froze Israeli-Egyptian hostility for a time. It was a diplomatic coup of huge proportions, it won Pearson the Nobel Peace Prize, and it helped the Liberals lose the election of 1957. Many Canadian voters still looked to London as the fount of all international wisdom and resented Pearson's heroics, which they completely misinterpreted as anti-British.

The defeat nonetheless provided Pearson with an opportunity. His Nobel Prize gave him the Liberal leadership in 1958, but his party was slaughtered by John Diefenbaker in the election that year. Not until 1963 did Pearson, tougher and more aware of the requirements of domestic politics, take power at the head of a minority government that pledged "Sixty Days of Decision."

His government was neither decisive nor pretty in its operations. There were continual crises and scandals, Diefenbaker offered an unprincipled but tenacious opposition, and Pearson's seemingly diplomatic desire for compromise on every contentious issue left his ministers constantly disappointed—or dangling precariously out on a limb. Yet the government's record was unquestionably as impressive as that produced by prime ministers who governed longer with safe majorities. There was a distinctive Canadian flag at last; the completion of the welfare state, with the Canada Pension Plan and Medicare; improved but still difficult relations with the United States, then plunging into the morass of Vietnam; and the first serious efforts to make Canada a bilingual nation. Pearson's government also unified the armed forces and continued to play a critical leadership role in peace-keeping, not least in Cyprus.

The record *was* impressive. Weaving and bobbing, stumbling and lurching, Herr Zigzag somehow had carried it off. Still, the definitive statement on Pearson as prime minister came from cartoonist Duncan Macpherson, who drew Pearson as a baseball player fumbling the ball two or three times before scrambling to catch it just before it hit the ground. "The Old Smoothie," Macpherson's half-admiring but devastating caption, said it all.

THE OLD SMOOTHIE

70

Emily Murphy

BORN: Cookstown, Ontario • 14 March 1868
DIED: Edmonton, Alberta • 27 October 1933

Emily Murphy's destiny as one of Canada's
most important reformers was probably sealed on a
summer's day in 1916. It was her first day presiding
over an Edmonton court as a police magistrate—
she was the first woman so elevated in the British
Empire—and an overbearing barrister was already
giving her trouble. "You have no right to be holding
court," he exclaimed at last. "You're not even a
person." This was a startling taunt, but also a legal
argument of some merit at the time. According to
British common law tradition, women were not
"persons" in many areas of the law, and there was
some question whether Murphy was actually eligible
for her post. Eventually the courts ruled she was, and
the empire's first woman judge went on to a
successful fifteen-year career on the bench. She did
not forget the incident, however, and Murphy's name
soon became associated with a legal struggle aimed
at giving a desperately simple question a conclusive
answer: Were women "persons" under the law?

Murphy was already a reformer of some renown
when she accepted her appointment to the bench.
The wife of an Ontario minister, she had followed
her husband's missionary work around Canada
and England for several years before settling in
Edmonton in 1907. A talented and independent
woman who intended to leave her own mark on

society, Murphy had built a prominent career as a freelance journalist and author. *The Impressions of Janey Canuck Abroad* (1902) was especially popular in both Canada and Britain. In Edmonton, Murphy led several municipal reform initiatives and was the prime mover behind the Alberta Dower Act of 1911, which protected the claims of widows to their deceased husbands' estates.

An appointment to the bench came about by accident after Murphy made inquiries on behalf of women who were barred from police court because they were women. Though she had no formal training in the law, she overcame initial scepticism and became a respected judge. Magistrate Murphy was especially known for her unbending approach to narcotics cases, and she published a book in 1922 that became the standard Canadian text on the drug trade for a generation.

Her growing familiarity with the law led her in 1927 to initiate the case for which she is most famous. Under the Supreme Court of Canada Act, any five Canadians had the right to ask Parliament to refer a constitutional question to the country's highest court. Murphy enlisted four other women activists to petition the Liberal government to ask the court if women were "persons" eligible for appointment to the Canadian Senate. Mackenzie King's Liberals agreed to ask the question, but the Supreme Court's answer in 1928 was a setback. Persons, the court held, meant men—that was the intention of the Fathers of Confederation, and that was how it ought to be. Murphy and the others pressed the case to the highest court in the empire, and a voice of sanity was heard at last in 1929. The Judicial Committee of the Privy Council ruled that "the word persons includes members of the male and female sex." It was an undiluted victory: Canadian women were at last legally guaranteed political

equality, and the empire's highest appeal court had made its
first avowedly pro-woman statement.

Many expected that Emily Murphy would be the first
women appointed to the Senate, but Prime Minister King
gave that honour to well-known Liberal Cairine Wilson in
1930. Murphy was disappointed, but she used the fame won
by the court case to campaign across Canada for the rights of
women. Before she died suddenly in 1933, few "persons" of
either sex could claim to have made such a difference.

71

Jean-Victor Allard

BORN: Saint-Monique de Nicolet, Quebec • 12 June 1913

DIED: Trois-Rivières, Quebec • 22 April 1996

"I AM A GOOD CANADIAN, ONE OF THOSE WHO feel at ease anywhere between the Pacific and the Atlantic," said General Jean Allard in his memoirs. He was that, and a brave man too. But Allard was pre-eminently a French Canadian, one who made his career in the armed forces, an institution that, for most of his life, was largely alien to Québécois.

Orphaned at an early age, educated in Quebec and Ontario, Allard was an independent-minded

man. That undoubtedly led him to join the militia in his home town of Trois-Rivières in 1933 and to remain in it, despite its low status, through the Depression. A major in an ill-equipped armoured regiment at the outbreak of war in 1939, Allard pushed to get overseas and then cajoled his way to Italy as second-in-command of the famous Van Doos. Soon he had a Distinguished Service Order won in action on the Arielli, the command of his regiment, a second DSO for his leadership in the cracking of the Gothic Line, the command of a brigade in Holland, and then an almost unprecedented third DSO. His record in action was second to none, and he stayed in the regular army with the peace.

Allard went to Moscow as military attaché in 1945 and, because Soviet suspicions meant that he never could get to see the Red Army, he occupied himself in learning Russian and developing an appreciation for serious music and ballet. During the Korean War he commanded the Canadian infantry brigade fighting in that United Nations "police action," and his developing friendship with the British commander of the Commonwealth Division there led in 1961 to his unprecedented appointment as general officer commanding Britain's 4th Infantry Division in Germany. His obvious concern for the troops, his willingness to lead by example, made him a huge success, and when Lester Pearson's defence minister, Paul Hellyer, began to move to integrate and then unify the Canadian Armed Forces, Allard was a natural choice for the highest ranks.

First he became a lieutenant-general, the highest rank ever held by a French-Canadian soldier, in command of Mobile Command. Then in 1966, with senior officers resigning *en masse* as unification and the elimination of service uniforms and traditions loomed, Hellyer tapped him to be chief of the Defence Staff and a four-star general.

Shrewd and calculating, Allard told the minister that he was grateful for the offer but had some conditions. Would the government undertake to ensure that all barriers to the advancement of francophones in the armed forces were eliminated? Would the minister support the establishment of FLUs—French Language Units? Hellyer gulped but agreed, and the deed was done. The bilingualization of the Canadian Armed Forces moved ahead, and before Allard's term was over, French language fighter squadrons, ships, and armoured and artillery regiments were in place. The adoption of the new green uniforms sported by the unified forces simultaneously hit at many of the remnants of British traditionalism that had kept the military an Anglo bastion. General Jean-Victor Allard had revolutionized and Canadianized the armed forces. At the same time, by creating FLUs, he had laid the groundwork for the armed forces of an independent Quebec nation, though this was never his intention.

Allard, a true believer, also had the difficult task of selling unification to sceptical officers and men. He tackled the job the same way he had done everything in his life—straight on. "I spoke to many men. I told them that this was not just a question of integration, but modernization and change. I told them if they didn't accept the challenge I didn't want them." Some left, but most of those who remained came to appreciate the merits of a unified military.

A good Canadian, a brave man, a leader. But in his memoirs, published in 1985, Allard looked at the position of his francophone compatriots in the military and in Canada as a whole and said bluntly: "To my infinite regret," if the situation does not improve, "Quebec will probably have no choice but to follow its own path." The French Language Units he was instrumental in establishing would likely be available to protect that path, if necessary. When he died in 1996 after a long illness, the referendum of 1995 had brought Quebec close to independence. How, or if, Jean-Victor Allard voted in the referendum remains unknown.

72

Glenn Gould

BORN: Toronto, Ontario • 25 September 1932

DIED: Toronto, Ontario • 4 October 1982

Fans and friends, intimates and strangers could all agree on one thing about Glenn Gould: he was more than a little weird. He often wore winter gloves, a hat, and an overcoat on hot summer days. He liked to sleep during the day and record music all night. He lived for days on nothing but milk-shakes and custard. His friends rarely saw him, but he would often call them on the telephone late at night and talk for hours at a time. He was, in short, one of the great Canadian eccentrics of all time.

Less extraordinary but more important, he was also one of the great musical geniuses of his era. His interpretations of pieces performed thousands of times before were nothing short of revolutionary; his infrequent live performances are still talked about; and his achievements in recorded music were ahead of his time.

It was apparent early on that Gould had a head start on becoming both an eccentric and a genius. At three, he could read music and had perfect pitch. He showed a passion for the piano immediately on being introduced to it. At school, meanwhile, he was mostly withdrawn and self-absorbed; friends remember him vigorously conducting silent symphonies on the walk home. Despite his parents' concern that Gould not be rushed into public performance, it soon became clear that they had a child prodigy on their hands. His debut at the age of thirteen attracted rave notices, and, a year later, Gould was concerto soloist with the Toronto Symphony Orchestra. He was a regular on CBC radio before he was twenty.

When he first took the stage in the United States in January 1955, the response was overwhelming: Gould's passion for every note he played, evidenced in his extreme

shifts of tempo and intensity, made the works he performed unfamiliar to many who had heard them before. He signed a recording contract almost immediately and embarked on a world tour. The same year, Gould's recorded version of Bach's Goldberg Variations—his first major album—was received as a milestone accomplishment. Bach's careful, measured harmonies seemed to take on a life of their own.

In no time he gained the celebrity status that most classical musicians could only dream about. It helped that, talent aside, Gould cut an unforgettable figure every second he was on the stage. He hummed aloud; he often appeared bewildered and distracted; his hair was unruly and his clothes often rumpled; his piano stool was so low that he seemed to be reaching up to the keyboard.

The media's obsession with his quirky character traits made Gould's performances sometimes seem like a circus act. Certainly he felt that way and often threatened to leave the concert stage forever. Finally, he made up his mind. "The concert is dead," Gould announced after a show in Chicago on Easter Sunday in 1964, with typical determination but uncharacteristic clarity. Nobody believed him at first, but at the age of thirty-one, his performance career was over for good.

His life at the keyboard was just beginning, however. Gould's self-absorption had always been about perfecting the music, and the recording studio gave him the opportunity to aim for perfection. Typically, he recorded a piece from start to finish, then slowed the tape down and painstakingly fixed every possible flaw. No classical artist had ever approached recording this way, and Gould's experiments with microphone placements, balancing, and editing were far ahead of his time. The results, measured in reviews and record sales, were spectacular.

Though a reclusive figure from the mid-1960s, Gould developed a sideline career in radio. He starred in several documentaries and produced others on his own. He was on the verge of giving serious attention to becoming a regular conductor when he died suddenly of a massive stroke, not long after his fiftieth birthday. By then Gould had recorded more than eighty albums that, combined, sold over 1.2 million copies.

Of course, Glenn Gould's live and recorded piano performances were only as good as the individual listeners thought they were. Many were stunned, some even awed, at the way this Canadian played the piano. But there remained those who were unimpressed, claiming that Gould was recklessly extravagant in his musical interpretation and more crazy than brilliant. Either way, the world of live and recorded classical music that he left was far different from the one he found.

73

Louis Robichaud

ALL ACROSS CANADA, ORANGEMEN WERE PREPARING for their annual celebration of King Billy's victory over the Irish Catholics that morning of 12 July 1960. But in Fredericton there was more than a tinge of gloom over the arrival of the Glorious Twelfth. That very day a French-speaking Roman Catholic Acadian would become premier of the province, and the thought chilled the descendants of the Loyalists who had governed for so many years.

Louis Robichaud, though one of ten children of a sawmill operator, village postmaster, and strong Liberal, had opportunities most Acadians did not. He went to school, to a classical college, to university, and he articled with a local lawyer. In 1952, a fervent Acadian turned social reformer by his schooling at Université Laval, he was called to the bar and opened his law office in Richibucto.

That same year, short but sturdy and still in his twenties, he won the nomination to run for the Liberal Party in Kent, a seat that had been Liberal for fifty years. He won easily and his rise was spectacular, as he demonstrated a capacity to get re-elected and to impress his party colleagues. In 1958 the province's Liberals selected him as their leader, and in the election two years later, after a brilliant campaign that saw him cover 50,000 miles, shake what seemed like a million hands, and deliver his passionate speeches in

virtually every schoolhouse and auditorium, he won power on 27 June 1960, the youngest premier in his province's long history. He had campaigned against New Brunswick's archaic liquor laws, against a compulsory hospital insurance tax, and Tory government corruption. Expectations were high.

Robichaud lived up to them. He set out to ensure that

Acadians, living in the poorest parts of New Brunswick with the weakest schools, received their due. "We want to stop the outward flow of our people," he said, perhaps thinking of his family members who had emigrated to Maine. "This is no time to be firmly entrenched in the past." He brought francophone civil servants to Fredericton; he set out actively to recruit industry for his province; and he adopted the recommendations of a royal commission that transferred the costs and controls of the municipalities to his government in areas of education, public housing, welfare, justice, and public utilities. The aim was to provide a minimum acceptable level of services to every New Brunswicker.

This "Program of Equal Opportunity for All" was quickly denounced by many English-speaking New Brunswickers and by the newspapers controlled by K.C. Irving, the province's wealthiest citizen, as a scheme to make the Anglo majority subsidize the Acadians. The plan, the Opposition argued as it launched a filibuster against "King Louis," would "rob Peter to pay Pierre," an all but open attempt to fan the flames of anti-French bigotry. Robichaud persisted, however, forcing his plan through. "New Brunswick has no pockets of poverty," he argued, "we have only pockets of prosperity." There could be no doubt that the province's premier had begun the process of equalizing opportunity for francophone New Brunswick.

Skilfully, he persuaded an Ottawa that was anxious over Quebec's restiveness to provide funds to speed New Brunswick's economic transformation and to help weld Acadians to Canada. He was no separatist, he said, and "there is not one separatist among us," but Ottawa wanted to be certain. The result was a ten-year program, with 75 per cent of the funding provided by the federal government, to improve life in rural, depressed areas, to upgrade education and vocational training, and to build public housing and roads. "We are not afraid of change if it is due," the premier claimed, "and believe me in New Brunswick it is long overdue."

But change frightens people and, although he retained power in the 1963 and 1967 elections, a tired and depressed Robichaud fell before Richard Hatfield and the Conservatives in the election of 1970. Strikingly, Hatfield was no typical Tory. He moved to reinforce the efforts Robichaud had made to improve life for the Acadians of the poorest parts of the province and, before the end of his long time in office, he made New Brunswick officially bilingual.

Robichaud had pushed and pulled New Brunswick into the present, providing equal rights for all and setting his province on the road to equal opportunity. In his decade in power, he left an indelible stamp on the country. His subsequent service on the International Joint Commission and in the Senate must have seemed anticlimactic to a man who had accomplished his best work by the age of forty-five, but Robichaud's achievements had been impressive by any standard.

Frank Stronach

74

BORN: Weiz, Austria • 6 September 1932

Hᴇ ʟɪᴋᴇʟʏ ᴅɪᴅ ɴᴏᴛ ʀᴇᴀʟɪᴢᴇ ɪᴛ ᴀᴛ ᴛʜᴇ ᴛɪᴍᴇ, ʙᴜᴛ the seeds of Frank Stronach's success were sown in 1965. That year a comprehensive trade treaty between Canada and the United States on manufacturing cars came into effect. The "Autopact" created a free-trade zone in car-making between the two countries and guaranteed Canadian jobs in a mammoth industry that was almost wholly foreign-owned. For Canadian business the Autopact was an opportunity; nobody took more advantage of that opportunity than Stronach.

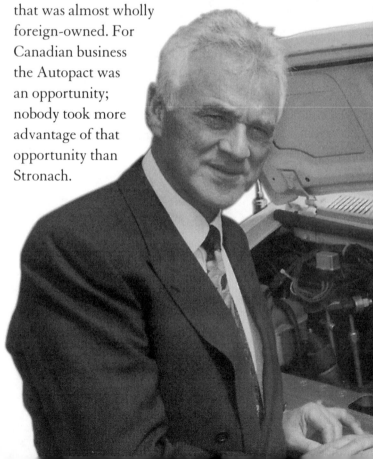

He was born Frank Strohsack in a worn-down Austria still in the clutches of the Great Depression and soon to be annexed by the Third Reich. At fourteen, he apprenticed as a tool-and-die maker, but left his Allied-occupied homeland four years later for Switzerland and a job as a machinist. Europe after the war held little hope for someone with boundless ambition, and promises of fortunes to be made in the new world drew him to Canada in 1954.

He became Frank Stronach—a name he decided was easier to pronounce—and took a series of odd jobs before settling in Toronto at a machine shop. By the late 1950s he had his own shop, financed with the aid of a fellow Austrian immigrant. Stronach built his outfit into a ten-person operation specializing in cutting-tools, but in 1959 received his first order for auto parts: a door bracket contract for industry monolith General Motors. The marriage of auto parts and Frank Stronach, it was soon clear, was made in heaven.

In 1969 Stronach merged his company with Magna Electronics Corp., a smallish defence supplier. He was in full control of the new company, Magna International Ltd., a year later. With his chief customers the Big Three American car-makers, the business grew rapidly. Magna took advantage of southern Ontario's proximity to Detroit and the lower wages of Canadian workers to build a competitive advantage in the economic sector that had long been the province's industrial core. It also gained business by using its own technical expertise to solve design and assembly problems for the auto manufacturers. With Stronach insisting on a decentralized organization that rewarded managers and employees involved in successful plants, Magna exploded in size during the 1970s. By 1984 it operated forty-three mostly Canadian plants and sold nearly $500 million in car parts.

By then, Stronach was a multimillionaire, and Magna

was the major player in the sometimes fragile Canadian automotive sector. When the Canada–U.S. Free Trade Agreement was approved, he pledged to enter politics to derail the deal. He failed to win a seat for the Liberals in 1988, however, and Stronach had to turn to saving his faltering empire.

Magna's continued expansion had left its management overstretched and its debts mounting. As Japanese imports cut into the market share of North American manufacturers and overall car sales became sluggish, few analysts concluded that Magna could survive. But Stronach closed plants, sold others, and restructured his company to concentrate on its core business. By the mid-1990s he was on top again, capitalizing on rebounding car sales and a push in the industry to contract out production to cheaper suppliers. This initiative, which could see Magna explode in size again in the next decade, has often been viewed as a strategic end-run around the unionized plants of the Big Three to un-unionized workers in Stronach's empire. But the Canadian entrepreneur is quick to defend his policy of discouraging unions by giving employees a significant share in Magna's profits.

Today those profits are astounding: in 1995 Magna earned over $300 million on sales of nearly $5 billion. It is impossible to imagine the Canadian automotive sector without Magna. Indeed, without Stronach, there is no doubt that many of his company's jobs would exist instead in Michigan or Louisiana.

Stronach's is a kind of Canadian success story that has been repeated thousands of times. He came to this country as a poor immigrant and, through hard work and good timing, built his own successful business. What makes Stronach different is the degree of his success.

75

Floyd Chalmers

BORN: Chicago, Illinois • 14 September 1898
DIED: Toronto, Ontario • 26 April 1993

CLOSE TO HIS NINETIETH BIRTHDAY FLOYD CHALMERS
took time to reflect on a life of arts patronage and
concluded: "I don't think I've ever made a bad investment in the arts." Every project and every plan he
supported, Chalmers remembered, was a worthwhile
effort. He admitted to only one peculiar regret: he
never learned to play the piano. "And after all these
years of loving music, being so closely involved with
it, could I tell you where middle C is?" he wondered
aloud. "Maybe—but I doubt it."

Here was a comment that summed up perfectly
the irony of Chalmers' life: this was a man who
donated thousands of hours and millions of dollars
to fields of endeavour about which he had only superficial knowledge. But to legions of Canadian artists,
and to succeeding generations who would value their
efforts, Chalmers' admitted lack of expertise never
mattered. When he died, his contribution to the arts
spoke for itself.

Unlike most philanthropists of renown, Chalmers
did not enjoy a privileged upbringing. Born in the
United States, Chalmers' working-class family
migrated to Orillia and then, when Floyd was a boy,
to Toronto. A stint in the Canadian Army during the
1914 war confirmed his Canadianness, and Chalmers
returned from Europe eager to earn a living in
Toronto. He found a job at the *Financial Post*, a

division of the Maclean Publishing Company, and worked initially as a reporter and ad salesman at the business newspaper. He showed an uncommon knack for securing the confidence of the most important Canadian business leaders and gained the *Post* a steady supply of inside information. In 1925 the precocious journalist was named editor of the paper.

Chalmers rose quickly through the ranks of what became the Maclean-Hunter publishing empire. In 1952 he started a twelve-year stint as company president; they were crucial years, as Maclean-Hunter expanded its operations and became the single most important media group in the country. Chalmers became chairman of the board in 1964, and remained a company adviser well into his retirement.

While building his career, Chalmers fell increasingly in love with the arts—or more precisely, with the idea of helping the arts. He began modestly, volunteering with the Toronto Conservatory of Music and helping to found what would become the Canadian Opera Company. In 1951 he offered spirited encouragement to Tom Patterson's plan for an annual Shakespearean festival in Stratford, and later became the drama company's most important fundraiser. But if these early activities were important, they paled in comparison with the money that Chalmers began to distribute personally in 1964. That year, Maclean-Hunter made a public share offering for the first time and Chalmers, who had gradually accumulated a 22 per cent interest in the company, decided to sell a big chunk of his stake. Shares were snapped up by investors, and Chalmers made a multi-million dollar profit overnight.

Only a fraction of the windfall was signed over to the Chalmers Foundation at first, but the retired businessmen soon discovered that he enjoyed doling out money whenever he found a deserving artistic project. For Canadian artists, it was too good to be true: Chalmers typically sought expert advice on potential projects, then left project design and implementation to the artists themselves. He seldom inter-fered, and lacked all the pretensions that often must be indulged in patrons. Chalmers insisted only that his aid be directed to Canadians and that the highest standards be maintained.

The results, measured in buildings and achievement, litter the Canadian artistic landscape. Chalmers himself paid for the Centennial opera *Louis Riel*, the *Encyclopedia of Music in Canada*, and dozens of endowed awards in theatre, music, and dance. Major contributions were made to Stratford, the Canadian Opera Company, the National Ballet, and the St Lawrence Centre for the Arts in Toronto. He also ensured that his influence would outlive him: first through the Ontario Arts Council, and, more recently, through his daughter Joan, family money has continued to find its way into artists' hands,

Chalmers, given the gift of long life, expressed approval for the culture he had wrought but never seemed interested in injecting himself into the projects he supported. He spent, observed, and approved, but forever remained the businessman who could not find middle C.

76

Richard Pound

BORN: St Catharines, Ontario • 22 March 1942

THE TIME IS 1894; THE PLACE IS PARIS. A HANDFUL of aristocrats are hatching plans for the modern Olympic Games with a spirit so remote from today's games that, in hindsight, they seem hopelessly naive. The games, they announce, will feature world-class competition, but above all they will be friendly and stress good sportsmanship. Gentleman amateurs will compete under national colours; professionals will not

be welcome. Sport for sport's sake will be stressed. The first Olympic Games is scheduled for Athens in 1896, the home of the ancient competitions. About 245 athletes from fourteen countries will take part.

Fast forward to 1996. In Atlanta the centennial Olympic Games are the biggest cultural event ever staged. They are a capitalist carnival: the budget is $1.5 billion and garish advertisements assault the senses from every direction. Television cameras record everyone's every move. About 10,000 athletes take part, representing 197 countries. Many have become rich from sport. Almost all, in some form or other, are corporate-sponsored: by shoe companies, film companies, soft-drink companies. The Olympic Games have become one of the biggest businesses on earth.

A good deal of the credit—or blame—for that development rests on the shoulders of Montreal tax lawyer and IOC vice-president Dick Pound. For Pound, the climb up the Olympic greasy pole began in the swimming pool. After his family moved to Montreal when he was fourteen, he joined a swim club and in short order was the fastest 100 metre swimmer in the country. His athletic career peaked with a sixth-place finish in that event at the 1960 Olympics in Rome. He quit competitive swimming in 1962 and proceeded to speed through law school and chartered accountancy exams. With his professional life just starting to take shape in 1968, he accepted a volunteer post with the Canadian Olympic Association.

By then the Olympics were a good deal bigger than their founders ever imagined, but they had failed to live up to some of their loftier goals. They were also in a lot of trouble. The IOC was chronically broke and, increasingly, political protests were stealing headlines away from the competition itself. Questions about the purported "amateur" status of Eastern-bloc athletes were also harming the event's credibility.

As Pound grew up with the Canadian Olympic movement, things went from bad to worse: the 1972 Munich Games were marred by murderous terrorism, and the 1976 Montreal Games were skipped by much of Africa. A U.S.–led boycott of the 1980 Moscow Games threatened to sabotage the Olympics for good.

That year, Juan Antonio Samaranch of Spain was elected president of the IOC with a mandate for reform. To help in this task, he enlisted Dick Pound—by 1980 head of the COA and a rising young tax lawyer in Quebec. Pound was unusual among the volunteer IOC brass: young, middle class, and a former Olympian himself, he seemed well suited to help modernize the games.

The tonic that Pound found for the games was television. In 1984 Los Angeles hosted the summer Olympics that no other city wanted—and, against the odds, turned a tidy profit. On their own initiative, local organizers staged the first commercial games by finding advertisers to pump millions into the operating budget. The real target of the ads was the U.S. television market, and Pound's job was to keep the dollars coming in. Though the Olympics had been on television in some manner for thirty years, the trick now was to turn the games into a truly made-for-TV event. Accordingly, Pound supervised an Olympian change in approach. Professionals were gradually welcomed to the games to create events that people around the world wanted to watch. Schedules and events were geared to the at-home audience—less entertaining sports were gradually ditched, and events of dubious stature such as beach volleyball were added. Then, all Pound had to do was open up the bidding for the right to televise the Olympics. By 1996 he had sold

TV packages to networks around the world, increasing the games' revenue ten- and twentyfold. Already, the American network NBC has paid $2.3 billion for the right to televise the games in 2004, 2006, and 2008.

Television was only the beginning: Pound also successfully built up IOC revenues in non-Olympic years. In 1986 he launched the "The Olympic Program," a marketing scheme that allowed major sponsors to associate their products with the games for a four-year period. For what now amounts to $40 million apiece, several companies have lined up to give the IOC their money.

The Olympics have travelled a long road from 1894 to today. No one talks about gentleman amateurs anymore, and sport for sport's sake is a creed useful more in the saying than the doing. The games are just another big entertainment production, now on a global scale, and TV ratings seem as important as medals and competition. For better or for worse, however, the only significant quadrennial international athletic competition in the world has survived. For Richard Pound, now favoured by some to be the next IOC president, it has been a job well done.

77

BORN: near Beardmore, Ontario • 14 March 1932

Norval Morrisseau

NATIVE AND NON-NATIVE CANADIANS HAVE LIVED
separate lives in the twentieth century. Technological
and cultural differences between natives and
newcomers made coexistence tricky at first, but
governments that continually shunted aboriginals
onto reserves made sure that natives would live this
century mostly outside mainstream Canadian life.
The glaring cultural gap persists, but native painter
Norval Morrisseau was the first to bridge it in a
meaningful way. In so doing, he emerged as the
catalyst behind a collective reassessment of native
Canadian culture.

The place between native and white societies has
often been a lonely, troubling one for Morrisseau. He
was born on the Sand Point Reserve in northwestern
Ontario to Ojibwa parents. His French name came
from his grandfather, but Morrisseau was raised in
a fashion typical for natives in mid-century Canada:
formal education was intermittent, and exposure to
cultural trends from the south almost non-existent.
His life was filled with the sort of poverty and
despair common on reserves, and he battled a booze
addiction than began when he was a child. What
Toronto art dealer Jack Pollock saw when he
"discovered" Morrisseau in 1962, therefore, was
nothing short of stunning.

In the remote Ontario bush, Pollock found bold,

colourful pictographs on birchbark and paper that made
Ojibwa legends come alive. People and spirits commingled
in Morrisseau's drawings in a stark, unprecedented way.
The pictures were remarkable in themselves but were made
more so because, for the first time, authentically native paintings were created that could be hung on walls: previously,
native legends were executed on rock formations or everyday
objects. Thus, Morrisseau's vision was perfectly suited for a
Western-style exhibition. Pollock quickly arranged a
Toronto showing for his new client, and the paintings were
an overnight success. In a matter of days, the careers of both
Morrisseau and Pollock were made. Suddenly the native
artist who lived in a shack beside a garbage dump in
Ontario's far north was the toast of the urbane, white
world of the south.

Not surprisingly, the ride from reserve to art exhibition
was a bumpy one. Morrisseau was charting a new path and
had to endure the celebrity that came with being famous: to
white society, natives had long been respected craftmakers,
but Ojibwa paintings that were chic were real news.
Morrisseau coped by drinking away most of the money he
made. Later, he faced painful, humiliating denunciations
from tribal elders, who decided his paintings denigrated
native myths by putting them on public display. But
Morrisseau continued to paint. His reputation as the best-
known native painter was sealed in 1967 when his specially
commissioned painting for Expo 67 in Montreal brought
acclaim from a world audience.

This sort of success created a new interest in native
society and culture in the rest of Canada. Morrisseau's
works pointed to the sophistication and distinctiveness of
aboriginal nations. Other native artists copied him, and
Morrisseau's genre even acquired the prestige of its own

name when he became known as the leader of the
"Woodland" style. Academic and political studies of native
Canadians in the 1970s and 1980s reflected this change: more
and more, "tribes" were viewed as "nations," and a new
respect for native society was evident. Prevailing assump-
tions about the "primitiveness" of native culture seemed
on the way out at last.

It is impossible, of course, to credit Morrisseau exclusively with all these developments. The years he spent in the 1970s and 1980s in a blurry alcoholic haze and his reluctance to assume any overtly political role make his connection to these changes an apparently tenuous one. Yet no other native had a similar profile in the arts community, and no one else engendered such sustained examination of the native myths and traditions he depicted.

Morrisseau has been widely criticized in recent years for not developing his style further, and his tentative examination of mystical and Christian themes has been rejected by many. He doubtless is far less influential than he once was. History will remember him, however, as the most important single person in bringing Canadian native culture a measure of acceptance on its own terms.

78

T.C. Douglas

BORN: Falkirk, Scotland • 20 October 1904
DIED: Ottawa, Ontario • 24 February 1986

A VERY GOOD BOXER IN HIS YOUTH, TOMMY DOUGLAS believed in fighting his battles all out but shaking hands after the match. In 1944, when he led the Co-operative Commonwealth Federation to victory in Saskatchewan and made himself health minister as well as premier, he met the outgoing Liberal minister. "Have you any suggestions for a man taking over the Department of Public Health?" he asked courteously. "You made the promises, you know all the answers," came the reply, "go ahead and see what you can do." Never one to be intimidated, Douglas shot back, "That is precisely what we intend to do...we plan to do more in the next four years than you've done in the last twenty-five." And he did.

Douglas came to Winnipeg in 1910 with his family, but his iron-moulder father returned home to join a Scots regiment on the outbreak of war. The family followed, and it was not until 1919 that they were all reunited in Manitoba. There was little money, much Baptist religion, and for the cocky Douglas an apprenticeship as a printer. But the church called and, just out of his teens, he went to Brandon College for six years, leaving in 1930 as an ordained Baptist preacher and nascent socialist.

Douglas arrived at his parish in Weyburn, Saskatchewan, just after the Depression had devastated global markets, a plague multiplied in force in

Saskatchewan by the combination of drought, wind, and grasshoppers. Quickly he came to the realization that the kingdom of God could not be achieved on earth without political action, and he joined the newly created CCF. He ran in 1934 in a provincial election, lost, and ran once more in the 1935 federal election. This time he won, and for nine years he sat in Ottawa as the CCF's "agricultural specialist," an honour indeed for a man who had never farmed a day in his life. Earning a reputation as one of the best debaters in the

House for his humorous, pointed, frequently self-deprecating and sarcastic style, Douglas and the tiny CCF caucus pressed for social legislation without much success. In 1944 the young MP returned to Saskatchewan, became CCF provincial leader, and, in the next general election, overcame a Liberal campaign that slandered the CCF as national socialists and won a huge majority. The first social-democratic government in North America was in power.

Hard-working, a taskmaster, and not one to suffer calmly the incompetence of ministers, aides, the Opposition, or the press, Douglas understood that the party leader's task was that of the orchestra conductor: to keep everybody playing the same score while he beat time. His tempo was fast as he set out to implement his campaign slogan of "Humanity First." His first budget allocated 70 per cent of expenditure to social services, granting old age pensioners free medical, hospital, and dental care, and taking over all costs for the treatment of cancer, tuberculosis, mental illness, and venereal disease. In 1947 health minister Douglas introduced universal hospital insurance, fulfilling his promise to the electorate. As a child, Douglas had suffered from osteomyelitis, a bone disease, and his leg had been saved only through a combination of charity and good fortune. He wanted others to have a right to care, and not to be forced to rely on good fortune. At mid-century in Canada, these were still almost revolutionary ideas.

In 1960 he decided on Medicare. Running in a vicious election campaign against Ross Thatcher's Liberals, the folksy orator pulled out all the stops. Laughing at himself, jabbing at his opponents with corny jokes and biblical allusions, his natural but studied speaking style was at its best as he promised to put a universal medical care plan into effect and, moreover, one that would satisfy doctors and patients.

He easily won his government's fourth successive election and moved to negotiate with the doctors, who were fearful of their rights, prerogatives, and incomes. The bill to put universal medical care in place was introduced in the legislature a few weeks before Douglas resigned as premier to lead the newly created federal New Democratic Party. It fell to his successor, Woodrow Lloyd, to implement Medicare in the face of a long, bitter doctors' strike and to lose power to Thatcher in 1964. Significantly, the Liberals dared not repeal Medicare, and the federal Liberal government, before the decade was out, made it a national program. This was Tommy Douglas' enduring gift to Canada.

For Douglas, the NDP national leadership was no bed of roses. He lost a 1962 by-election in his home province, a residue of the bitterness over Medicare, and the anticipation felt by social democrats over the NDP's marriage of farmers and labour turned to ashes. His high point in Ottawa came when he led his party in opposition to the Trudeau government's imposition of the War Measures Act in the October 1970 FLQ crisis. That principled stand won him few friends then, but kudos years later.

Wounded but not slain by his failure to translate his Saskatchewan success onto the national scene, Douglas remained leader until 1971, and he stayed an MP until 1979. Injured when he was hit by a bus in Ottawa in 1984 and suffering from cancer, Douglas succumbed in his eighty-first year. Praised in Parliament, hailed as the great social visionary he was, Douglas would have laughed to hear his virtues intoned by those who had fought him. "There is nothing the upper classes are so fond of," he once noted shrewdly, "as a dead radical."

79

Gaétan Dugas

BORN: Ancienne-Lorette, Quebec • 28 February 1953
DIED: Quebec City, Quebec • 30 March 1984

I<small>T IS DIFFICULT TO PINPOINT EXACTLY WHY, BUT</small> there was something un-Canadian about Gaétan Dugas. Perhaps he was too brash and too confident. Maybe he was more fearless than Canadians are said to be. Certainly he was more flashy and seductive in a way that most of us never aspire to—even in our raunchiest dreams. But typical or not, this Canadian, in a tragic, bizarre way, had an impact on the lives of untold thousands around the world.

Born in a village just outside Quebec City in the 1950s, Gaétan Dugas grew up feeling he did not quite belong. When he discovered he had been adopted as an infant, he decided that was the explanation. Dugas resolved, however, to find a world where he would fit it. He first worked as a hairdresser in his home province. Then he landed his dream job in the mid-1970s when he was hired as a flight attendant with Air Canada. The young Québécois was outgoing by nature and enjoyed the work. It was the fringe benefits, though, that made flying really worthwhile: the free overseas travel made Dugas a frequent visitor to large cities across Europe and the United States. He met people easily and fell in love with breathtaking frequency. For someone young, strikingly attractive, and single, life was good.

It all started going terribly wrong in 1980. Dugas was diagnosed with a rare form of skin cancer—an unusual condition in itself, but made more so by the fact that doctors were finding the same disease with unusual frequency among young homosexual men in San Francisco and New York. Within a year, researchers identified the cancer as a symptom of a baffling new syndrome with many names but no cure: "gay cancer," GRID (Gay Related Immune Deficiency), or ACIDS (Acquired Community Immune Deficiency Syndrome) were all descriptions of the same thing.

Dugas was one of the first North Americans to contract what we now call AIDS. He was almost certainly the first Canadian to be diagnosed with it. Before the extent of the AIDS epidemic was fully realized, Dugas endured a debilitating, painful series of AIDS-related diseases. He died—wholly unknown in his own country—in Quebec City early in 1984.

The extent to which this private tragedy was a public health question came to light only in 1987. That year, American journalist Randy Shilts published the first detailed account of the earliest days of the AIDS crisis. For Canadians, Shilts reached a stunning conclusion: Gaétan Dugas was likely the first North American to contract AIDS, and, further, that he passed the virus to perhaps thousands of homosexual lovers. In the jargon doctors use to analyse epidemics, Dugas was "Patient Zero."

This was a controversial and ultimately unprovable claim. And whether Dugas brought the AIDS virus to North America first or not is probably irrelevant. If Dugas did not, someone else did—someone else was Patient Zero. What really mattered was this Canadian's cooperation with medical researchers at a vital point: for it was Dugas and his sexual history, Shilts showed, that gave scientists in 1981 and 1982 a breakthrough understanding of the way AIDS was transmitted. Dugas admitted to thousands of sexual partners, and when hundreds of these men were tracked down, it was clear to researchers for the first time that the AIDS virus might be sexually transmitted. Once laboratory research confirmed this theory, the first real anti-AIDS education was started. In a bizarre irony, Dugas' cooperation with researchers saved the lives of many—even though he had likely infected hundreds of others himself.

But, sadly, the short sad life of Gaétan Dugas left very little legacy of hope. Blood agencies and health authorities responded to the disease with glacial speed. Prevailing prejudices against homosexual lifestyles stifled scientific inquiry in the beginning, and gay organizations initially resisted attempts to educate their community about the disease. Of course, for Gaétan Dugas and the thousands he directly or indirectly infected with the killer virus, none of that really mattered.

80

Lawren Harris

BORN: Brantford, Ontario • 23 October 1885

DIED: Vancouver, British Columbia • 29 January 1970

CANADA WAS AT BEST A FUZZY IDEA BEFORE A gaggle of Toronto painters came together in 1920 and called themselves the Group of Seven. In politics, art, and culture, mainstream tastes were almost always borrowed from Britain, Europe, and the United States. In attitude and outlook, the dominion was profoundly colonial.

Lawren Harris, the heir to a family fortune made in the Canadian farm machinery business, hoped to change this attitude. He was deeply troubled by Canada's cultural dependence when he returned from four years of studying art abroad in 1908. As he became reacquainted with the arts community in Toronto, he met other painters who were also frustrated with the general conservatism of bourgeois Canada. Inspired by a young commercial artist, Tom Thomson, Harris and others turned increasingly to northern Ontario as the subject of their work.

In 1913 Harris joined forces with local doctor and art patron James MacCallum to found the Studio Building, a three-storey workspace in the city where like-minded artists could meet and paint. As the artists were increasingly drawn to the north, Harris provided the means for them to spend sustained periods in the wilderness, where they discovered a national spirit. The studio and the trips north developed their collective identity, and they vowed to make a bold public statement with their work.

The Group of Seven burst onto the art scene in 1920. Thomson had died tragically in 1917, but Franklin Carmichael, Lawren Harris, A.Y. Jackson, Franz Johnston, Arthur Lismer, J.E.H. MacDonald, and F.H. Varley mounted a joint exhibition in Toronto. Their ambitious goal was made clear in the group's first exhibition catalogue: "An Art must grow and flower in the land before the country will be a real home for its people." Their paintings—passionate, vivid depictions of the northern Ontario landscape—were an immediate sensation. The group positioned its members as rebels by declaring war on the mainstream aesthetic, which valued traditional European masters and nineteenth-century naturalism, but they were not outsiders for long. Harris, especially, had moneyed connections in the Toronto philan-thropic community, and the group began to sell a lot of paintings in the 1920s. The time was right, it seemed, for a distinctively Canadian approach to visual art. Harris, who alone among the group could open doors and pay the most pressing bills, was the *de facto* leader. He was also the creator of some of its most memorable works. His paintings have been described as unfeelingly cold, but stripped of detail, at once brilliantly lit but suggesting a powerful gloom, they have become enduring national symbols.

Harris spent much of the 1930s painting and teaching in the United States. He returned to Canada in 1940, moved to Vancouver, and almost alone among the Group of Seven began turning to more abstract projects. Nature remained his inspiration, and his towering reputation in the Canadian art community gave nascent Canadian abstractionism an impor-tant endorsement.

Harris' real place in history was at the heart of the group, however, and as early as 1930 its nationalist project could be dubbed a success. Its bold, modernist canvases had dragged Canadian painting into the twentieth century. And by passionately representing the Canadianness of the nation's north, the group offered stirring visual evidence of a viable Canadian culture.

It seems more than a little imprecise to untangle one individual from the Group of Seven and judge him particularly influential. In its approach, and its impact, the group was a collective exercise. "In a sense the Group re-invented Canada," one observer suggested. Lawren Harris, more than any other, had invented the group.

81

BORN: Brantford, Ontario • 26 January 1961

Wayne Gretzky

AT ONE SECOND BEFORE MIDNIGHT ON 31 DECEMBER 1999, Wayne Gretzky will be nearly thirty-nine years old. He will have perhaps half his life still ahead of him. That makes him the youngest person on this list, and the only one born later than the 1950s. In a remarkably short time, his influence has been profound.

To suggest that Gretzky is among the best players ever to play hockey is suggesting the obvious. He owns every significant scoring record in National Hockey League history. He dominated the professional and international game for ten years in the 1980s, a feat no one before or since can claim. Along the way, he inspired and captivated millions. What truly puts him in his own league, however, is the impact he had on his sport: hockey after Gretzky is a much different game from hockey before him.

Gretzky's achievements are all the more impressive because he has lived his life in the media spotlight. He was born and raised in southwestern Ontario, a hockey hothouse if ever there was one. His father was his coach and, according to legend, the son could skate before he could walk. When he was ten, he scored 378 goals for his Brantford league team and immediately was featured in dozens of Canadian newspapers and magazines. One writer labelled him "The Great Gretzky," and any pretense of a normal life for the child hockey star disappeared.

Since then, Gretzky's life has been a succession of great expectations. He has met or surpassed them almost always. A brief career in the now-defunct World Hockey Association was followed in 1979–80 by his debut season in the NHL. He tied for the league lead in scoring that year with 137 points, then proceeded to win the title outright for the next seven consecutive years. In 1985–86, he smashed his own single season record with 215 points—an incredible 60 points better than any other player had ever achieved. Loaded with offensive weapons fired by Gretzky, his Edmonton Oilers won four Stanley Cups, and Gretzky was judged "most valuable player" of the league in every year of the decade except one. No one could remember a player who dominated a professional sport in quite the same way.

It seemed improbable. Gretzky was a skinny kid who was a good skater, but not nearly the best. His chief advantage lay in a kind of sixth sense; he anticipated the lightning quick pace of hockey better than anyone who ever played. And his perfect passing, which often surprised his teammates as much as his opponents, was a joy to behold.

As the records tumbled and the awards piled up, Gretzky's unaffected "aw shucksism" made him a national icon while he was still in his twenties. He was pure Canadian, the commentators gushed: modest, soft-spoken, even heroic. Accordingly, the outcry when he was traded from Edmonton to the Los Angeles Kings on 9 August 1988 was predictable. From coast to coast the angst was palpable, and only one conclusion was possible: the Americans had stolen a national treasure.

For the game, however, No. 99's relocation was hugely important. Hockey has always had an ambivalent relationship with the United States: while it was intensely popular in localized northern pockets, in the rest of the country it was a sideshow that could never compete with baseball or basketball. Gretzky in LA began to change that. In California, where entertainment is created and tastes established, professional hockey had always been greeted with indifference, but Gretzky brought the game unprecedented exposure. On the ice, he was not the dominant player in the 1990s that he had been the decade before; still, late night talk shows and major magazines lined up to make Gretzky a household name. And sponsorship deals with giants like Nike, Nissan, and Coke put him and hockey on the American stage for the first time. Within six years of the trade, two more NHL teams sprouted in California, and a long-sought U.S. television deal was signed.

In the mid-1990s, as he aged and his skills slipped,

Gretzky's star began to tarnish. He was overpaid, some complained. He was a one-dimensional player, others said. Many wondered whether he really was the best ever. But players' salaries had grown threefold or more since his debut; owners were cashing in on the fame he had made; and fans could reflect on the faster, more exciting style of hockey he had originated. They all owed him much.

82

Norman Jewison

BORN: Toronto, Ontario • 21 July 1926

"GROWING UP A METHODIST WITH A JEWISH NAME in the east end of Toronto," Norman Jewison said, "gave me a very Canadian outlook. I think I was more objective because I was Canadian. We look at things with a slightly cocked eye. It makes our films more sardonic."

The most important and prolific Canadian film-maker, Jewison grew up in lower-middle-class Toronto, his father the owner of a small dry-goods store. After high school, he joined the Royal Canadian Navy in 1944 and, using his Veterans Charter benefits, went to the University of Toronto following his discharge. Taking his life's savings of $140, in 1950 he went to London to scramble for work with the BBC as a script writer and bit-part actor until 1952, when he returned home to join the Canadian Broadcasting Corporation. He quickly made his name as the TV director for Wayne and Shuster, among others. Impressed with his fresh approach to variety programming, New York called, and Jewison began to work for CBS, rejuvenating *Your Hit Parade* and building a reputation for directing specials for Andy Williams, Harry Belafonte, Judy Garland, and similar stars.

Frustrated by TV's ratings wars and the stress of working on live TV in "heart attack city," Jewison moved to Los Angeles and carved out a place for himself in film. "Feature films are the literature of our generation," he says. "They express the social conscience of a country; films are forever." Although his first directorial efforts included frothy Doris Day romances, he had his chance in 1965 to put his Canadian-formed social conscience on film with *The Cincinnati Kid*, a gritty film about pool hustlers that became a critical success. Then *The Russians Are Coming, The Russians Are Coming*, perhaps the first Cold War comedy and certainly the first to humanize the Russians and denounce America's patriotic extremism, topped the charts. Even *Pravda* approved what Jewison called "my version of *War and Peace*" and, remarkably, so did the U.S. Senate. *In the Heat of the Night*, his next winner, explored contemporary racial tensions in the South in the guise of a thriller; the film received seven Academy Award nominations and won five.

The Vietnam War and the assassinations of Robert Kennedy and Martin Luther King turned Jewison completely against America. He had remained a Canadian citizen throughout his time in the United States, but in 1970 he mailed his green card back to Washington and went to England to work and live. When he began to direct and produce in Hollywood again, he was determined to get and keep artistic control over everything he directed. "I have always fought against ever having to work for someone else," he explained. His independent streak and his eye for what an audience wanted were perhaps best seen in 1987's wildly successful *Moonstruck*. Still, some Americans remember and resent Jewison's constant carping about American politics. "I wish Norman would shut up," his Los Angeles agent complains. "He's known as a Canadian here...all the anti-American statements he made in the 1960s really hurt him in this town."

Jewison had long had a 280-acre farm in the Caledon Hills north of Toronto where he raised Herefords and

produced maple syrup, and in 1978 he returned to Canada
to live. He was the founder and co-chair of the Canadian
Centre for Advanced Film Studies (now the Canadian Film
Centre) in Toronto, a gift to his native land and to the
promotion and improvement of the craft in Canada. But he
was never a nationalist. Canadian corporate donors were
stingy, and he refused to believe that he or anyone had to

produce films glorifying Canada and Canadian heroes. "The world is not interested in hearing about your heroes. They want you to entertain them, move them," he argued. Nor did he apologize for working in Hollywood—money has no personality, he said bluntly—or for making Toronto streets look like New York: "Film is always pretending to be somewhere else. A stage is a stage." Jewison admitted up front that he made his films for people to see. "If I were a 'pure' artist making movies only for me," that would be one thing. "But I'm not a pure artist in that sense—I'm a storyteller and I make movies for an audience." The audience, for Jewison, is always right, and the first Canadian to score huge commercial success has irrefutably demonstrated that one can educate and entertain at the same time.

83

Joseph Flavelle

BORN: Peterborough, Canada West • 15 February 1858
DIED: Palm Beach, Florida • 7 March 1939

In his day he was Canada's great capitalist success story. Joe Flavelle, a poor boy from Peterborough, came to Toronto to seek his fortune in 1887. He found it in butter, eggs, but most of all bacon, and by 1900 was the head of the biggest pork-packing operation in the British Empire. A rich but also a deeply religious man, he donated hundreds of thousands of dollars to worthy charitable causes. His manner was suitably reserved and his tastes temperate, and Flavelle happily served his country during the Great War—he had the biggest job and was the biggest success. Some said he could have been prime minister, if only he had the requisite ambition. For Flavelle, it must all have seemed too good to be true. As it turned out, it was. By the time he died in 1939, Sir Joseph Flavelle was no longer regarded as a model by anyone.

Flavelle's life and career were made—and unmade—during the First World War. As the president of the William Davies Co., he had more than enough work to do. The slaughterhouse and associated bacon exporting operation had earned Toronto its "Hogtown" label and made Flavelle rich. And as Britain and its colonies prepared to send millions of men onto the field of battle, the market for pork products was booming. Additional responsibilities as chairman of the Bank of Commerce, National Trust, and Simpson's made Flavelle one of the busiest capitalists in the empire. Still, when the British government asked him to take over the procurement and manufacture of munitions in Canada in late 1915, Flavelle was ready to serve.

Everyone else had made a mess of the job up to then. A loosely organized Canadian Shell Committee had overspent, filled few orders, and turned the dominion's professed commitment to aid the British war effort into a national shame. But Flavelle quickly turned things around when he imposed strict procurement and profit rules and made what he could not buy in government factories. Old factories were refitted, and new ones built; in a little over a year, Flavelle was over-seeing 600 plants and 250,000 workers. Combined, they were spending $50 million per month and churning out 100,000 shells per day. His Imperial Munitions Board was the largest enterprise that had ever existed in Canada. And, except for the sacrifice of the 230,000 Canadians killed or wounded, the

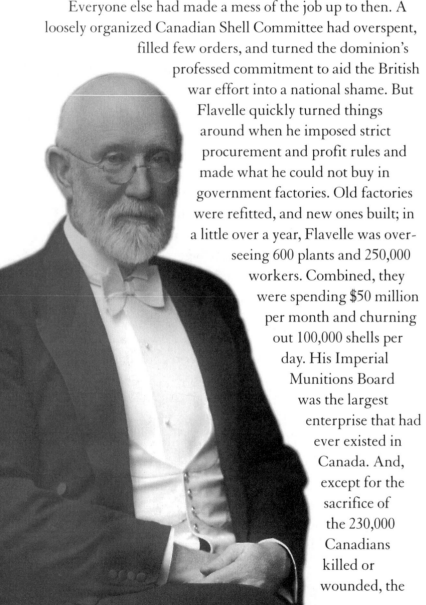

IMB represented Canada's most important contribution to the eventual Allied victory.

The British rewarded Flavelle's efforts with a baronetcy in 1917; from then on, he would be Sir Joseph. Most Canadians were pleased. Though there was a growing feeling that hereditary titles did not suit Canada's new world democratic pretensions, there was general agreement that Sir Joseph had earned his title.

That changed quickly in July 1917 when questions were publicly raised about the extent to which Flavelle and others had profited from the wartime emergency. It was an issue that had simmered throughout the war, but, up to then, no one had been able to put a face to the rumours about who was making money on all the sacrifice and death. But now, according to the screaming headlines, all was clear: Sir Joseph, while seemingly a national hero for delivering shells to the Allies, had been making windfall profits on the bacon trade. A leaked government report about profit margins that started the story was widely misinterpreted, and Flavelle eventually was able to prove he had done nothing wrong. Quite simply, bacon prices had gone up and his company was the best positioned to take advantage. But no worker in a shell factory, no mother who had lost a son on the Somme, no farmer's son facing conscription into the service could see beyond the reported profit figures that Flavelle admitted were true: his William Davies Co. made returns on capital of 43 per cent, 80 per cent, and 57 per cent in the first three years of the war. A nation weary of sacrifice had at last found the ugly face of capitalism, and Flavelle's good name was in ruins.

Flavelle—now scorned as the Baron of Bacon—could do nothing to repair the reputation he acquired during a few fateful months in wartime. He continued as a major figure in Canadian business and, as before, was a national leader in

322 • Joseph Flavelle

charitable giving. But the public could not forgive him for apparently making the wrong kind of killing on the war.

Somehow, this fall from grace marked a tangible change in the personality of the nation. Large-scale capitalism was still a new thing in the early years of the century, and the rise and fall of Joseph Flavelle proved to Canadians that business needed to be closely watched. Gradually, taxes and regulations were created that made sure there could never be such war profiteering again. And the most visible symbol of Flavelle's success was publicly discredited: never again would a Canadian living in Canada receive a hereditary title.

Joseph Flavelle was a good man by all accounts. He was certainly generous to a fault. But he was also a symbol of an age when one class making millions off the labour of others would no longer be acceptable in Canada. At least, no one would be caught in his position again.

84

BORN: Natashquan, Quebec • 27 October 1928

Gilles Vigneault

"*M*ON PAYS, CE N'EST PAS UN PAYS, C'EST L'HIVER
[My country, it's not a country, it's the winter]," Gilles
Vigneault sang in his most famous song, the *chanson*
that is the virtual national anthem of Quebec. But it is
more than that—it is also a popular hymn to winter
in all of Canada, a fact that explains the popular
outrage when Patsy Gallant took Vigneault's tune
in 1976 and crassly de-Canadianized it. The
Americanized "From New York to L.A.," with its
disco beat, damaged her career near fatally, so revered
was "Mon Pays."

Born in an isolated North Shore fishing village,
1300 kilometres from Montreal, Vigneault received a
good education at the Rimouski seminary and at
Université Laval. His first instincts were towards
poetry, and throughout the 1950s he produced poems,
stories, and what he called monologues with indifferent success. Married, with a growing family, he
supported himself as an algebra teacher, publicist,
and clerk while simultaneously becoming involved
in theatre. In 1959 he founded a literary magazine,
published a collection of his poetry, and saw the first
of his songs recorded. The next year, in L'Arlequin,
the coffee house he founded in Quebec City, he was
pressed by friends to sing his own work, and a star
was born. After some successful concerts, his first
recording appeared in 1962.

Vigneault was no conventional balladeer. His voice was hard, rough, "a voice that hurts," one critic said. But after a few minutes, the force of the personality grabbed the audience tightly and listeners forgot about his gangling, awkward body to become wholly absorbed by the mood he created. His work was distinctively Québécois, nurtured in and shaped by the rhythms of the old folk songs. "I lived in a world where they still sang drinking songs and where they still liked to square dance," he recalled. He achieved the status of a Quebec icon when "Mon Pays," sung by Monique Leyrac, won the International Song Festival in 1965. Quickly adopted by separatists, "Mon Pays," in fact, was not written to be nationalist or even patriotic, but simply as a lament for the coldness of so many who were unable to share their love.

From the 1970s onwards, however, Vigneault became an active supporter of the Parti Québécois, one who regularly appeared at huge concerts on Saint-Jean Baptiste Day (one in Montreal drew 300,000 people) and sang on every nationalist TV spectacle. His 1976 song "Gens du Pays" quickly became the PQ's own anthem, sung with pride and many tears after referendum defeats in 1980 and 1995. In his person, Vigneault seemed to link the cultural past and the nationalist present.

Best known as a balladeer in Canada and abroad, Vigneault was also prominent in Quebec as a poet. One of his collections won the Governor General's Literary Award in 1965, and his poetry focused on his North Shore homeland, the characters who inhabited it, and the travails of love, solitude, and the inexorable passage of time. Like his songs, Vigneault's writings drew on the folk culture of Quebec, and Louis Dudek called him "the most gifted poet in Canada since Emile Nelligan, whether in English or French." That might even be true, but Vigneault's most

significant contribution was his popularizing of traditional
values that could still guide and shape the future in Quebec.
His "sense of country and values," one literary critic noted,
"helps explain the emotional appeal of Vigneault's songs
[and] poems," an appeal "that goes beyond even their technical skill and which gives his contemporary and traditional
roles...such social force."

Now close to seventy, Vigneault is still hugely popular,
still a devoted *indépendantiste*. He can attack English Canada

for its approach to Quebec, he can sneer at Jean Chrétien as "Trudeau coming back, minus the intelligence and culture," but he will sing in English because he supports himself on his concert and record sales. His second marriage produced three children to go along with the four of his first, and he has bills to pay.

And, as with so many Québécois, there is in him yet a sense of yearning towards Canada. "It would be so exciting to make Canada," he said during the Meech Lake debacle, an agreement that he opposed. "But this is not interesting. I don't want to marry someone who has a revolver to her head." He added, "I am sorry for Anglo Canadians who believe that the problem will be solved" by Meech Lake. There were few enough of those, in truth, and the relations of Québécois and Canadians may yet turn out to be insoluble. Still, every Canadian can enjoy Vigneault's songs and be moved by "Mon Pays/My Country."

85

BORN: Chatsworth, Ontario • 20 October 1873

DIED: Victoria, British Columbia • 1 September 1951

Nellie McClung

SHE WAS BORN ON A SMALL ONTARIO FARM AND, AS a child, Nellie Mooney moved west with the tide of settlers hoping to find prosperity on the Canadian prairie. It was a pioneering life in Manitoba in the closing years of the nineteenth century, and Nellie did not see the inside of a school until she was ten. She married, becoming Mrs Wes McClung in 1896. There was not much in this typical Canadian upbringing to suggest that Nellie McClung would ever become one of the most influential social activists in Canadian history.

Her mother was the first to notice something unusual. She often rebuked her adolescent daughter for being a "show-off"; it seems Nellie loved to talk to anyone who would listen, she acted in school plays at every opportunity, and, most appalling, she played boys' games. It was all too unladylike for proper Mrs Mooney. Her mother's anxiety caused Nellie's first conflict with the social expectations she was not prepared to live up to.

For McClung, a fight for women's rights in society thus began as a practical rather than a theoretical matter. Forced to forego a teaching career after she married, she was nevertheless determined to maintain a life independent of home and family in Manitou, Manitoba. She built a modest career as a writer and enjoyed her greatest success with the

romantic rural novel *Sowing Seeds in Danny*. It was only after
the family followed her husband's job to Winnipeg in 1911
that McClung embarked on a truly public career.

To promote her books, McClung had always done some
public speaking. Recitations, as they were known then, were a
popular form of entertainment—especially in remote parts of
the country. In Winnipeg, McClung began adding political
commentary to her less serious themes. She had become a
passionate advocate for temperance, since it was women, in
her view, who usually paid the price for the widespread abuse
of alcohol. McClung was soon a leading representative of the
burgeoning Woman's Christian Temperance Union, and
her speeches were the reason: no one else could entertain and
educate an audience as she could. She was funny, not preachy,
and soon people actually paid to see McClung. When the
WCTU decided that women needed the vote to achieve a
booze-free society, McClung attacked that cause with a passion.

She was the ideal person to lead the fight. People enjoyed
listening to McClung and, in a world where nobody knew
what a feminist was, her demands for suffrage seemed
like common sense. The family moved to Alberta in 1915,
and McClung continued her campaign for the WCTU.
Manitoba, Alberta, Saskatchewan, and British Columbia
finally granted women the vote in 1916, and politicians and
newspapers justly credited McClung with leading the
successful fight. Voters showed their approval by electing
her to the Alberta legislature in 1921.

By then Nellie McClung was a leading figure in the
women's rights movement around the English-speaking world,
and she was often persuaded to give speeches in faraway places.
Invariably, she was warmly received. Into the 1930s and 1940s,
her place as Canada's most famous feminist was assured.

In recent years historians often have drawn a distinction

between the "maternal" feminism of reformers like McClung and more recent "equal rights" feminism. The argument goes something like this: because McClung did not directly challenge the traditional view of the family, she and others like her represented a more primitive, less progressive challenge to the *status quo*. It was not until the 1960s, according to this view, when mainstream Canadian feminist organizations began a campaign for complete social and legal equality, that the women's movement really arrived. But this analysis is either mistaken or irrelevant. The fact is that McClung frequently made very clear demands for complete equality of the sexes. Even if Canada's first feminist was a strong believer in the importance of home and family, this does not diminish her very tangible accomplishments. That more recent generations of women began their battle for equality from a point far beyond women's status in 1900 was due in large part to Nellie McClung.

86

Harold Johns

BORN: Chengtu, West China • 4 July 1915

THE ODDS WERE LONG ON HAROLD JOHNS EVER
having much to do with Canada, let alone becoming
an influential Canadian. Born to missionary parents
from Toronto in the Szechuan province of West
China in 1915, Johns spent his formative years
learning to speak Chinese. His parents taught and
preached at a local university, and were content to
continue doing so. Mounting political and social
turmoil in China, however, forced the family to
return to Canada just in time for Johns to attend high

school. He ended up at McMaster University, then
in Toronto, where he earned a doctorate in physics
in 1939. A postdoctoral fellowship at Cambridge beckoned,
but the war in Europe dashed these plans and Johns settled
for a teaching position at the University of Alberta. After the
war Johns was appointed assistant professor of physics at the
University of Saskatchewan. Saskatoon was a long way from
anywhere in 1945—especially for a young scientist keen on
working on a pathbreaking project. Yet circumstances were
auspicious for a medical breakthrough. The Saskatchewan
government, perennially Canada's leader in progressive
reform, had established North America's first government-
sponsored cancer clinic in 1931. By the 1940s the province
was something of an authority on the treatment of cancerous
tumours with radiation beams. Doctors enjoyed limited
success with some cancers, but there were continuing problems associated with radiation therapy. Not the least of these
was the enormous expense and potential danger of radium,
the radioactive element used to create the healing beam. Soon
after arriving in Saskatchewan, Johns persuaded his supe-
riors to fund his research on finding another source of radiation for the treatment of cancer. Premier Tommy Douglas
personally approved the expensive research and, improbably,
Johns was on his way to making a significant discovery.

The key to the puzzle was cobalt-60. The world's source
of this radioactive element was a nuclear reactor at Chalk
River, Ontario, at a facility created by the Canadian government for Second World War nuclear research. Johns
convinced scientists there, fresh from a top-secret role in the
Manhattan Project, to prepare small quantities of cobalt-60 for
his experiments. At the same time, he set to work designing
and building a treatment machine that could exploit cobalt-60.
When it was finished, the results were spectacular: Johns'

machine was infinitely cheaper and vastly more powerful than anything else in existence. The media, which inevitably associated any sort of radiation research with Hiroshima, dubbed the new invention the "cobalt bomb." And the way cancer patients were treated was vastly improved almost overnight.

Johns was still a young man after the first cancer patient was treated with the new cobalt-60 machine in 1951. Most of his scientific career lay ahead of him. At first he concentrated on experiments designed to calculate the appropriate doses of radiation to be delivered from his machine for specific kinds of cancer. Through a vast body of published research, he and his growing cadre of graduate students made Saskatchewan a leading centre for advances related to radiation doses. He continued his internationally recognized work in Toronto at Princess Margaret Hospital and the Ontario Cancer Institute in 1956, and in 1958 created the Graduate Department in Medical Biophysics at the University of Toronto. A permanent place in the university now was established for the recruitment of physicists to attack the problems associated with treating cancer with radiation.

Today more than 3000 "cobalt bomb" machines are used to treat cancer in over seventy countries. Perhaps 7 million patients have been treated with Johns' brainchild. Most of these machines are Canadian-built. But even with improved techniques, Johns' invention is not a miracle cure: doctors and scientists around the world continue to be frustrated by their inability to find a permanent cure for the killer disease. Yet in combination with surgery and drug treatment, cobalt-60 radiotherapy bought time and, in millions of cases, new life for patients around the world. It is that, combined with an international legacy of research and discovery, which makes this Chinese-born Canadian among the most influential scientists his country has produced.

87

BORN: Montreal, Quebec • 4 August 1921

Maurice Richard

To GRASP THE ENDURING SIGNIFICANCE OF THE LIFE of Maurice "Rocket" Richard, one must understand a little about his longtime employer, Le Club de Hockey Canadien. Known as the Montreal Canadiens, this now-legendary hockey team was founded in 1909 so that French Canadians might compete against the English-speaking Montreal Wanderers of the National Hockey Association. These early years of the century were momentous ones for hockey: surging crowds and professionalization were turning the ice game into big business. In 1917 the best teams in Canada and the United States, including the Canadiens, formed an élite professional association, and the new National

Hockey League ushered in the era of big-time hockey.

The Canadiens performed indifferently at the beginning. By 1942 the team had won four Stanley Cups; a respectable record to be sure, but hardly a sign that the Canadiens would ever be the most successful team in their own city, let alone the entire league. What sustained the club when local rivals the Wanderers and the Maroons went bankrupt was its Frenchness. The Canadiens' stars were not always *français*, but most of their supporters were. The team went out of its way to secure the services of French players, and local sons Newsy Lalonde and Georges Vézina became revered stars. Accordingly, the French identity of the team—an island in a sea of English-Canadian and American clubs—was assured.

It was entirely predictable that Montreal-born francophone Maurice Richard would play for the Canadiens when he joined the NHL in 1942. He was barely noticed at first, but in the 1943–44 season he became a formidable goal scorer and led the Canadiens to the Stanley Cup. A year later his scoring prowess became the stuff of legend when he smashed the single-season goals record with fifty in fifty games.

From then on, the goals came in bunches for Richard. But more amazing than all the goals was the way he scored them. There was a glorious excitement to the way the Rocket played the game. As a goal-scorer, he was an artist: his trademark charge from the right wing to the net, when blazing speed and dazzling stick-work blended to make a goal a thing of beauty, left fans and defenders in awe. His was a sublime talent, and it was combined with a passionate ferocity: no one ever doubted that the Rocket wanted to win every game more than anybody else. His glowering, black-eyed stare was proof of that. When on-ice pushes led to shoves, Richard would fight all comers, and always give at least as good as he got. He was fierce, proud, and dominating, capable of altering the outcome of a game single-handedly.

But it was not a goal that boosted the Rocket from the ranks of ordinary hockey stars to the singular status of Canadian legend. Instead, it was an ugly brawl that erupted in a game in Boston on 13 March 1955. Naturally, accounts of the incident vary, but there is little doubt that the Rocket lost his temper in frightening fashion: all agreed that Richard cracked more than one stick across a Bruin's back and then slugged a linesman who was trying to subdue him.

Richard was thrown out of that game, but the real penalty came a few days later when NHL president Clarence Campbell suspended him for the remaining three games of the regular season and the entire playoffs. This was a staggering blow to the team and its fans. Montreal's Stanley Cup chances hinged on the Rocket and, nearly as important, the Canadiens' leader was on the verge of the NHL scoring championship.

The entire city was outraged and Campbell's life was threatened. On 17 March, as the team prepared for a home game the day the suspension was announced, raucous demonstrations against the decision were held in front of the Montreal Forum. As the match began at 8:30 p.m., fury was thick in the air. When Campbell himself arrived at the game mid-way through the first period, the rage boiled over: spectators attempted to attack him, and, finally, in circumstances that remain unclear, a tear gas canister went off within a few feet of the league president.

Police quickly evacuated the building, and the game was forfeited to the visitors. Choking fans from inside left the rink and met the crowds who were milling outside. Then the rioting began. Everything that was not nailed down was tossed at the Forum. Police cars and buses were attacked and destroyed and order was not restored until early the next morning. The city awoke to find its main streets a river of broken glass. The mayor blamed Campbell for inciting disorder, but a shaken Richard went on radio and television to urge calm. Though bitter frustration remained, the violence was over. That spring, the exiled Richard lost the scoring championship, and the Canadiens lost the Stanley Cup.

The league, and perhaps even the country, would never be the same. A Quebec player playing for a Montreal team had been suspended by the English-speaking president of an English-speaking league—whatever the facts of the case, this was the only thing that really mattered. For millions of French Canadians, the Richard Riot was proof of something that many suspected all along: to be French Canadian in North America meant a raw deal. Some historians would later date the beginning of Quebec's Quiet Revolution to that winter's night in 1955.

From then on, Rocket Richard was the Canadiens; at once he symbolized their greatness but also their otherness. He and his mates turned their bitterness towards the league into unprecedented success and, from 1956 to 1960, the Canadiens won an amazing five consecutive Stanley Cups, a feat not equalled before or since. Richard continued to score the most goals, the most important goals, and the most memorable goals for Montreal. He retired a hero in 1960.

After Richard, the team continued to win: Stanley Cup championships in the 1960s, 1970s, 1980s, and 1990s made the Canadiens perhaps the most successful professional sports franchise on the continent. No team has won more championships. And today, the Montreal Canadiens and the Rocket, the greatest team and its greatest star, are so united in popular memory that they are virtually inseparable. They remain cultural icons, emblematic of the spirit and success of Canada's game, but also of the gulf that has and always will separate some of us from *les autres*.

88

David Suzuki

BORN: Vancouver, British Columbia • 24 March 1936

H E HATES THE COMPARISON, BUT WHEN PRESSED, David Suzuki will admit that he is a boy crying wolf. The rainforest is disappearing faster every day, and humans will soon be gasping for breath. Many Canadian rivers and lakes are poisoned beyond hope. The planet is so overcrowded that the biosphere is on the verge of complete collapse. Today, these claims are outlandish at worst, debatable at best. But Suzuki remains defiant: "The whole point of the parable," he says, "is that in the end, the wolf did come." One sure thing is that if (when?) the wolf does come, and humankind's contamination of the natural environment begins to choke off life on Earth, the world will not have David Suzuki to blame. He is not the first to make saving the world from itself a career, but, worldwide, few have done it better.

It is tempting to find the well-spring of Suzuki's drive in an ugly chapter in Canadian history during his childhood. In 1942 the federal government responded to wartime hysteria by forcibly removing Japanese nationals and Canadians of Japanese ancentry from the British Columbia coast. Suzuki's father was assigned to a road crew in the province, and the rest of the family was moved to an inland camp. At war's end, this Canadian family was relocated to Ontario. For a child who already felt like an alien in the country of his birth, the war experience left Suzuki with memories of fear and self-loathing that would not soon fade.

In a hostile world, he grew up needing to prove himself. A brilliant student, Suzuki breezed though university in the United States. His passion was genetics, and he was a professor of zoology at the University of British Columbia when he was barely out of his twenties. Pathbreaking research on fruit flies gained him an international reputation,

but his real gift was teaching: his lectures were captivating, and he earned a cult following among students as the professor who was in love with his subject.

There were more than a few scientists and students who were disappointed when Suzuki gradually gave up research and teaching in the 1970s. First radio, and then television, offered opportunities to bring his passion for science to the masses. And in Suzuki, Canadians came to know a most unusual scientist: down to earth but sophisticated, credible yet accessible. In a series of CBC programs, he became the best-known Canadian scientist ever.

Shows like *Quirks and Quarks*, *Earthwatch*, and *Discovery* also made Suzuki's name outside Canada when the programs were aired around the world. By the early 1980s, however, Suzuki began to lose his faith in science as an unqualified source of good. The television special *A Planet for the Taking* in 1985 confirmed his belief that the biggest threat facing the human species was its own desecration of the environment, much of that brought about by technological advances. Apparently, many people agreed. His shows were some of the most watched in Canadian history and were rebroadcast worldwide in dozens of languages. In the spotlight as never before, Suzuki had discovered his life's work.

His most recent television series, *The Nature of Things*, is concerned almost exclusively with environmental themes. In 1995 it was watched in more than fifty countries. That makes Suzuki a world figure, and he has seldom hesitated to lend his fame to save rivers, forests, and the ozone layer. He is now something of his own industry: his books, children's programs, and foundation are all many people know of environmentalism. At the end of the twentieth century, he is perhaps the most recognized living Canadian on the planet.

89

Pierre Péladeau

BORN: Outremont, Quebec • 11 April 1925

THE IDEA OF HAVING PIERRE PÉLADEAU FOR A BOSS, wrote the sometimes humorous Allan Fotheringham in a column in 1996, "would be too much to stomach... He is, for starters, an ex-alcoholic, a closet separatist, and has slurred Jews." Diane Francis added in her *Financial Post* column: "I don't want a separatist like Pierre Péladeau buying the Sun news-paper chain... Péladeau may be able to legally buy this chain but he won't own a single soul who works here." No man is a hero to his valet, to be sure, but the vehemence with which Péladeau's never-to-be consummated interest in the Sun chain was greeted was unusual for ordinarily placid Canadians. But then, so too is Pierre Péladeau.

Péladeau's father made and lost fortunes in the lumber business but died broke, leaving a large family to be raised in debt. Péladeau nonetheless received a good education, first at the Collège Jean-de-Brebeuf, where he believed he was the only poor student, followed by Université de Montréal and the McGill University law school, from which he gradu-ated in 1950. That same year he purchased a small weekly newspaper with a borrowed $1500. The foun-dations of the empire had been laid.

By 1954 he owned five weeklies and, annoyed by difficulties with his printers, he invested in presses and branched out into printing. In 1964, when

journalists at *La Presse*, Montreal's biggest daily, went on strike, Péladeau seized the opportunity, pulled together a makeshift editorial and production staff from his weeklies, and established *Le Journal de Montréal*—an instant sucess. When the strike ended and *La Presse* went back on the street, however, circulation for the upstart paper plummeted. Advised to take his money and run, Péladeau hung in, gradually rebuilt circulation, and learned to cater to the lowest common denominator with a steady diet of scandals, murder, and sports; he was also shrewd enough to get Parti Québécois leader René Lévesque as a columnist, a great boost for sales. *Le Journal de Montréal* today has 320,000 readers, second only to *La Presse*.

Péladeau continued buying newspapers and magazines. His attempts to go public with his company in 1972 to finance expansion were initially foiled when the Montreal financial houses, perhaps upset with the elfin Péladeau's hell-raising flamboyance and alleged womanizing, priced his offering too low. Undeterred, Péladeau raised his funds in New York City, and he continues to own more than 50 per cent of his holding company, Québecor Inc. The company owns newspapers in Winnipeg, Quebec, and New Brunswick, book publishing companies, 218 printing houses that produce everything from telephone books to comic books to the *Reader's Digest*, and pulp and paper plants. Revenues in 1996 were above $6 billion, and Péladeau is now owner of one of the fastest-growing printing firms anywhere. His businesses are at the forefront of technology, he prices aggressively, and offers a high quality of service.

This is raw power, in Quebec ranking only after the Caisse du dépôt, Hydro-Québec, Bombardier, and the Groupe Desjardins, and almost equal in Canada to Conrad Black and Ted Rogers. Thus, what Péladeau says has weight, and what he says sometimes disturbs. He has made controversial remarks that were widely interpreted as sexist and anti-Semitic, he has expressed admiration for Germany's discipline under the Nazis, he voted "Oui" in 1980, and, despite wearing the Order of Canada's pin in his lapel and chairing a Canada Day celebration in 1987, he suggested in 1990 that he had confidence in Quebec's ability to thrive as an independent nation. "The question now is, do we have the will?" There is a petulant bluntness about him that verges on the eccentric, though those who know him suggest he has been mellowed by his participation in Alcoholics Anonymous, his new-found belief in God, his love for Beethoven, and his affection for the works of Balzac.

Whatever he may be, Péladeau is rich. His companies have been a huge success and, as *Sun* columnist Peter Worthington noted, one of the reasons Péladeau is "every *Sun* journalist's worst nightmare...is that he's efficient, and any newspaper that gets an efficient proprietor has a lot of people worried." Likely so, and Péladeau's efficiency— and his vast holdings—have now turned him into a well-regarded and omnipresent business force in Quebec, friendly with everyone from Claude Béland to Brian Mulroney. On the other hand, his anti-Semitic remarks were one factor that led Université de Montréal to refuse him an honorary degree. Mavericks, even rich, influential ones, make people nervous, and Pierre Péladeau makes many Canadians very nervous indeed.

90

Bobbie Rosenfeld

BORN, Russia • 28 December 1905
DIED, Toronto, Ontario • 14 November 1969

PRECISELY WHEN THE YOUNG WOMAN WHO GREW up just north of Toronto decided to call herself Bobbie, rather than her given name Fanny, is not clear, but it was a characteristic decision. Rosenfeld spent her entire life charting her own course, and in the process she blazed new paths for Canadian women.

Bobbie Rosenfeld was the best woman athlete Canada ever produced, but it was the hurdles she overcame in society to achieve that designation which made her influential by example. Born in Russia to Jewish parents, Rosenfeld came to Canada as a baby when her family settled in Barrie, Ontario. Although she showed uncommon athletic prowess as a child, everybody was shocked when, barely a teenager, she beat the reigning Canadian champion in a 100-yard sprint. At once the nation realized that Barrie had produced a child prodigy. When the town could not supply the calibre of competition Rosenfeld required, however, she moved to Toronto at the age of sixteen.

Women's sport in Canada was just then reaching a crucial juncture. The Olympics had not yet found room for women, and there were few international opportunities for accomplished female athletes to face each other. But locally, women in several sports were becoming mini-celebrities in Toronto. Rosenfeld was easily the best of them all. After working days at a local chocolate factory, she filled her spare time playing basketball, softball, and hockey. Invariably, she dominated whatever sport she played. Her greatest success came as an individual in track and field. At various points in the 1920s she held Canadian records in the 100-yard and 220-yard sprints, and was the best in the country in the long jump, shot put, and discus.

By 1925 Rosenfeld was a national figure and a world-ranked track star. The Canadian public viewed this development cautiously: women's sports were undoubtedly thrilling to watch, and Rosenfeld was a one-in-a-million talent, but there remained a sense that sports violated the strict unwritten code of feminine behaviour prevalent in buttoned-up Canadian society. Athletics might "loosen ladies' morals," one observer complained. Accepted opinion was best summed up by the comment that many men keenly watched what they

would not allow their own daughters to participate in. Rosenfeld, an immigrant daughter perhaps unburdened by the gender guilt of the upper and middle classes, ignored the debate, and continued to run and jump faster and higher.

The 1928 Olympics in Amsterdam were the first to include women. Rosenfeld's performance in several events made her the best-known Canadian woman of her time and gained her the mantle of national heroine. The key to this acceptance was success: Rosenfeld narrowly missed winning the 100 metre final, but she led the Canadian team to a gold medal and world record in the 100 metre relay. She also placed fifth in the 800 metre race, an event she had not prepared for. Overall, in the few events open to them, the Canadian women dominated the games. For a country only tentatively asserting its identity, the success of Rosenfeld and her team-mates produced a burst of national pride. A jubilant crowd of 300,000 greeted the team's return to Toronto. And an unspoken lesson had been learned: athletics and women sports put Canada on the international stage, so perhaps the combination was not such a terrible thing after all.

Rosenfeld retired in 1933 and later gained a job as a sports reporter and columnist with a Toronto newspaper. She was not the first woman sports journalist in Canada, but she was the most famous. She was always opinionated and occasionally controversial. Her views mattered, and whether it was women's sports or men's, people remembered who Rosenfeld was and paid attention to what she wrote.

Poor health ended her newspaper career prematurely in 1966. Canada was a different place for women by then. Rosenfeld, though hardly an activist for women's rights, had something to do with the change. As a successful athlete and journalist in a time when these endeavours were the domain of men, her influence came from deeds, not words.

91

BORN: Neepawa, Manitoba • 18 July 1926
DIED: Lakefield, Ontario • 5 January 1987

Margaret Laurence

THE ENTRY ON MARGARET LAURENCE IN *THE Oxford Companion to Canadian Literature* opens by referring to her as "Canada's most successful novelist." Whether this is still true is a matter for debate, depending on how "successful" is defined. What is beyond doubt is that Laurence brought Canadian fiction out of the shadows and into the full sun, and that her strong female characters and her own example galvanized women writers.

Margaret Wemyss' parents died when she was very young and she was raised by her mother's sister in a household above a funeral parlour dominated by her repressive, authoritarian grandfather. Escape came at United College in Winnipeg where, broke, she went to the book department at the Hudson's Bay Company and read new fiction, a chapter at a time, hoping the salesclerks would not throw her out. Soon she began to publish her own writing: "Writing is an addiction with me," she said later. At the same time, she immersed herself in the city's rich political stew, emerging imbued with the fashionable leftist views of late wartime Canada. She married Jack Laurence, an engineer, in 1948, and accompanied him to England and to Africa. The couple spent two years in British Somaliland and five years on the Gold Coast (now Ghana), both colonial societies quite different in character but beginning to contemplate independence.

Her first works emerged out of these years—a translation of Somalian poetry, a sensuous novel set in Africa, and a memoir of her Somalian experience. Her sense of "social awareness, [her] feelings of anti-imperialism, anti-colonialism, anti-authoritarianism" all flowered in Africa and were evident in her writing.

The marriage did not survive long after the family returned to Canada. In 1962 Laurence left her husband and took her two children to England, set up house in the countryside, and began to mine her Canadian experiences. *The Stone Angel* (1964) was the first of her novels to be set in Manawaka, the mythical prairie town populated by Scots-Irish Presbyterians that resembled her own birthplace. Its nonagenarian heroine, the indomitable Hagar Shipley, instantly became one of the great survivors and enduring characters in Canadian fiction. Hagar's humorous, ironic recounting of her struggle for self in a masculine-dominated world struck a chord across the country, especially with women. In 1969 Laurence returned to Canada, and she began to receive the honours and awards that ultimately included two Governor General's Awards for Fiction, a Companionship in the Order of Canada, and a bushel of honorary degrees.

More books followed in a steady stream: *A Jest of God*, which was made into the successful Hollywood film *Rachel, Rachel*; *A Bird in the House*, a collection of short stories that verged on the autobiographical; *The Fire-Dwellers*; and, most notably, *The Diviners*, which completed her Manawaka saga. *The Diviners* featured another strong female character, Morag Gunn, and raised questions of social ostracism, racism, and sexuality. Before long, angry parents tried to ban the novel from schools in Peterborough, close by the Ontario town of Lakefield where Laurence resided, claiming that the book endorsed immorality.

Her writing aside, Laurence was an active participant in Canadian life and letters, not least as the first head of the Writers' Union of Canada. She did stints as writer-in-residence at Canadian universities, served as a much-loved chancellor of Trent University, and spoke out feelingly— some might say naively—on questions of social policy and nuclear disarmament. She was, she proclaimed, "a Christian, a woman, a writer, a parent, a member of humanity and a sharer in life itself, a life I believe to be informed and infused with the holy spirit." Curiously, Laurence had left out from that list that she was a Canadian, but her writing had already made that obvious to herself and her fellow citizens.

92

Joey Smallwood

BORN: Gambo, Newfoundland • 24 December 1900

DIED: St John's, Newfoundland • 17 December 1991

In the late 1950s, or so the story goes, federal Liberals approached Joey Smallwood to ask him to seek the leadership of their party. Why should he do such a thing, the Newfoundland premier asked. "I am king of my own little island, and that's all I've ever wanted to be."

Born into poverty, Smallwood pulled himself up by dint of his extraordinary energy. With the help of a prosperous uncle, he attended Bishop Feild College as the "poorest boy in the school, from the poorest family," and he emerged a socialist after a truncated academic career. He worked for newspapers in Newfoundland, in Boston, and later in New York, where he lived in flophouses while he developed his mesmerizing oratorical style by preaching the socialist gospel in countless meeting halls. Then it was back to Newfoundland as an indifferently successful union organizer, newspaper editor, aspiring political wheeler-dealer, and, after a brief stay in England, an unsuccessful Liberal Party candidate.

The Great Depression hit Newfoundland very hard, and the dominion was obliged to abandon its self-governing status for a British-appointed Commission of Government that ruled through the Second World War. Smallwood passed these years writing the encyclopedic *Book of Newfoundland*, establishing himself as a popular six-nights-a-week

broadcaster, and running pig farms near St John's and
Gander. The end of the war saw Britain, itself financially
strapped, anxious to be rid of the Newfoundland burden, and
London decreed that a national convention should be called
to decide on the island's future. Smallwood soon decided that
confederation with Canada was the only answer to his
country's problems, and, as the sole out-and-out confederate,
he won election to the convention.

Badly outnumbered, Smallwood still dominated the
convention, thanks largely to his effective stump debating
style and the radio coverage of the sessions. The convoluted

history of events between 1946 and 1948 included negotiations with Ottawa, two referenda, and constant political infighting, but Smallwood triumphed against the odds, achieved confederation on good terms, and became Newfoundland's premier in 1949. He had ensured his place in history for moving Canada's boundaries eastward into the North Atlantic.

Thus began an extraordinary political career. Capitalizing on the money that flowed from Ottawa and his long and close relationship with Liberal minister Jack Pickersgill, Smallwood won the affection and improved the life of the "toiling masses" in six elections. He remained in power for twenty-three years and created an extraordinarily effective political and patronage machine. He tried every conceivable method to bring Newfoundland out of poverty, forcing measures on the population that he knew would be beneficial, whether they wanted them or not. His methods were rough and almost never effective, as he naively chased after the god of industrialization, only to see his great projects end in scandal or failure. He sought to move people from the outports to more viable settlements, with the result, too often, that he transferred proud and independent fishermen from isolated poverty to urban slums. In 1969 he struck a deal to sell the hydroelectric power of Labrador's Churchill Falls to Quebec, but the sixty-five-year contract, though it seemed favourable at the time, turned out to be a drain on Newfoundland's public finances.

Inevitably, by the late 1960s Smallwood's long reign had created the impression that he was simultaneously "a deadly serious clown," a bullying dictator, and yesterday's man. Knowing full well that he was telling a humorous truth, he told Prime Minister Mike Pearson to wave as their car passed a cemetery: "Some of your most faithful voters are in there."

With less fun and more ruthlessness, the old socialist used the power of the state in 1959 to crush a loggers' union; the educated class he had created by building up Memorial University increasingly viewed him as an anachronistic throwback. He stayed too long, and after the October 1971 election Joey was gone—following an agonizing and intrigue-filled campaign. He resigned in February 1972 but tried to come back, his efforts succeeding only in scuppering his successor's chances to form a government. In 1977 he retired from politics once more and turned to the publication of the *Encyclopedia of Newfoundland and Labrador*. This great, expensive project nearly ended in tragic farce when Smallwood, felled by a stroke that cruelly left him without the power of speech in 1984, was slapped with writs for the printer's bills. Friends rallied and raised money to complete the project, but Joey died in 1991 after only three of the projected five volumes had been published.

Smallwood's energy, passion, and strong streak of puritanism had combined to create a unique political genius. This last father of Confederation was one of a kind in his oratorical flair, his passion for books and learning, his political unscrupulousness, and his devotion to Newfoundland and "Great Canada." We shall not see his like again.

Lise Bissonnette

FEMINIST AND NATIONALIST, WITHOUT DOUBT. Separatist? Increasingly so, but sightly less certain, though she supported the Parti Québécois, the Bloc Québécois, and the "Oui" in the 1995 Quebec referendum. As publisher of *Le Devoir*, the powerful newspaper of the Quebec francophone élite, Lise Bissonnette may not always set the agenda, but what she writes and says helps determine how Quebec reacts to it.

Born in Rouyn in the hard-scrabble mining country of the Abitibi, Bissonnette was one of seven children in a lower-middle-class family that was firmly in second or third place compared with the Anglo mining executives who lived in the adjacent community of Noranda. Smart, she sailed through high school with blinding speed, spent a few years in Hull on an educational course, and then attended Université de Montréal. After two years in France working on a never completed doctorate, she landed a job at Université du Québec à Montréal helping to develop the new university's programs.

Learning of an opening for an education reporter at *Le Devoir* in 1974, Bissonnette applied and virtually harassed editor Claude Ryan, the so-called Pope of Saint-Sacrement Street where the newspaper had its offices, into hiring her. She was an immediate success, her tough prose and work ethic propelling her onward in a newspaper that was not known to be friendly to women. Following stints in Quebec City and Ottawa, she joined the newspaper's editorial board. In 1982, after only eight years in the business, she was made editor-in-chief, a position that lasted for almost four years before she was fired in what she called "a sordid affair" orchestrated by the paper's publisher.

Redemption came in 1990 when, after she had written for the magazine *Forces* and done a weekly Quebec column in

the *Globe and Mail*, Bissonnette was appointed publisher of *Le Devoir*. Ever devoted to the task of fostering Canadian disunity and friction between the French and English speaking, the newspaper was in money-losing difficulty, its circulation stagnant at around 30,000 copies a day, and its advertising revenues sinking. In August 1993 Bissonnette, a personally charming individual with a steel inner core, suspended publication for two days and dealt toughly with the newspaper's unions while she raised money from business and organized labour.

Simultaneously, she again put her stamp on the editorial pages. Although Bissonette consistently resisted any effort by the Parti Québécois to take *Le Devoir* for granted, she almost invariably supported its policies with the faithfulness of a true believer. She had counselled a "Oui" vote in the 1980 referendum, although her editorial criticizing the PQ minister who had labelled female federalists as "Yvettes" played a role in galvanizing federalist support among francophone women. She denounced the fevered negotiations that produced a constitutional bargain without Quebec's concurrence in 1981, she declared herself in 1990 for "the maximum sovereignty for Quebec, with an organic entente with the rest of Canada," and she promoted the Bloc Québécois in the 1993 federal election and the PQ in the provincial vote the next year.

Despite Bissonnette's intellectual clarity, there is a rigidity and blindness in her views of federalists, Canada, and history. Press colleagues who were *féderastes* were self-righteous lapdogs frightened by free speech and independent thought. "Indépendantistes" were those who have "simply given up on a Canada that failed to meet their parents' aspirations," separatists who have "no connection with Canada" any longer. "It's a question of belonging," she said. "Canada isn't a bad idea. But if it asks me to like it, to say 'Canada is my country,' no, that doesn't correspond with reality"—or Bissonnette's version of reality.

In her vicious attacks on Mordecai Richler—who had dared to suggest the simple truth that *Le Devoir* had been anti-Semitic in the 1930s—Bissonnette showed nothing so much as her inability to read in context. "Such defamation," she wrote about Richler in 1992, "smears all those who are now associated with *Le Devoir*." And when Richler appeared on CBC's *The Journal*, Bissonnette wrote that "a more Rhodesian scene than that one would have been difficult to imagine," with Barbara Frum playing the part of a "high society matron serving tea in her Salisbury villa to a poor disaffected neighbour, who complains that the servants are ingrates." Too often, Bissonnette's blinkered view of the world through her *fleur-de-lys* spectacles allows her ire to run well ahead of her good sense.

Still, Bissonnette remains one of the major players in Quebec life. She is on television frequently, she appears in magazines, and she has even written two much praised novels. If Canada is to survive intact, it will not be because Lise Bissonnette has not done her best to push the country towards break-up.

94

Frederick Tisdall

BORN: Clinton, Ontario • 3 November 1893

DIED: Thornhill, Ontario • 23 April 1949

It used to be a lot tougher to be a kid in Canada. Even in the early years of the twentieth century, polio and diabetes were terrifying child-killers. And if you had the misfortune of being poor, it was always much worse: miserable things like rickets and chronic diarrhoea were a constant threat. Thousands of Canadian children died before their fourth birthdays.

Slowly, medical research scored the major break-throughs that were required to overcome some of these diseases; Fred Banting's discovery of insulin was just the best known. A much less dramatic but crucial step towards improved infant mortality rates came only a few years later in the form of a flavourless, lumpy mush. It was 1931 and Dr Fred Tisdall, working out of a laboratory at Toronto's Hospital for Sick Children, gave the world its first taste of pablum.

Pablum is known worldwide as the first scientifically engineered baby food, but its inventor is not known, evidence of Tisdall's pursuit of knowledge over fame. A standout student at the University of Toronto medical school, Tisdall graduated during the Great War before pursuing further training at Johns Hopkins and Harvard universities. He returned to Toronto in the 1920s and set his sights on curbing the country's infant mortality rate.

A dynamic personality and born salesman as well as an inspired researcher, Tisdall secured research funding for major investigative work in the area of nutrition. Heading a team of several doctors, Tisdall perfected a formula in early 1930 for a baked biscuit that contained wheat germ, milk, butter, and all the scientifically determined goodness he could cram into it. He worked out a deal with a cookie-maker so that the biscuit would be widely available, and his hospital received a portion of the proceeds for further research.

A cheap, durable food that would protect its consumers from malnutrition was a significant achievement, but it was not the big one. Biscuits were ideal for older children, but infants needed something that did not have to be chewed. A baby's need for a balanced diet, though still not perfectly understood, was deemed to be even greater than what the biscuit could provide. Experiments with vitamin-enriched, dehydrated cereal mixtures took time, but, finally, in 1931, pablum was ready for the market.

Tisdall knew the product would make an immediate impact if it was widely available, so he travelled to Chicago to find the right company to sell it. At the same time, he made sure that royalties would continue to flow to research at Sick Kids, which was fast gaining a world reputation as a centre for nutrition science. As the doctor predicted, Mead's Cereal—pablum's first tradename—was a huge seller around the globe in a matter of years. After all, here, for the first time, was a nearly perfect scientifically devised infant food.

The invention saved countless lives, but pablum also stood for something else: its universal popularity marked the triumph of the medicalization of birth and child-rearing. From the 1930s, mothers were no longer urged to trust their instincts when it came to having and raising babies. Doctors knew best, and each subsequent medical advance seemed to confirm what only a few dared question: that the scientific approach to having children was the only choice for responsible parents. Generations of children, especially in North America, would feel the effects.

Tisdall mostly dodged the credit for his discovery, but he continued to test recipes for nutritional foods in the years after pablum's discovery. He made sure that improvements quickly found their way to market, and he always turned the profits back into research.

In short, Fred Tisdall figured out what was required and how to sell it. His epitaph could have read "Millions and Millions Served—and Tens of Thousands Saved."

95

Kenojuak Ashevak

EVEN IF THEY KNOW ALMOST NOTHING OF THE North, Canadians still idealize it. "The true north strong and free" is part and parcel of our identity. In the last thirty-five years our vision of that vast, lone land has been created to an extraordinary extent by Inuit art. No Inuit artist has captured our imagination as firmly as Kenojuak, the best known of all the northern artists.

Born on Baffin Island, Kenojuak was raised in the traditional way of Inuit women, travelling with her family from camp to camp. Married in 1946, she soon developed tuberculosis and was confined to a sanitarium at Quebec, a terrible period during which her two eldest children died of botulism. What turned her life around was art. "One day, while I was getting provisions in Cape Dorset," she said in her oral autobiography, James Houston, a government worker who was trusted by the Inuit, "gave me paper and pencils, wrapped in a plastic bag...I was uncertain what I should draw, but he suggested that I draw whatever was in my mind." It turned out that her mind was full of images, both traditional and wholly original. "I just take these things out of my thoughts," she said, "and out of my imagination, and I don't really give any weight to the idea of its being an image of something...I am just concentrating on placing it down on paper in a way that is pleasing to

my own eye." That, she maintained, was the way she started
and that is the way she remained.

Dazzled, Houston arranged for the creation of artistic
cooperatives that would transfer the drawings produced by
Kenojuak and others, including her husband, onto
silkscreens, and, beginning in 1959, Kenojuak's art burst
upon the world. There was immediate acclaim in Canada
and abroad, enough that the National Film Board in 1962
made her the subject of a documentary. Her limited edition
prints quickly commanded high prices. One of her first
images, "Enchanted Owl," appeared on the postage stamp
issued in 1970 to commemorate the centennial of the
Northwest Territories, and the owl, grave but decorative
with its staring eyes and gripping claws, has been a much
reiterated theme in her work. The owl, as she said, "drives
away the darkness," and for the Inuit, living without sun for
half the year, no image could be more meaningful. Soon she
was scratching her art directly onto copper plates carried
from camp to camp, bringing the completed work to Cape
Dorset for reproduction.

In all, Kenojuak produced some two hundred prints,
most in the annual Cape Dorset print collections. There were
additional commissions from the World Wildlife Fund and
the federal government, to commemorate the 1990 signing of
Inuit land settlements.

Astonishingly, Kenojuak proved adept in the medium of
sculpture, too. Until her hands became too weak to work in
stone, she produced a flood of superb soapstone pieces. With
her husband, Johnniebo, she undertook a huge twenty-five
panel green and white mosaic plaster mural for the Canadian
Pavilion at Expo 70 in Osaka, Japan. Characteristically, a
huge owl was at the centre, surrounded by symbolic repre-
sentations of the sun, igloos, polar bears, and dog sleds.

Honoured by her government and her people, Kenojuak continued her work, producing prints, sculptures, and, in the early 1990s, perhaps because the print market seemed to be drying up, coloured pencil and ink drawings. Less vigorous in her old age, she continues to draw, though less frequently. "I continue to do so primarily for the future these works of art will guarantee for my children," she said. "Therefore, I am grateful to those people who are interested in, and admire, my work. When I am dead, I am sure there will still be people discussing my art." Kenojuak's art has provided a rich legacy not only for her children but for all Canadians.

Douglas Cardinal

BORN: Red Deer, Alberta • 7 March 1934

Eᴠᴇʀ sɪɴᴄᴇ 1943, ᴡʜᴇɴ Aʏɴ Rᴀɴᴅ ᴍᴀᴅᴇ ᴀɴ individualistic, independent architect the hero of her novel *The Fountainhead*, the creators of plans for great buildings have enjoyed the status of stormy petrels. Most architects are ordinary individuals producing ordinary designs in ordinary ways, but there are those who rage against their critics and battle for the purity of designs and concepts. Douglas Cardinal might have sprung full blown from the mind of Ayn Rand.

A Métis, the son of a game warden and forest ranger, Cardinal received his architectural training in Texas after he fell out with the University of British Columbia, but returned to Alberta to apprentice. Soon he was on his own in Edmonton, and his first commissions established his original approach. His designs were unusual in the way they blended organically into the landscape—so unconventional that contractors claimed they could not build his "soaring curves, serpentine walls, strata-like masses and irregular plans." His "geology, not geometry" designs frequently ran into opposition from government clients, not least when cost overruns arose.

Cardinal's aboriginal heritage is usually cited as the explanation for his organic approach. But Cardinal himself has observed that his artistic vision antedated his involvement with native causes. His

1968 swirling St Mary's Church at Red Deer with its arresting suspended roof, the first of his designs to attract national attention, was completed well before his renewed consciousness of traditional native culture. "I built the church in Red Deer," Cardinal said, "because I did not realize it was impossible to do." Only by pioneering the use of computers in design was he able to work out the technical problems posed by his fluid concepts.

Cardinal insists on the integrity of design in his buildings and will fight to preserve it. He was furious when his 1974 Grande Prairie Regional College, northwest of Edmonton, was dramatically changed by a $54 million renovation that attached a graceless large addition to his design and gutted the original structure. "It's just not my work," he said, denouncing the college's board of governors for its "illegal act" of disfigurement. "I always thought that if a building has merit, the public will protect it," he said, with a certain naivety. When St Mary's planned renovations in the late 1980s without consulting him, he dissuaded the church by threat of a suit.

His best-known building in Canada is the Canadian Museum of Civilization in Hull, Quebec, across the river from the Parliament Buildings. Instantly recognizable, it is one of the masterworks of Canadian architecture. The 1985 design obliged him to deal with government, both politicians with cronies to reward and stuffy bureaucrats. But as costs skyrocketed to $250 million, the pressure for change was understandable. Begun under the Trudeau government and completed under Mulroney, Cardinal's plan had its critics. "When the Tories came on board," he recalled, "there was a sort of campaign to modify the design and degrade all the materials...There was always someone with another product, another agenda, coming up. I wouldn't accept that." For years Cardinal fought for his concept, and he prevailed. The museum is one of the national capital's great structures.

Cardinal's most recent works include the Institute for American Indian Arts in Santa Fe, New Mexico, and village buildings and housing for the Cree of Ouje-Bougamou in Quebec. His northern town features energy-efficient houses dominated by their roof line, with light and open space shaping the interiors. The village is circular, with a meeting place in the centre and community buildings in an interior ring. There are no boxes, no imposing walls, and traditional Cree culture is reflected in every line. No architect has ever interpreted aboriginal ideas better in his work to both natives and all Canadians.

Cardinal's triumph in the north and in Ottawa-Hull has led to what is potentially his greatest commission—the $110 million, 250,000-square-foot National Museum of the American Indian on Washington's National Mall, scheduled to open in 2002. "For all my life," Cardinal said, "my Indian background has been used against me. Here's an opportunity for it to be used as a benefit, for it to work for me." The Americans, he adds, are easy to deal with, straight up, and they don't mess with the figures. "I don't have to play Horatio at the bridge like I did in Ottawa." In Washington, he ruminates bitterly, "it's okay to be an Indian. In Canada, it isn't."

97

Robert Borden

BORN: Grand Pré, Nova Scotia • 26 June 1854
DIED: Ottawa, Ontario • 10 June 1937

PERHAPS ONE CANADIAN IN A THOUSAND COULD properly identify Sir Robert Borden today. But there once was a time when this determined man, so fixed on victory, led Canada through war prepared to destroy his own country in order to save it.

A lawyer, Borden had practised in Halifax from 1878. A Conservative, he ran for the House of Commons in 1896, a bad year for Tories, and won election in Halifax. A man without much evident ambition or demonstrated political talent, he reluctantly accepted the party leadership in 1901 when no one appeared to want it. An unhappy leader, he repeatedly offered to resign, only to see his political enemies draw back for fear that another, more distasteful leader would claim the prize.

Although Borden had pledged to clean up government corruption, he struck an alliance in 1911 with the "Toronto Eighteen," large manufacturers who were opposed to Sir Wilfrid Laurier's reciprocity agreement with the United States. Borden, the man of principle, not only agreed to give the leaders of Toronto business a big say in choosing his Cabinet but he accepted their demand that he put French Canada in its place and that Canada's relations with the empire be enhanced. In return, the Conservatives had all the money and all the newspaper support they needed to defeat the Liberals. Robert Borden, the

unlikely leader, was in power at last, and free trade with the Americans was dead.

Borden honoured his deal with business. He put Thomas White, the Toronto Eighteen's candidate, in Cabinet as minister of finance, and he offered Britain money to build two huge dreadnaughts, only to see the Liberal-dominated Senate derail his proposal to strengthen the Royal Navy. Quebec received little from him, scarcely even the back of his hand, and the *nationalistes* who had supported him in 1911 because of their hatred for Laurier fell away quickly.

When war came in August 1914, Borden's government was already deeply unpopular. As the nation mobilized and as patronage scandals rocked the House of Commons, Borden's leadership again was weak. But Canada's army grew strong overseas and, its reputation spread quickly, though casualties mounted ever higher. Could the nation sustain its strength at the front through voluntary methods? Should Quebec, low on enthusiasm for military adventures abroad and the British Empire, be permitted to send so few of its sons to the front? Or should "equality of sacrifice" be the ideal?

Returning to Canada in May 1917 after a trip to the front, Borden determined that conscription had to be imposed to sustain the Canadian Corps' strength in the line. Quebec's opposition was fierce, but Borden tried to bring Laurier onside by offering to take him into the government. Laurier refused. Borden then began to woo Liberals in the provinces, holding out the prospect of a Union Government to fight the election that was expected before the end of 1917. Again, there was reluctance, so Borden's government passed the Military Voters Act and the Wartime Elections Act. The first measure gave the vote to soldiers, which none disagreed with, though it tacked on powers to allocate votes to constituencies which blatantly corrupted the electoral system. The second act took away the votes of naturalized "enemy" aliens, believed to be Liberal voters, and gave the franchise to the female relatives of soldiers, a group that might confidently be expected to support conscription to reinforce the men overseas. The two gerrymandering bills tilted the balance in favour of the government and propelled conscriptionist Liberals into the Union. To guarantee his electoral victory, two weeks before the election Borden exempted farmers, cool to military service, from conscription. His government swept to power once more, winning scarcely a seat in French Canada and splitting the two solitudes.

Canada was divided as never before. The government's conscription measure led thousands of call-ups to flee into the bush, provoked riots in the streets of Quebec City (put down by troops rushed from Toronto), and led to calls for secession in the Quebec legislature. Unmoved, Borden pressed ahead and, when the Germans launched a huge offensive in March 1918, he rescinded the farmers' exemption from conscription. Tough and determined, Borden brooked no opposition. Neither past pledges nor electoral honesty could sway him from his goal.

Borden's triumphs left his Conservative Party in ruins and his country scarred. Not until 1958 would *bleus* again do well in Quebec, and never again would Québécois truly trust an English-speaking leader. Not until 1944, after five years of war, would Canada impose a measure of conscription to reinforce its hard-pressed infantry in Northwest Europe and Italy. Not until 1988 would free trade with the United States be put into effect. The dour Nova Scotian with a will of iron had set his nation's course for the future.

98

Robert Coats

BORN: Clinton, Ontario • 25 July 1874

DIED: Ottawa, Ontario • 7 February 1960

Nations, like corporations, must collect data. How many were born and died, and where? How many came to the country or emigrated? How much was produced, how many were out of work, how much did prices rise? Numbers are an essential tool of nationhood, of planning, and of government.

Robert H. Coats was Canada's man of numbers, the creator of the Dominion Bureau of Statistics.

A graduate of the University of Toronto in 1896 who had worked as a journalist in Toronto, he was brought to Ottawa in 1902 by his classmate, Mackenzie King, then deputy minister of labour, to be assistant editor of the *Labour Gazette*. He stayed with the Department of Labour for the next fourteen years as chief statistician, spending much of his time collecting data on prices, studying the cost of living, and becoming truly alarmed by the haphazard state of the information available to the government. Statistics had to be collected regularly and in a uniform manner, Coats believed, and he made this argument forcibly to Sir George Foster, the minister of trade and commerce in the Borden government. Impressed, Foster had Coats made dominion statistician and commissioner of the census in 1915 and assigned him to direct the 1916 census of the Prairie provinces. Most important for his and the nation's future, Coats prepared the draft of the Statistics Act of 1918. In May 1918 the government established the Dominion Bureau of Statistics, which Coats led until his retirement in 1942.

Setting statistical norms was no easy task. Various departments in Ottawa collected—and protected—their data; provincial governments did the same, all in different ways; and municipalities across the land number-crunched too. Coats' first task was to get Canada's vital statistics made uniform. He accomplished this by calling a conference, mastering provincial statutes, and cajoling jealous bureaucrats into cooperation. By 1926 every province operated with uniform definitions and asked standard questions on birth and death certificates. Simple, but essential. That success led Coats to expand his gaze into other areas, and the result was similar Ottawa-directed uniformity in data relating to agriculture, foreign and domestic trade, industrial and mining production, and education. At last, government could confidently measure the gross national product and assess sectoral performance. By the 1930s his now well-established Dominion Bureau of Statistics was undertaking regular surveys of business statistics and the wholesale and retail trades, using the most advanced techniques of the day. Such data helped government become more professional, and business more profitable.

As the data poured in, Coats' command of the numbers increased his usefulness to the government. With Prime Minister Mackenzie King and his key foreign policy adviser, O.D. Skelton, he worked at imperial conferences to bolster the dominion's arguments. He also coordinated international gatherings and played a major role at meetings of statisticians at the League of Nations in Geneva. Just as important, in the patronage-ridden public service of drones that ordinarily ran the dominion until the mid-1930s, Coats' easy, casual style and his sharp wit impressed all who met him. So too did his willingness to find and encourage the bright young men and women who came to work in the capital. Coats helped to create the basis for the public service mandarinate that, using the DBS data, let Canada fight the Second World War with vastly greater domestic efficiency than had been possible in 1914.

Robert Coats was the architect of the Dominion Bureau of Statistics, the essential foundation-stone of effective, efficient government in Canada. Little known at the time outside Ottawa, remembered by only a few today, Coats' professionalism and the reliability of the systems he put in place made a difference.

99

BORN: Maple, Ontario • 25 May 1879
DIED: Cherkley, Mickleham, United Kingdom • 9 June 1964

Maxwell Aitken

Were he still around, Max Aitken would be convinced that he belongs in this book. If he was never connected with a specific outstanding achievement, and if he never quite made it to the pinnacle of a particular profession, Aitken nevertheless believed that many of the momentous events of the twentieth century involved him intimately. Modesty was obviously not one of Aitken's personality traits, and there was much exaggerated self-importance to just about everything he did. Yet over the course of his long life, whatever he was up to, Aitken could never be ignored.

Capitalist, politician, journalist, publisher, and author were Aitken's best-known public roles, but beneath it all, seduction was his real craft. He simply had an exceptional knack for ingratiating himself with people. Though born in Ontario, Aitken's Presbyterian minister father moved the family to New Brunswick when he was an infant, and Aitken would call the Maritime province home for the rest of his life. From the start, Aitken made friends effortlessly: he had a way with strangers that allowed him to accumulate business partners and money with breathtaking ease. A millionaire in his twenties, he rapidly rose to prominence by choreographing major industrial mergers such as those that created Stelco and Canada Cement. By then he was one of the few Canadian financiers who mattered.

Business brought him to England before the 1914–18 war, and Aitken stepped easily into the British ruling classes. He seemed an unlikely fit with the sundry lords and ladies of the aristocracy; he was, after all, a poor man's son, a businessman, and a Canadian. And his often-commented-upon appearance—short, ugly, with an apparently permanent self-satisfied grin—won him few admirers. But Aitken possessed charm in abundance and even more money, and he liked to lavish both on himself and his friends. Men and women of all stations fell under his spell. Of course, being rich was never enough for Aitken; he needed to plunk himself near the centre of the action to remain content. England seemed to be the place for that in those years, so he decided to stay. He befriended another Canadian in London, Andrew Bonar Law, and emerged as an overnight insider within the Conservative Party to make his compatriot British prime minister. Aitken himself entered politics briefly and was elevated to the House of Lords in 1917. From then on, he was Lord Beaverbrook.

After the war, Canada's most renowned baron became a newspaper owner. The press was just a sideline at first, but he quickly realized how much power newspapers wielded in a democracy. Soon Beaverbrook was an obsessive publisher with a knack for the great crusade: he wrote editorials, super-vised coverage, and boosted circulation at his flagship *Daily Express* until readership was over 4 million. More than ever his opinions mattered. He campaigned for issues he viewed as particularly important to Canada—a plan for imperial free trade, for example, though never successful, was a cause he alone kept in the public eye. Beaverbrook could not be disre-garded, and kings and prime ministers routinely sought his advice. When they did not, it was proffered anyway.

By 1939, though Beaverbrook still cultivated his Canadian identity, he was one of the most important people in British politics. He was a close confidant of Winston Churchill, and he joined the prime minister's Cabinet for most of the war. "He did not fail. This was his hour," Churchill remembered of Beaverbrook's wartime contribu-tion. His lordship was in the middle of struggles to increase war production, and in secret meetings with international leaders at the highest level. But the Canadian, too used to getting his own way in his personal affairs and newspapers, was not well suited for the compromise-filled world of politics. He retired before the war was over and returned to the carousing life of a fabulously rich press lord.

Late in life Beaverbrook took to recording the public events of his lifetime. These memoirs were usually self-serving and sometimes mean-spirited, but, combined, his books offer a unique first-hand glimpse inside important moments in mid-century history; they are required reading for a full understanding of the period. He spent more and more of his time in his home province in his declining years, and the University of New Brunswick and the Beaverbrook Art Gallery in Fredericton were just the most notable recipients of millions in donations. What it all added up to was a continuing obsession with his place in history: Beaverbrook hoped to charm future generations of historians as completely as he had many of his contemporaries. But in most of his roles, Beaverbrook was a supporting player rather than a star. He lurked for over fifty years on the very edge of power; highly influential, but rarely able to change events decisively on his own.

Lucien Bouchard

BORN: Saint-Coeur-de-Marie, Quebec • 22 December 1938

Lucien Bouchard is a man Canadians love to despise. The occasionally temperate *Globe and Mail* noted that Bouchard is Canada's chameleon, with a short but mercurial career in public life. "He has shed more skins than the average snake," the newspaper noted, pointing to Bouchard's successive political affiliations: Union National, Liberal, Parti Québécois, Progressive Conservative, Bloc Québécois, and Parti Québécois. No principle here, but a "means of ascent, fed by the oxygen of ambition."

Born to a working-class family in the Lac St-Jean area, the cerebral Bouchard went to the classical college run by the Oblate Fathers at Jonquière, and then to Université Laval. He took his law degree in the same class as Brian Mulroney in Quebec City and the two ambitious poor boys became fast friends, a fateful pairing for Canada if ever there was one. In 1974 Mulroney brought Bouchard onto the staff of the Cliche commission investigating construction industry corruption in Quebec and, for the first time, gave him public notice. Then, although Bouchard was an open Péquiste and a campaigner for the "Oui" in the 1980 referendum in Quebec, Mulroney, elected Tory leader in 1983, called on his crony to advise him during the 1984 election that brought the Tories to power. As his reward for advice that markedly softened Mulroney's hitherto strong federalist/centralist approach, Bouchard became ambassador to France in 1985, a blatant patronage appointment.

But unlike most political ambassadors, Bouchard did well. The French liked the darkly handsome Bouchard's reputation for womanizing, they knew that he had Mulroney's ear, and they went along with his efforts to push the French-speaking commonwealth, La francophonie, as a vehicle to serve Canadian interests.

Then it was the federal Cabinet in 1988, initially as secretary of state and then as environment minister. Most important, Bouchard became Mulroney's Quebec lieutenant, the controller of patronage and the head of the party's then-powerful Quebec caucus. The Meech Lake accord was running aground by 1990, and the prime minister was twisting arms, modifying and changing text, and pulling out all the stops to save it. Fearing that Quebec's interests were about to be sacrificed, Bouchard dramatically broke with his old friend, left the government and party, and, within a short period, gathered a group of former Tory and Liberal MPs around him as the Bloc Québécois. The old friendship was destroyed, and the prime minister gloomily watched his classmate become the *de facto* leader of Quebec separatism. "I don't think there is anyone," Mulroney said in Parliament, "who would believe that we have lessons to learn from [Bouchard] in the area of truth and loyalty." In the 1993 election, Bouchard's Bloc won 54 seats in Quebec, becoming the official Opposition in Ottawa; the Tories under Mulroney's successor were reduced to one seat in Quebec and one in New Brunswick.

Effective in opposition, Bouchard won national sympathy in December 1994 when he fought off necrotizing myositis, the flesh-eating disease, but at the cost of a leg. His near-martyr status helped greatly when Bouchard's defining

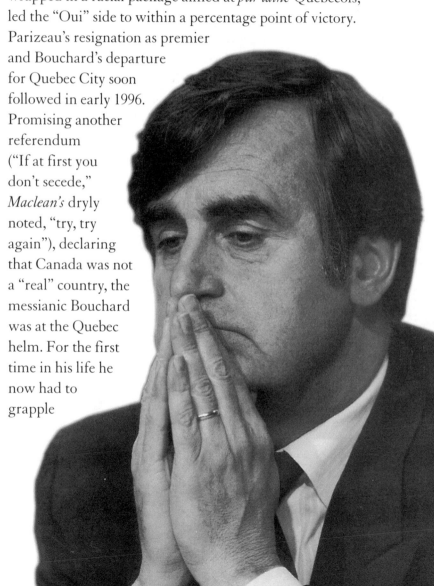

moment came during the 1995 Quebec referendum on independence. With the campaign led by PQ premier Jacques Parizeau faltering, Bouchard stepped in to take the lead, waving his "magic wand" and promising to create a "beautiful vista" for the province. This charismatic twaddle, wrapped in a racial package aimed at *pur laine* Québécois, led the "Oui" side to within a percentage point of victory. Parizeau's resignation as premier and Bouchard's departure for Quebec City soon followed in early 1996. Promising another referendum ("If at first you don't secede," *Maclean's* dryly noted, "try, try again"), declaring that Canada was not a "real" country, the messianic Bouchard was at the Quebec helm. For the first time in his life he now had to grapple with the reality of deficits, debt, unemployment, and foreign bondholders.

Bouchard's stock in trade was the "humiliation" the Québécois nation had suffered at the hands of the "maudits anglais"—through three centuries of history, in the 1981 constitutional negotiations, during Meech and Charlottetown, in the Montreal federalist rally in the 1995 referendum, and yesterday, today, and tomorrow. His black hair dropping over his forehead, his orations resonating with passion and fervour as he rang the changes on the litany of federalist Canada's sins, he resembled nothing so much as a leader in search of a white horse to ride at the head of a mob crying "liberté"—and trampling on the rights of everyone else. A dangerous demagogue, Bouchard will destroy Canada or paralyse it. Unless, of course, the ambitious snake sheds his skin one more time and emerges again as...a reluctant federalist?

p. 16   National Archives of Canada
p. 21   National Archives of Canada
p. 25   National Archives of Canada
p. 28   National Archives of Canada
p. 31   National Archives of Canada / Harry Palmer
p. 34   National Archives of Canada
p. 38   *The Toronto Star* / Loek
p. 43   National Archives of Canada
p. 47   National Archives of Canada
p. 48   National Archives of Canada / *The Toronto Star* / Macpherson
p. 51   *The Ottawa Citizen* / Paul Latour
p. 54   National Archives of Canada
p. 59   *The Ottawa Citizen* / John Major
p. 60   National Archives of Canada
p. 63   National Archives of Canada
p. 66   National Archives of Canada
p. 69   National Archives of Canada
p. 73   *The Ottawa Citizen* / Lynn Ball
p. 77   The Supreme Court of Canada
p. 80   National Archives of Canada
p. 84   National Archives of Canada
p. 89   National Archives of Canada
p. 92   Canapress Photo Service / Bill Becker
p. 95   University of Toronto Archives
p. 98   CBC Radio's *Morningside*
p. 105 *The Ottawa Citizen* / Chris Mikula
p. 111 *The Ottawa Citizen* / Paul Latour
p. 115 *The Ottawa Citizen*
p. 118 Canapress Photo Service
p. 123 National Gallery of Canada / Victoria City Archives
p. 127 McClelland & Stewart Inc.
p. 130 Canada's Sports Hall of Fame / Wamboldt-Waterfield
p. 134 *The Toronto Star* / R. Innell
p. 141 Ontario Hydro Archives
p. 144 National Archives of Canada
p. 147 Musée J. Armand Bombardier
p. 151 *The Ottawa Citizen* / John Major
p. 156 National Archives of Canada
p. 159 The National Gallery of Canada / Taconis
p. 162 *The Ottawa Citizen*
p. 167 *The Bulletin* / University of Toronto / Robert Lansdale
p. 171 Dalhousie Art Gallery / Simon Elwes
p. 174 *The Ottawa Citizen* / Bruno Schlumberger
p. 179 National Archives of Canada
p. 182 National Archives of Canada
p. 185 University of Toronto Archives
p. 190 *The Ottawa Citizen* / Bruno Schlumberger
p. 197 *The Globe and Mail*
p. 201 National Archives of Canada
p. 207 National Gallery of Canada / National Film Board of Canada /
        Jacques Godbout Film
p. 211 National Archives of Canada
p. 215 National Archives of Canada
p. 218 *The Ottawa Citizen* / Chris Mikula
p. 223 *The Ottawa Citizen* / Rod MacIvor
p. 225 National Archives of Canada / Karsh
p. 230 *The Bulletin* / University of Toronto / David Lloyd
p. 234 Robert Lansdale
p. 239 *The Ottawa Citizen* / Wayne Cuddington